FEMINIST
STUDIES

CRITICAL
STUDIES

Feminist Studies / Critical Studies
is Volume 8 in the series
THEORIES OF CONTEMPORARY CULTURE
Center for Twentieth Century Studies
University of Wisconsin-Milwaukee

General Editor, KATHLEEN WOODWARD

FEMINIST STUDIES

CRITICAL STUDIES

EDITED BY

TERESA

de LAURETIS

INDIANA UNIVERSITY PRESS
BLOOMINGTON

Manufactured in the United States of America

Library of Congress Cataloging-in-Publication Data
Feminist studies, critical studies.
(Theories of contemporary culture; v. 8)
Papers presented at a conference in April 1985 at
the Center for Twentieth Century Studies of the
University of Wisconsin-Milwaukee.
Includes bibliographical references.
1. Feminism—Congresses. 2. Criticism (Philosophy)—
Congresses. I. De Lauretis, Teresa. II. University of
Wisconsin-Milwaukee. Center for Twentieth Century
Studies. III. Series.
HQ1154.F4473   1986   305.4'2   85-45981
ISBN 0-253-32171-9
ISBN 0-253-20386-4 (pbk.)

CONTENTS

PREFACE

The Center for Twentieth Century Studies at the University of Wisconsin–Milwaukee is a crossdisciplinary research institute devoted to the study of contemporary culture from the point of view of the humanities and with an emphasis on critical theory. *Theories of Contemporary Culture,* the Center's book series with Indiana University Press, represents the Center's commitment to crossdisciplinary, collective research in contemporary cultural studies. Subjects of Center books that have already appeared over the past ten years include performance in postmodern culture, technology and culture, aging and psychoanalysis, mass culture, and deconstruction and displacement, among others. Research is planned in television/video studies and social theory. I am pleased to announce that in the future *Theories of Contemporary Culture* will also include single-authored collections of essays.

This volume, *Feminist Studies/Critical Studies,* the eighth in the series, had its beginnings in a conference of the University of Wisconsin–Milwaukee conceived and organized by Teresa de Lauretis and held at the Center in April 1985. To my former colleague, whose presence I very much miss at the Center, I owe my warmest thanks. I would also like to thank Dean William F. Halloran of the College of Letters and Science and Dean George Keulks of The Graduate School of the University of Wisconsin–Milwaukee for their ongoing support of the work of the Center, which has flourished under their administrations. Most importantly, Teresa de Lauretis and I would like to thank all those at the Center without whom this book would not have assumed tangible form. To Jean Lile and Carol Tennessen, to Shirley Reinhold, Jon Erickson, Laura Roskos, Ed Schelb, and Debra Vest, we extend our affection and gratitude.

Kathleen Woodward
Director, Center for Twentieth Century Studies
General Editor, *Theories of Contemporary Culture*

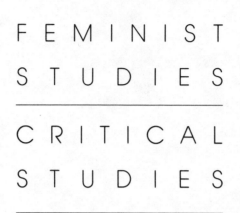

FEMINIST
STUDIES

CRITICAL
STUDIES

Feminist Studies/Critical Studies: Issues, Terms, and Contexts

Teresa de Lauretis

"It is by now clear that a feminist renaissance is under way . . . a shift in perspective far more extraordinary and influential than the shift from theology to humanism of the European Renaissance."[1] Like feminism itself, these words of Adrienne Rich, written in 1973, bear reevaluation; not so much, perhaps, to discuss the validity of their assessment or the extensiveness of its claim as to examine the manner of the shift, to analyze, articulate, address the terms of this other perspective.

For just such a purpose was a conference held, in April 1985, at the Center for Twentieth Century Studies of the University of Wisconsin-Milwaukee on the topic "Feminist Studies: Reconstituting Knowledge." This volume may be read as one record of that conference, or better, as one text of many that could have been written or heard from it.* The conference focused on feminist work in the fields of history, science, literary writing, criticism, and theory, with the relation of feminist politics to critical studies (and thus also to each and all of these disciplinary areas) as its general and overarching concern. Its project was outlined in a letter to participants, as follows:

> The intellectual presence of feminist studies has been felt in the academy for well over a decade. The work of feminist scholars in literary and social criticism, theory, and history has significantly altered the configuration of critical studies in this country. But while the results of feminist scholarship—ranging from the (re)discovery of forgotten writ-

---

*All the contributions to this volume are revised and/or expanded versions of papers presented at the conference, with the exception of the essays by Modleski, Moraga, and Martin and Mohanty. These contributors, however, were also invited to participate, and, but for Moraga, who was unable to attend due to prior commitments, did take part in the conference.

I wish to thank Elaine Marks, who generously and graciously shared with me the task of opening and directing the three-day conference.

ers, artists, and cultural figures to the revision of the canon and the "rewriting" of history—are acknowledged as an important achievement, there are a general uncertainty and, among feminists, serious differences as to what the specific concerns, values and methods of feminist critical work are, or ought to be.

If it is true, as many claim, that feminist studies have proposed new ways of thinking about culture, language, morality, or knowledge itself, then it is timely and necessary to arrive at a more precise understanding of the epistemological framework and critical foundations of feminist studies. Or if it is true, as some feminist critics maintain, that feminist theory has reached an impasse, notably on the issue of essentialism (the idea of an innate femininity, an essential nature of woman, whether biologically or philosophically defined); or if it is true that feminist thought is stalemated in the debate concerning culturalism vs. biologism, then it is vital that we look around the room and ask: are there any new faces, any different perspectives, any possibilities of theoretical break-through?

At a time when the women's movement is being both integrated and quietly suffocated within the institutions, when the feminist critique is partially accommodated within some academic disciplines and emar-ginated otherwise, when feminism is nudged into the pockets of the economy with one hand, and of the intelligentsia with the other, it seems important and even crucial to assess the intellectual and political role of feminist studies in the production, reproduction and transfor-mation of social discourses and knowledges.

Focusing mainly on three areas—social history, literary criticism and cultural theory—speakers will seek to identify the specificity of feminism as a critical theory, its methods, goals and analytic framework(s), its epistemological and ideological foundations. The approach will be speculative and theoretical, rather than empirical or quantitative. Par-ticipants will include leading scholars both within and outside feminist studies, younger scholars whose training was influenced by Women's Studies programs, and scholars who are also active in professional fields such as publishing, psychotherapy, and community work. The sessions will consist of papers and responses, in the manner of a dialogue, deal-ing with areas of study where the feminist discourse has articulated specific issues, themes or questions: papers will survey those areas of research and outline critical concepts, problems and directions; re-sponses will focus on one or two aspects of those areas, giving a sharper, if narrower, critical view of the issues involved and sketching out further directions for analysis. The panels will address areas and problems not yet sufficiently articulated within feminist theory, questions that arise at the boundaries of feminism and other critical practices or mark the limits of current feminist thought.

The project of the conference was conceived in the awareness of the very differences, contradictions, even impasses that—precisely—made it necessary, that made such a meeting crucial, as well as timely. One of those contradictions was purposely inscribed in the title of the conference: "Feminist Studies" are a kind of feminist activity that takes place primarily within the academic institution, the university, which is an institution of formal knowledge and an institution of the state. Feminism, on the other hand, is not an institution, nor is it—or, better, nor does it seem to be—a matter of formal knowledge. And to the extent that pressure is exercised in the direction of "mainstreaming," to the extent that pressure is felt to yield to an increasing institutionalization of feminist knowledge and critical activity, the project of the conference was to resist that pressure, to resist the institution.

The second phrase of the title also contained something of an ambiguity, a double drift. In one sense, it demanded consideration of whether and to what extent feminist studies have been "Reconstituting Knowledge"; whether they have produced new forms and methods of knowledge, or, even more directly, have produced new knowledges, and thus reshaped at once the field and the object of knowledge, as well as the conditions of knowing. Read the other way, however, the title suggested that the knowledges produced by feminist studies have been reconstituting women—women as social subject, as subject of both knowledge and knowing; and consequently it demanded consideration of whether and to what extent those knowledges and epistemological frames have redefined what counts as knowledge, and thus effectively resist the established canons.

The notion of resistance, however, is itself not unambiguous. It too can mean—and has meant historically—rather diverse things, translating into different practices and strategies that must be assessed and developed each in its concrete sociohistorical situation. Resistance has been armed or unarmed, for instance (though never disarmed, if it was really resistance). It can be socially organized in group action or lived subjectively as a personal commitment, and often is both. But by the very nature of power and of the mechanisms that harness power to institutions, rather than individuals, resistance tends to be cast as op-position, tends to be seen as locked in an opposite position, or what the media call an "opposing viewpoint." Thus, it is not just accommodated but in fact anticipated, and so effectively neutralized, particularly by democratic institutions. That is the pressure, the move to mainstream feminism to which I alluded earlier. But it would be naive to think that only we, teachers and writers, are working within and against institutional constraints, and other feminists are not. Even a separatist commune of women living off the land, so to speak, has to contend, though in more mediated ways, with the state.

The ways of resistance in feminism are many. In our own lives as scholars, students, and writers, we know the complex mediations and daily negotiations required of women who will not abide in silence, and who will read and write. Women have written books, to say nothing of diaries and letters and drawersful of words, about how much it takes to be able to write, at best, and how many other women do not have even that much. We have written books about our writing and the suppression of our writing; we have written about silence and madness, marginality and invisibility, negativity and difference. But we have also written of femininity and feminine writing, of identities, differences, and commonalities, affirming what Audre Lorde has called "the interdependency of different strengths" in feminism.[2] In sum, it is now possible, as Sheila Rowbotham put it, "to look back at ourselves through our own cultural creations, our actions, our ideas, our pamphlets, our organizations, our history, our theory."[3] That is precisely one of the aims of this volume.

It is not only possible, I believe, but necessary, for two reasons: one internal to feminism, the other external. The first has to do with the definition of feminism, which is certainly not a point of consensus; the second with that pressure toward institutionalization that I already mentioned and on which, I would think, there is a measure of consensus. Obviously, the two are related, since there is no real boundary between feminism and what is external to it; no boundary separates or insulates feminism from other social practices or makes it impervious to the institutions of civil society. There are, however, discursive boundaries: not only specific terms, concepts, and rhetorical strategies that distinguish feminist writing and speech from the others, but also certain shared assumptions, interpretive paths, inferences drawn from events and behaviors, and unstated premises—unstated because they no longer need to be stated, having become, one might say, "part of the discourse." These discursive boundaries—by which I do not mean simply constraints but also configurations, discursive configurations— delineate a set of possible meanings, or what I would rather call a horizon of meaning (for example, the horizon of meaning or range of experiential contents conveyed by the single English word *mother-hood* has been significantly expanded and shifted by Adrienne Rich's book *Of Woman Born*).

The notion of a feminist discourse, a configuration of rhetorical and interpretive strategies, a horizon of possible meanings that may be agreed upon as constituting and defining feminism at a given historical juncture, is important in view of the tendency to equate women and feminism to which most of us have acquiesced, feminists and not, if for different reasons. As Linda Gordon states in her essay in this volume, femaleness and feminist consciousness are not equivalent terms:

"There are traditions of female thought, women's culture, and female consciousness that are not feminist. . . . The female is ourselves, our bodies and our socially constructed experience. It is not the same as feminism, which is not a 'natural' excretion of that experience but a controversial political interpretation and struggle, by no means universal to women."

However, if we take seriously the implications of one of the original insights of the women's movement (and one of the terms of the feminist discourse), that the personal is political, that there is a direct relation, however complex it may be, between sociality and subjectivity, between language and consciousness, or between institutions and individuals—in other words, if the political is also personal, then the discursive boundaries of feminism must correspond for each and all of us, according to our histories, to certain subjective limits.[4] Again I do not mean just limitations, but rather configurations of subjectivity, patterns by which experiential and emotional contents, feelings, images, and memories are organized to form one's self-image, one's sense of self and others, and of our possibilities of existence. Thus, to return and add to Gordon's statement, if feminism is not a "natural" consequence of being female (and surely it is not), it nevertheless may contribute, as a social discourse and a political practice, to the "socially constructed experience" of women. The relation of experience to discourse, finally, is what is at issue in the definition of feminism.

In this respect, going back to the semantic shift in the term *motherhood*, I would offer as an example the further shift accomplished by Alice Walker's essay "A Child of One's Own," as it resonates within Virginia Woolf's *Room of One's Own* and expands it beyond the confines of an alternative—either children or writing—that most women not only are forced to make but deeply believe we are forced to make.[5] And Jessica Benjamin, in her essay in this volume, again reshapes the configuration of feminist discourse as she answers the famous question, What does the woman want? with "A Desire of One's Own." Elaborating the relation of mothering to intersubjective space, Benjamin proposes it as a nonphallic model of psychic organization in which woman's desire may be more adequately accounted for. Of course, one's possibilities of existence are not simply the effect of one's subjective limits and discursive boundaries; but neither can they be simply attributed to an immutable deployment of socioeconomic forces that will be changed some day when conditions are right. The change must occur now, indeed is occurring now, if we look to see it; that is to say, if we consider the notion of change at certain levels of abstraction and not others. And one way in which change can be seen to occur, though not necessarily in the direction one expected or wants, is through discourses and representations, which actually and concretely affect the lives of people.

In a paper delivered at the Modern Language Association in 1978 and subsequently published with the title "The Straight Mind," Monique Wittig argued that if the discourses of modern theory and social science exert a power upon us, it is because they work with "concepts which closely touch us."

> These discourses speak about us and claim to say the truth in an apolitical field, as if anything of that which signifies could escape the political in this moment of history, and as if, in what concerns us, politically insignificant signs could exist. These discourses of heterosexuality oppress us in the sense that they prevent us from speaking unless we speak in their terms. Everything which puts them into question is at once disregarded as elementary. Our refusal of the totalizing interpretation of psychoanalysis makes the theoreticians say that we neglect the symbolic dimension. These discourses deny us every possibility of creating our own categories. But their most ferocious action is the unrelenting tyranny that they exert upon our physical and mental selves.
>
> When we use the overgeneralizing term "ideology" to designate all the discourses of the dominating group, we relegate these discourses to the domain of Irreal Ideas, we forget the material (physical) violence that they directly do to the oppressed people, a violence produced by the abstract and "scientific" discourses as well as by the discourses of the mass media. I would like to insist on the material oppression of individuals by discourses.[6]

Wittig's lucid analysis makes altogether apparent why the definition of feminism and the effects of institutionalization (both the pressure and the resistance to it) are related and very important issues for feminists to address. There are, of course, many other pressing issues for feminists, and they are being addressed in other contexts (through the courts, in the media, in the workplace, in communities and neighborhoods), and they are being addressed with other tactics, with different forms of resistance to different kinds of pressure. But for those of us who work with words, ideas, and other tools of formal knowledge, who know both the high price and the negotiability of discourses (that is to say, how discourses—including those of feminism or attributed to feminism—can be traded in the intellectual stock exchange), for us, then, it is imperative that we confront these issues.

What are feminist studies, really? What constitutes a feminist critical framework? Is feminism a mode of production of knowledge—social, aesthetic, and formal knowledge, as well as personal or common knowledge? Is there one feminist discourse, and if so, what characterizes it, and can it too be materially oppressive to some women? Or are there, rather, a variety of discourses, several "feminisms," as many now prefer to say? But if so, the question still remains, What indeed makes them feminist? And finally, how is feminist theory—a term that is used both loosely and narrowly to designate several distinct views and political positions—implicated in institutional discourses, power relations, and ideology?

These are the larger questions under which come more specific areas of debate: the debate on culturalism vs. biologism in the social sciences, where nature and culture continue to up the antes on each other; the issue of "identity politics" with the attendant problems of racism and anti-Semitism in the representation and definition of feminism; the difficult relation of feminist scholarship to the practice-oriented component of the women's movement, a relation often summed up (falsely, in my opinion) as an opposition of theory to practice; or the even more insidious opposition between theoreticism and empiricism, where accusations of jargon, bad writing, or elitism from one camp are met with counteraccusations of essentialism and unsophisticated thinking by the other.

These debates make us uncomfortable because they give incontrovertible evidence that sisterhood is powerful but difficult, and not achieved; that feminism itself, the most original of what we can call "our own cultural creations," is not a secure or stable ground but a highly permeable terrain infiltrated by subterranean waterways that cause it to shift under our feet and sometimes to turn into a swamp. The conflicting claims that are made for feminism, no less than the appropriation of feminist strategies and conceptual frames within "legitimate" discourses or by other critical theories, make us uncomfortable because we know and fear what they signal to us beyond a doubt: the constant drive on the part of institutions (in which, like it or not, feminists are also engaged) to deflect radical resistance and to recuperate it as liberal opposition. And the proven most effective means to that end is what Flo Kennedy, speaking in Milwaukee a few months ago, called "horizontal violence," the in-fighting among members of an oppressed group. Granted that, among women, such horizontal violence is verbal rather than physical, and that the fine line between in-fighting and critical debate is often too fine to know for sure; nevertheless, Wittig's point on "the material oppression of individuals by discourses" must apply here, as well, and should be kept on the front burner of a feminist political consciousness in one with the issue of power.[7]

In the final instance, however, within the discursive boundaries of feminism, these debates seem to me ultimately productive, because they sustain and nourish the practice of self-criticism, or better, perhaps, self-consciousness, as the Italian feminists call what in the United States we used to call "consciousness raising" and have now abandoned since that term, too, has been appropriated and devalued by the media. But the practice of self-consciousness, which, according to Catharine MacKinnon, is the "critical method" of feminism, its specific mode of knowledge as political apprehension of self in reality, continues to be essential to feminism.[8] It continues to be essential, that is, if feminism is to continue to be a political critique of society. Even more important, or more to the immediate point, the practice of self-consciousness—of reading, speaking, and listening to one another—is the best way we have precisely to resist horizontal violence without acquiescing to institutional recuperation, the best way we know to analyze our differences and contradictions even as we accept, as we must, the liberal allocation of a tiny amount of "equal" time in which to present our "opposing viewpoint."

As the history of revolutionary movements in this century has shown, and as the most recent developments in feminist theory confirm beyond a doubt (developments that have been prompted by the writings of women of color, Jewish women, and lesbians, and that can be sustained only by a serious, critical, and self-critical attention to the issues they raise), consciousness is not the result but the term of a process. Consciousness of self, like class consciousness or race consciousness (e.g., my consciousness of being white), is a particular configuration of subjectivity, or subjective limits, produced at the intersection of meaning with experience. (I have never, before coming to this country, been conscious of being white; and the meaning, the sense of what it means to be white has changed for me greatly over the years.) In other words, these different forms of consciousness are grounded, to be sure, in one's personal history; but that history—one's identity—is interpreted or reconstructed by each of us within the horizon of meanings and knowledges available in the culture at given historical moments, a horizon that also includes modes of political commitment and struggle. Self and identity, in other words, are always grasped and understood within particular discursive configurations. Consciousness, therefore, is never fixed, never attained once and for all, because discursive boundaries change with historical conditions.

In this perspective, the very notion of identity undergoes a shift: identity is not the goal but rather the point of departure of the process of self-consciousness, a process by which one begins to know that and how the personal is political, that and how the subject is specifically and materially en-gendered in its social conditions and possibilities of existence. As it is articulated in the context of the debate on identity politics, and most vividly in the essays by Elly Bulkin, Minnie Bruce Pratt, and Barbara Smith in *Yours in Struggle,* this feminist concept of identity is not at all the statement of an essential nature of Woman, whether defined biologically or philosophically, but rather a political-personal strategy of survival and resistance that is also, at the same time, a critical practice *and* a mode of knowledge. As Biddy Martin and Chandra Mohanty show in their "Feminist Politics: What's Home Got to Do with It?", a close reading of Pratt's autobiographical essay, the search for identity may be, in fact, a "rewriting" of self "in relation to shifting interpersonal and political contexts": in other words, a recasting of the notion that the personal is political which does not simply equate and collapse the two ("the personal is the same as the political," which in practice translates into "the personal instead of the political") but maintains the tension between them precisely through the understanding of identity as multiple and even self-contradictory.

It seems to me that this notion of identity points to a more useful conception of the subject than the one proposed by neo-Freudian psychoanalysis and poststructuralist theories. For it is not the fragmented, or intermittent, identity of a subject constructed in division by language alone, an "I" continuously prefigured and preempted in an unchangeable symbolic order. It is neither, in short, the imaginary identity of the individualist, bourgeois subject, which is male and white; nor the "flickering" of the posthumanist Lacanian subject, which is too nearly white and at best (fe)male. What is emerging in feminist writings is, instead, the concept of a multiple, shifting, and often self-contradictory identity, a subject that is not divided in, but rather at odds with, language; an identity made up of heterogeneous and heteronomous representations of gender, race, and class, and often indeed across languages and cultures; an identity that one decides to reclaim from a history of multiple assimilations, and that one insists on as a strategy: "I think," writes Elly Bulkin, "of all the women [of mixed heritage] who, told to choose between or among identities, insist on selecting all."[9] Representing the conditions of existence of those subjects who are muted, elided, or unrepresentable in dominant discourses, this new understanding of the nature of identity actually opens up the possibility to "set about creating something else to be," as Toni Morrison writes of her two heroines in *Sula*: "Because each had discovered years before that they were neither white nor male, and that all freedom and triumph was forbidden to them, they had set about creating something else to be."[10]

The emergent conception of a gendered and heteronomous subject (subject in the two senses of the term: both subject-ed to social constraint and yet subject in the active sense of maker as well as user of culture, intent on self-definition and self-determination), and of a subject that is *initially* defined by its consciousness of oppression (of multiple oppression), is an instance of the epistemological shift effected by feminism. By epistemological shift I mean a new way of thinking about culture, language, art, experience, and knowledge itself that, in redefining the nature and boundaries of the political, at once addresses women as social subject and en-genders the subject as political.

Here is where, to my mind, feminism differs from other contemporary modes of radical, critical or creative thinking, such as postmodernism and philosophical antihumanism: feminism defines itself as a political instance, not merely a sexual politics but a politics of experience, of everyday life, which later then in turn enters the public sphere of expression and creative practice, displacing aesthetic hierarchies and generic categories, and which thus establishes the semiotic ground for a different production of reference and meaning. That we see in feminist critical writings and other artistic practices, such as women's filmmaking. I would argue, in this regard, that the feminist critical text, the rereading against the grain of the "master works" of Western culture and the textual construction (written, filmic, etc.) of discursive spaces in which not Woman but women are represented and addressed as subjects, possessed of both a specificity (gender) and a history, is an original "cultural creation" of feminism; more, perhaps, than a new genre of (critical/fictional) creative expression, it can be thought of as a new aesthetic, a rewriting of culture.[11]

As we look back on the history of feminism over the past two decades, then, we can trace the permanence of certain critical terms, such as the emphasis on subjectivity and the centrality of gender to any account of social processes, but we can also see developments or shifts in them, as well as other, equally fundamental concepts. Identity and consciousness are being redefined substantially, as I have briefly indicated. The notion of a gendered, heterogeneous, and heteronomous subject, which has been worked through initially in relation to questions of spectatorship (in feminist film theory) and of reading and writing as women (in literary theory and criticism), is achieving definition in the retelling of stories: retelling well-known stories in order to destabilize the literary and scientific myths of origin, as Gilbert and Gubar do in *The Madwoman in the Attic,* for example, or as Donna Haraway does in her critique of primatology; and in the telling of new stories so as to inscribe into the picture of reality characters and events and resolutions that were previously invisible, untold, unspoken (and so unthinkable, unimaginable, "impossible").[12]

Another crucial point of revision in the history of feminist thought is, of course, the notions of sexuality and sexual difference, which have been all along the basis of the critique of representation, not just in the media and the visual arts but also in scientific discourses, jurisprudence, and so forth. Currently, the question of sexuality and the terms in which the question should be posed are one of the areas of least consensus among feminists. While I shall not attempt to outline this particular debate, as it is not directly addressed in the volume, still a couple of remarks may be in order. First, among the many critical issues raised by feminism, sexuality or sexual difference and subjectivity are the ones that other critical discourses have more readily engaged or taken up—not to say appropriated, which I suspect is the correct way to put it. I will suggest, in a moment, that proper distinctions should be maintained. Second, I strongly feel that even within the discursive boundaries of feminism, the notion of sexual difference needs to be seriously reconsidered. And this second point is in part a consequence of the first.

The specificity of feminism as a political-theoretical project becomes apparent as we compare it with other current discourses on sexuality and subjectivity, from the Foucauldian notion of the "technology of sex" to the various antioedipal desiring machines, libidinal economies, and postmodern antiaesthetics: discourses that, not unlike traditional Marxist humanism, regard "the woman question" as merely one moment of a broader movement for "human" liberation. But much less rigorously than the latter, and indeed with amazing facility, these discourses lump women together with children and slaves, madmen and poets, and go so far as to include in such chaotic typology the entire "Third World."

My guess is that, if antihumanism so badly needs to claim feminism in its ranks, it is because of that epistemological priority which feminism has located in the personal, the subjective, the body, the symptomatic, the quotidian, as the very site of material inscription of the ideological; that is to say, the ground where socio-political determinations take hold and are real-ized. That, in the last instance, is what is at stake in the critique of humanism, liberal or Marxist, a stake that both feminism and antihumanism have in common. But for feminism, and for women, the centrality of subjectivity and sexuality is not merely the sign of a crisis of reason, a proof of the failure of instrumental rationality in late capitalism; nor is "the end of politics" a useful feminist conceit. On the contrary, while it may be served by the critique of humanism and of its institutions, from metaphysics to metadiscourse, feminism differs from philosophical antihumanism in that it remains very much a politics of everyday life. The edge is there: the sense of struggle, the weight of oppression and contradiction. The stakes, for women, are rooted in the body—which is not to say that the body escapes representation, but quite the opposite.

The body is continually and inevitably caught up in representation. It is, of course, the supreme object of representation for the visual arts, the medical sciences, the capitalist media industry, and several related social practices from organized sports to individual jogging; even the unconscious and its drives cannot be grasped except in their particular processes of representation through the body. But, again, what is at stake for women in the received representations of the body, no less than in representations of the subject or subjectivity, is the definition of the pivotal notion that supports them all, the definition of sexual difference.

In the view currently popular, the meaning of sexual difference is posed in terms of an opposition—nature or culture, biology or socialization—that seems progressive or "liberated" but is, in fact, only inches away from the infamous anatomy-destiny idea. For merely to say that sexual difference is "cultural" allows no greater understanding of female subjectivity, and of women's actual and real differences, than to believe it to be "natural." And that is so since all accepted definitions of cultural, social, and subjective processes start from the same assumption: that sexual difference is the difference from man, the difference of woman from man—man being the measure, standard, or term of reference of all legitimated discourse. See, in this regard, Mary Russo's discussion in this volume of recent theories of masquerade, carnival, and performance which, on the one hand, hinge on the idea of femininity and the representation of the female body, while, on the other, they either disregard the social implications of gender or claim femininity as a mask, style, or support of male subjectivity. Put another way, even as they assert that sexual difference is culturally produced, the discourses of science, philosophy, and literary and critical theory concern themselves, finally, only with the production of Oedipus (or anti-Oedipus).

That is precisely what Wittig, in the essay I cited earlier, refers to as "the straight mind": the kind of thinking that "produces the difference between the sexes as a political and philosophical dogma." The "heterosexual contract," in her terms, or what Adrienne Rich has called "compulsory heterosexuality," is not merely a question of who's sleeping with whom, but the deeply held and embedded assumption that "what founds society, any society, is heterosexuality."[13] No matter that in recent theories, Wittig writes, "there is no such thing as nature, that everything is culture. There remains within that culture a core of nature which defies examination, a relationship excluded from the social in the analysis—a relationship whose characteristic is its ineluctability in culture, as well as nature, [and that is] the obligatory social relation between 'man' and 'woman' " (p. 107).

A feminist frame of reference, therefore, it seems to me, cannot be either "man" or "woman," for both of these are constructs of a male-centered discourse, both are products of "the straight mind." If the goal of feminist theory is to define sexual difference for women, to understand how one becomes a woman, and what gives femaleness (rather than femininity) its meaning as the experience of a female subject, then the starting point can be neither "man" nor "woman": neither the Man with the capital M of humanism, or the lower-case man of modernism; nor, on the other hand, woman as the opposite or the complement of man: Woman as Nature, Mother, Body, and Matter, or woman as style, figure, or metaphor of man's femininity.

As the discourse on sexuality becomes institutionalized in the academy, in the literary critical disciplines, Hortense Spillers has observed, the meaning of sexual difference "threatens to lose its living and palpable connection to training in the feelings and to become, rather, a mode of theatre for the dominating mythologies."[14] Sexuality is a term of power, Spillers says, and it belongs to the empowered. For this reason, the (white) feminist discourse on sexuality "flirts with the concealment of the activity of sex by way of an exquisite dance of textual priorities and successions, revisions and corrections." For this reason, it can ignore the compelling connection between sexuality and the requirements of survival that is the perceived reality of those women whom class and status do not protect. For insofar as we can speak or think of sexuality as something in itself, "as an isolated ontological detail" (in Spillers's phrase), we are to some extent protected. And it is women so protected by class or white-skin privilege who have laid out the terms of the critical discourse on sexuality along the tracks of a single option: either to perform (and yield to) the seductions of the father-text (in that "exquisite dance of textual priorities") or to stake out a territory in the wilderness and colonize it as an "empire of women."[15] For Spillers, neither of these models will do. I fully agree with her.

What that amounts to saying, in effect, is that an all-purpose feminist frame of reference does not exist, nor should it ever come prepackaged and ready-made. We need to keep building one, absolutely flexible and readjustable, from women's own experience of difference, of our difference from Woman and of the differences among women; differences which, as the essays by Sondra O'Neale, Sheila Radford-Hill, and Cherríe Moraga in this volume argue and document, are perceived as having as much (or more) to do with race, class, or ethnicity as with gender or sexuality per se.[16] However, if I am not mistaken in suggesting, as I did above, that a new conception of the subject is, in fact, emerging from feminist analyses of women's heterogeneous subjectivity and multiple identity, then I would further suggest that the differences among women may be better understood as differences within women. For if it is the case that the female subject is en-gendered across multiple representations of class, race, language, and social relations, it is also the case (and the essays document that, too) that gender is a common denominator: the female subject is always constructed and defined in gender, starting from gender. In this sense, therefore, if differences among women are also differences within women, not only does feminism exist despite those differences, but, most important, as we are just now beginning to realize, it cannot continue to exist without them.

Again I see a shift, a development, and I do hope I'm not mistaken, in the feminist understanding of female subjectivity: a shift from the earlier view of woman defined purely by sexual difference (i.e., in relation to man) to the more difficult and complex notion that the female subject is a site of differences; differences that are not only sexual or only racial, economic, or (sub)cultural, but all of these together, and often enough at odds with one another. These differences, which are no less intensely felt for being addressed or confronted, as they are now beginning to be, remain concretely embedded in social and power relations; they coexist concurrently with (though perhaps no longer in spite of) the provisional unity of any concerted political action or coalition. But once articulated and understood in their constitutive power—once it is understood, that is, that these differences not only constitute each woman's consciousness and subjective limits but all together define *the female subject of feminism* in its very specificity, its inherent and at least for now irreconcilable contradiction—these differences, then, cannot be again collapsed into a fixed identity, a sameness of all women as Woman, or a representation of Feminism as a coherent and available image.

The image of feminism as a coherent ideology, a set of dogmas and rules of conduct repressive to some and oppressive to others, has currency inside, as well as outside, the discursive boundaries of feminism. And this image, too, of a homogeneous, monolithic Feminism—whether white or black or Third World, whether mainstream or separatist, academic or activist—is something that must be resisted. Very importantly, for example, in their contribution to this volume, Martin and Mohanty challenge the assumption "that the terms of a totalizing feminist discourse *are adequate* [their emphasis] to the task of articulating the situation of white women in the West. We would contest that assumption and argue that the reproduction of such polarities [i.e., West/East, white/nonwhite] only serves to concede 'feminism' to the 'West' all over again."

For one thing, that "feminism" is a facile, reductive, easily saleable image, serving the purposes of those who stand outside or do not stand to gain from feminism. For another, however, it is built in part from ambiguities and actual conflicts internal to the women's movement; from the personal disaffection of some women, who have nevertheless remained politically active (black women such as Bell Hooks, white women such as Sheila Delany, for example); and from the writings of others who, keeping up with fashion, declare feminism outmoded and themselves "postfeminists." And, lastly, it has been buttressed by the self-complacency of the many feminists who would seem to wish to avoid the emotional and intellectual pains of contradiction and confrontation by averting eyes and ears from the surrounding world.[17]

Another aim of this volume, therefore, is to resist that image of Feminism by looking at the ambiguities, conflicts, and paradoxes that distinguish and differentiate women from men and from ourselves, and by articulating the various, interwoven strands of a tension, a condition of contradiction, that for the time being, at least, will not be reconciled.

The essays in this book are arranged in a sequence roughly following the contributors' primary areas of research: history, science, literary writing, criticism, and theory. Again, reflecting a marked emphasis of the conference project, the political dimension of feminist studies is an explicit concern throughout the volume, and, with regard to their concrete results or their political effectiveness, the opinions expressed vary from the more doubtful or cautionary to the more hopeful or encouraging. Different stances are taken, and arguments develop among essays within a single area, such as history or literary criticism, white and black; but there is also productive interchange or borrowing across disciplines, for instance, science from literary theory, literary criticism from history, and vice versa.

The relation of feminism to other critical discourses is specifically addressed in several of the essays. For example, what may distinguish a feminist understanding of "reading as a woman" from the meaning and ideological agenda the phrase has acquired in the discourse of deconstruction, is forcefully argued by Tania Modleski's essay on interpretation, itself a critical (one might say deconstructive) reading of feminist and other readings. Again for example, the effects of a double temporality of intellectual history, which unfolds concurrently—and discontinuously—in "women's time" of feminist criticism and in "the Eastern Standard time" of traditional scholarship, are keenly observed by Nancy K. Miller in her dual-language reading (so to speak) of Roland Barthes and Adrienne Rich. Or, again, the possibility that "psychoanalytic feminism" may have at last metamorphosed into a feminist psychoanalysis is not the least of the implications of Jessica Benjamin's painstaking review of that long-standing and uneasy relationship.

Whether or not the inscription of subjectivity in the text necessitates modernist or avant-garde techniques, as Kristeva and others claim, or whether realism is still alive in this postmodern age; how the scientific text can be seen as an open book and yet hide the secrets of an invisible voice; how language, class, and gender mutually affect one another; how feminism can provide a model for social change by redefining notions of home and family, community and liminality, self and other; whether sexuality may be redeployed against its own social technology (in Foucault's terms) for progressive political ends, or even whether "women on top" may be a viable model (in the words of Natalie Davis quoted by Mary Russo) of "riot and political disobedience for both men and women"—these are some of the other questions raised by the essays.

Rich and Barthes are by no means the only unlikely pairing to be encountered in these pages. Other unwonted connections are made, as well as references to names seldom indexed in volumes of critical studies. Freud is here, to be sure, as is Lacan, and so is Mitchell, but not at center stage; Bakhtin, on the other hand, has two curtain calls.

Alice Walker and Toni Morrison are cited more frequently than James Joyce, Irigaray more than Nietzsche, de Beauvoir (as might have been expected) more than Sartre. More equal time is given Elaine Showalter than Jonathan Culler; Rosalind Franklin receives at least as much attention as James Watson; and, rather unexpectedly, Derrida shares the last laugh with Yvonne Rainer. No mention is made of Hegel, Heidegger, or Althusser. That said, however, I want to conclude by briefly pointing out what this book does for me, its editor, and now reader.

Reading the essays again, in the completed manuscript, I am compelled to return to some of my earlier introductory statements, for in the meantime, it seems, the ground has shifted, and the text I thought I read from the conference has recomposed itself almost under my eyes. Themes and motifs, phrases, quotations, references recur from one essay to the others and resonate intertextually, insistently, taking on new possibilities of meaning, sketching the boundaries of a theoretical horizon not quite the same as before.

Differences. Identity. Take those two terms *mask* and *masquerade,* which reappear conspicuously and are both meant, worn as they are, as weapons of survival. But the former is there to represent a burden, imposed, constraining the expression of one's real identity; the latter is flaunted, or, if not, at least put on like a new dress which, even when required, does give some pleasure to the wearer. *Mask* and *masquerade* are the terms of different demands (though I will not say of different desires). Verisimilitude, realism, positive images are the demands that women of color make of their own writing as critical and political practice; white women demand instead simulation, textual performances, double displacements. That—considering that the political, the personal, and the tension between them are foregrounded by each and all of the critics in question—is difference indeed. However, I would not say that *mask* and *masquerade* are terms inscribing different desires; to me they both are signs of the same need for, and a very similar drive toward, the representation of a subjectivity that, however diverse its sociohistorical configurations and modes of expression, has come into its own as political consciousness.

Thus, it may be sobering for some of us, and even reassuring, after the topsy-turvy "carnival of theory," to be reminded that the signifier does not endlessly rush on toward the abyss of nonmeaning, and that there is a referent, the real world, after all. For others, perhaps, an inside view of the division, contradiction, and internal constraints that prompt the masquerade, or that make up even the images we may perceive as positive, may be empowering in some way. Or so I hope. That I would rather look, myself, to the kind of image of identity that Martin and Mohanty see in Pratt's political autobiography is undoubtedly the effect of my personal history, of my own cultural, geographic, social, and sexual displacements. And to the extent that I can see beyond and through that history by knowing the ways of other(s') histories, the project of this book has been, for me, empowering. It is more than editorial correctness, therefore, that makes me end this introduction with the words of others who have enabled me to see beyond my history through them:

> We don't have to be the same to have a movement, but we *do* have to admit our fear and pain and be accountable for our ignorance. In the end, finally, we must refuse to give up on each other.[18]

N O T E S

1. Adrienne Rich, "Toward a Woman-Centered University," in *On Lies, Secrets, and Silence: Selected Prose, 1966-1978* (New York: W. W. Norton, 1979), p. 126.

2. Audre Lorde, "The Master's Tools Will Never Dismantle the Master's House," in *Sister Outsider: Essays and Speeches* (Trumansburg, N. Y.: Crossing Press, 1984), p. 111.

3. Sheila Rowbotham, *Woman's Consciousness, Man's World* (Harmondsworth: Penguin Books, 1973), p. 28.

4. I owe the terms *discursive boundaries* and *subjective limits* to Kaja Silverman's analysis of the work of a West German feminist filmmaker. See Kaja Silverman, "Helke Sander and the Will to Change," *Discourse*, no. 6 (Fall 1983), pp. 10-30.

5. Alice Walker's essay, in her *In Search of Our Mothers' Gardens* (San Diego: Harcourt Brace Jovanovich, 1983), responds not only to Woolf but also to Tillie Olsen's analysis of writing and mothering in *Silences* (New York: Dell Publishing Co., 1965, 1972, 1978).

6. Monique Wittig, "The Straight Mind," *Feminist Issues* 1 (Summer 1980): 105-106.

7. A good example of how fine that line can be is the volume produced from the 1982 Barnard conference, "Towards a Politics of Sexuality," and appropriately titled *Pleasure and Danger: Exploring Female Sexuality,* ed. Carole S. Vance (Boston: Routledge and Kegan Paul, 1984).

8. Catharine A. MacKinnon, "Feminism, Marxism, Method, and the State: An Agenda for Theory," *Signs* 7, no. 3 (Spring 1982): 515-44. This particular point is made on p. 535.

9. Elly Bulkin, "Hard Ground: Jewish Identity, Racism, and Anti-Semitism," in Elly Bulkin, Minnie Bruce Pratt, and Barbara Smith, *Yours in Struggle: Three Feminist Perspectives on Anti-Semitism and Racism* (Brooklyn, N. Y.: Long Haul Press, 1984), p. 106.

10. Toni Morrison, *Sula* (New York: Bantam Books, 1975), p. 44.

11. I have begun developing these ideas, so far only in relation to feminist filmmaking in "Aesthetic and Feminist Theory: Rethinking Women's Cinema," *New German Critique*, no. 34 (Winter 1985), pp. 154–75.

12. Sandra Gilbert and Susan Gubar, *The Madwoman in the Attic: The Woman Writer and the Nineteenth-Century Literary Imagination* (New Haven: Yale University Press, 1979); Donna Haraway, "Teddy-Bear Patriarchy," *Social Text*, no. 11 (Winter 1984–85), pp. 20–64. As for the telling of new stories, suffice it to mention recent feminist fiction, such as Alice Walker's *The Color Purple*, autobiographical essays such as those of *Yours in Struggle,* or Audre Lorde's *Zami: A New Spelling of My Name,* and, of course, the feminist science fiction of Joanna Russ or Alice Sheldon (alias James Tiptree, Jr.).

13. Wittig, "Straight Mind," p. 105. Adrienne Rich, "Compulsory Hetero-sexuality and Lesbian Existence," *Signs* 5, no. 4 (1980): 631–60.

14. Hortense J. Spillers, "Interstices: A Small Drama of Words," in Vance, *Pleasure and Danger,* p. 79.

15. Spillers, "Interstices," p. 81. The latter project is outlined, for example, in Elaine Showalter, "Feminist Criticism in the Wilderness," *Critical Inquiry* special issue: *Writing and Sexual Difference,* ed. Elizabeth Abel, vol. 8, no. 2 (Winter 1981), pp. 179–205.

16. See also Gloria I. Joseph and Jill Lewis, *Common Differences: Conflicts in Black and White Feminist Perspectives* (Garden City, N. Y.: Anchor Books, 1981); *This Bridge Called My Back: Writings by Radical Women of Color,* ed. Cherríe Moraga and Gloria Anzaldúa (New York: Kitchen Table: Women of Color Press, 1983); *Nice Jewish Girls: A Lesbian Anthology,* ed. Evelyn Torton Beck (Trumansburg, N. Y.: Crossing Press, 1982); *All the Women Are White, All the Blacks Are Men, But Some of Us Are Brave: Black Women's Studies,* ed. Gloria T. Hull, Patricia Bell Scott, and Barbara Smith (Old Westbury, N. Y.: Feminist Press, 1982); E. Frances White, "Listening to the Voices of Black Feminism," *Radical America* 18, no. 2–3 (1984): 7–25; and Chela Sandoval, *Women Respond to Racism,* Occasional Paper Series "The Struggle Within," published by the Center for Third World Organizing, 4228 Telegraph Avenue, Oakland, CA 94609, n.d.

17. For Bell Hooks, see chap. 1 of *Feminist Theory: From Margin to Center* (Boston: South End Press, 1984); for Sheila Delany, see chap. 1 of *Writing Woman: Women Writers and Women in Literature, Medieval to Modern* (New York: Schocken Books, 1983). The last category is too large for this footnote, but some references will be given in the following essays. As for "postfem-inists," the reference would hardly be relevant to a volume such as this.

18. Cherríe Moraga, Julia Perez, Barbara Smith, and Beverly Smith, quoted by Elly Bulkin in Bulkin, Pratt, and Smith, *Yours in Struggle,* p. 151.

What's New in Women's History

Linda Gordon

1

The question raised by this conference brought me to a surprising conclusion: that the feminist reconstitution of knowledge no longer seems to me so radical a break as it once did. In history, and probably in other fields, as well, our critiques of old scholarship, and our attempts to construct a new scholarship, seem to me rather to follow in paths already opened. That does not, I think, belittle or weaken the feminist contribution. On the contrary, the emphasis on the uniqueness and novelty of what we are doing may reflect the bravado of inadequate confidence.

In attempting to reconstruct history, feminists do no more and no less than many groups battling for political power have done before. If history is the king of the political arts, its power to legitimate sovereignty is frequently under attack and must constantly be defended. From the classical world to Tudor England to the Reagan administration, ideologues write and rewrite histories of their imperialisms, successions, and legitimacy, with an eye to raising money for armies. Opponents counterattack, now scoring points as the rulers reveal their hypocrisy, now writhing in helplessness, unable to reach the masses with their counterarguments. The stakes may be higher today, but the ability of the dynasties to buy historians is greater, too.

Naming the new women's history "herstory" does us no favor. Implying that we are the first to fight this ideological battle deprives us of a history we already have. Indeed, I would venture to say that the rhetoric of the uniqueness of our intellectual project reflects a growing distance of scholars from the totalizing tendencies of a strong political feminist movement, and its desire to incorporate, even to subsume, other radical traditions. But most historiographical progress—perhaps most intellectual progress—proceeds by rearranging relationships within old stories, not by writing new stories. The old stories have been ours, too—women's, not only men's—although that is a contested point, and I will return to argue it shortly.

I hardly need to mention that the feminist retellings of the past are stimulated by feminist political challenges to present-day structures and relationships. I may, however, need to mention that there was a first wave of women's history in the late nineteenth and early twentieth centuries. If this first wave was forgotten, it was not because it was modest. Elizabeth Cady Stanton reinterpreted the Bible. Alice Clark began to rewrite the rise of capitalism. Their influence was negligible, but within the academy the evidence is not overwhelming that we have had much more influence in the last decade. I respond with a cold sweat when I remember how completely this first wave of history was suppressed. When I became a feminist and began, with a group of historians turned feminist, to find out something about women's situation in the past, I discovered these books, dusty, in the Widener library stacks, untouched for decades. It is not good for the ego to contemplate a similar fate for one's own work. Only the continued existence of a strong feminist movement will make our own work remembered long enough to contribute to other generations.

Because of the hiatus in the feminist political tradition, the new wave of women's historians had to regain some lost territory. For a second time we had first to render the invisible visible, the silent noisy, the motionless active. In doing so, we were answering a call from a massive and powerful women's liberation movement for useful myths and countermyths. Yet, and here is an optimistic sign, we left that task more quickly than our nineteenth-century ancestors did, they having produced scores of volumes of sketches of great women, descriptions of their country childhood, and tributes to their mothers. As historians, we were soon dissatisfied with myth making, perhaps because the movement that gave birth to us was less elite (as were, for many of us, our own social origins); we moved to less glorious and also more ambivalent analyses of the past. Very soon many women's historians, and no doubt other feminist scholars, experienced friction with (or, worse, distance from) the social movement that had given birth to their careers. It frequently happened to me that the women's movement offered questions and topics, but my answers did not confirm all the slogans I had helped write.

Existing in between a social movement and the academy, women's scholarship has a mistress and a master, and guess which one pays wages. Undermining to some extent the coopting effect of the academy, the rudeness with which women are treated there recreates some of the material conditions that provoked our social movement. But in history, at least, both academic and political impulses have been channeled at times into two different purposes, two poles of philosophical assumption and self-consciousness. One pole of energy, assimilated to the empiricism that dominated most history writing in this period, directed us to rectify past errors. Women's historians sought to proclaim a truth heretofore denied, disguised, distorted, defamed, and thereby to expose the meretricious lies of earlier mandarins. This goal, of course, presupposed the possibility of a truth, achieved through historical objectivity, and where this goal was dominant, women's historians used and assimilated the work of the new social history. Another pole, rejecting the possibility of objectivity and accepting the humanistic and story-telling function of history, stimulated us to create new myths to serve our aspirations.

I would like to find a method in between. This in-between would not imply resolution, careful balance of fact and myth, or synthesis of fact and interpretation. My sense of a liminal method is rather a condition of being constantly pulled, usually off balance, sometimes teetering wildly, almost always tense. The tension cannot be released. Indeed, the very desire to find a way to relax the tension is a temptation that must be avoided. Neither goal can be surrendered. It is wrong to conclude, as some have, that because there may be no objective truth possible, there are not objective lies. There may be no objective canons of historiography, but there are degrees of accuracy; there are better and worse pieces of history. The challenge is precisely to maintain this tension between accuracy and mythic power.

For the historian, the tension is further maintained by the nature of our sources. Among the particular constraints on the activity of producing history which embodies both truth and myth, is the finite, capricious, mottled nature of the evidence. Historians can be trained to creativity and imagination in the search for evidence, in sensitivity about what can constitute evidence, but we cannot always enlarge the available evidence through hard work or great intelligence. Moreover, we are not at ethical liberty to pick and choose among the shards available; our equivalent of the Hippocratic oath enjoins us to present all, or a representative sample, of the evidence relevant to a given inquiry; to search hard for the same; to seek out bits of evidence that might defeat our argument. These are neither outmoded nor unrealizable standards; nor are they standards inappropriate for feminists. They embody quite usefully the tension that we should seek to maintain between verifiable, fact-based truth and myth.

2

In our feminist version of this old task of reconstituting history, in negotiating between demands for truth and demands for myth, we encounter several issues at once old and new, feminist versions of traditional epistemological questions in history and politics. I would like to comment on four of them.

Domination and Resistance

In the history of women's history, the greatest of our contradictions has been that between domination and resistance. Sometimes we feel impelled to document oppression, diagram the structures of domination, specify the agents and authors of domination, mourn the damages. Sometimes we feel impelled to defend our honor and raise our spirits by documenting our struggles and identifying successes in mitigating the tyranny. Neither aspect corresponds uniquely to myth making; rather, we need different myths in different situations. In the history of women's history, Simone de Beauvoir and Mary Beard have stood respectively for each tendency, each with its shortcomings. In defining us as the other, de Beauvoir invited us to confront our pain, our jealousy of men, our humiliation. Her bravery was extraordinary. Mary Beard, much less well known, the clubwoman, the reformer, the no-nonsense capable matron, has been a far less attractive figure, because she wrote and embodied women's capability, not their fragility.

At other times the duality appears identified with the structure vs. agency debate in Marxism. This debate unfortunately has often been reduced to a schema in which structural analysis implies determination, while analysis in terms of human agency implies indeterminacy or contingency. Here, too, the dichotomy is not so neat. Usually it is the dominant groups who can have individual agency, while the subordinated appear locked in "structures." The feminist critique, like that of good labor history, demands the recognition of structure and agency on all sides of a power equation.

My impression is that despite the long history of this historiographical problem, historians today have difficulty writing interpretations of the past that encompass both domination and resistance. Structural analysis is presented as deterministic, while discussion of women's agency is misunderstood as victim blaming. Power itself becomes a pejorative. I remember some early second-wave feminist rhetoric and poetry calling for an end to power, indeed equating female beauty and kindness with the rejection of power; and I still read too many histories of female experience as powerless, which is false and impossible. To be less powerful is not to be power-less, or even to lose all the time. Analysis becomes moralistic rather than historical. Women's oppression is assumed to make us all angels, without character flaws.

Political or Social History: Redefining Power

A more recent contradiction in the new women's history is sometimes formulated as an argument between political and social history. To review a bit of the history of our discipline: once the only history was political or diplomatic (as studying interdynastic struggle has been called). It *was* history, by definition—the epics and apologia for kings. The age of democracy produced the so-called social history, a most revealing misnomer, for social means the *hoi polloi*, the commoners, we who have no individuality. At first social history was like imperialist, primitive anthropology: writers chronicled the quaint culinary, marital, and folk customs of the peasantry. Recently there have been a revival of social history and a contest for its meaning and purpose, in which historians on both ends of the continuum between fact and myth participate.

In the last few decades, particularly through developments in demography, social historians tended to study aspects of life seemingly removed from political domination. They studied household structure, marital patterns, friendships, childbirth. Political historians charged that the result was a romanticization of oppression. Eugene Genovese criticized some black history in this way. In women's history, the poles were identified as political and *cultural* history. Ellen DuBois, for example, criticized some of Carroll Smith-Rosenberg's work for photographing the positive aspects of the culture of the oppressed with a focus too close to show the framework: the prison bars.

Social or cultural historians have had several responses. One is, of course, that political historians still look only at the queens among us. Moreover, since the power of the rulers is far easier to see than the power of the ruled, the political/social history distinction tended to coincide with the domination/resistance dichotomy. Political historians charged that social history meant denial of oppression, constriction, suffering; social historians charged that political history missed the sources of popular cultural autonomy. It could hardly be true that the concept of a women's culture per se denies the problem of oppression. On the contrary, the imposition of concepts such as oppression often masks the specificity of women's own understanding of their condition.

Transcending this unproductive polarization requires, I think, that we integrate into the debate a critique of the definition of the political. If political is to do with power, there are ways in which the masses are involved in political activity and political relationships in their daily lives. There is no reason why questions of power, even the measurement of power, should not be fit into descriptions of, for example, women's writing, mothering, housework, or leisure. But here, too, I find that feminists cannot take unique credit for challenging definitions of the political as having to do with state power. Nonfeminist libertarian social theorists began the exposure of hidden forms of power, although male supremacy remained invisible to them; while many feminists have, as I just argued, denied power, which is just another way of mystifying and thus upholding it.

The responsibility to situate one's work in an adequate analysis of power relations is not merely a problem for historians. While all scholarly work, in these postencyclopedic days, requires some specialization and particularity, that does not mean that any scholarly topic, any unit of study, is legitimate. It is not legitimate to define a topic that by its very boundaries creates a distorted view of reality. I am reminded particularly of women's scholarship that begins with the caveat that only white, or only middle-class, women are here included, as if the statement justified the exclusion. Similarly, choosing topics or sources of information that allow us to see only domination or only areas of women's autonomy can be illegitimate. Our collective goal ought to be to advance a theoretical framework to our scholarship that transcends the victim/heroine, domination/resistance dualism and incorporates the varied experiences of women. We need, I think, work that insists on presenting the complexity of the sources of power and weakness in women's lives.

Difference

In the 1980s, perhaps the dominant emphasis in women's studies scholarship has been on what is generally called "difference." I have severe reservations about this emphasis because I fear that "difference" is becoming a substitute, an accommodating, affable, and even lazy substitute, for opposition.

A development of the single greatest theoretical contribution of second-wave feminism, the notion of gender, *difference* is a code word that has now taken on two meanings. The primary meaning is that women have, according to discipline, a different voice, a different muse, a different psychology, a different experience of love, work, family, and goal. To varying degrees, all the disciplines have been involved in demonstrating not only the existence of that difference in experience but also the difference that recognizing it makes in the whole picture.

"Difference" may be hegemonic today, but it is not without critics, and it has not always defined feminist work. Feminist scholarship has another edge, examining the imposition of difference—i.e., gender— as a squeezing of possibility, and protesting the exclusion and sub-ordination of women in the name of our uniqueness. Different but equal may be the gender version of separate but equal. Indeed, the very notion of difference can function to obscure domination, to imply a neutral asymmetry. The difference motif is not characteristic of all disciplines: strong in literature, psychology, and philosophy, it by no means dominates in history, sociology, or anthropology. Moreover, the difference motif does not seem to me to have the same meanings in all disciplines or in all pieces of work. In some, the discovery of hidden voices dominates; in others, it becomes a language of dis-tinction, of dualism; in still others, it is used to define the nature of the feminine. Indeed, the meanings of difference can range from the essential to the trivial. In much historical and social-science work, for example, we are identifying the varying forms of labor and relations that produce certain patterns of response, making the difference a derivative rather than a primary category. Moreover, in other contexts, difference takes on another meaning, that of difference *among* women, a meaning nearly opposite in implication—but more on that later.

If one uses the notion of "difference" as an organizing principle, one can periodize the entire history of feminism in terms of the dom-ination, in alternation, of an androgynous and a female-uniqueness view of women's subordination and liberation. The eighteenth- and early-nineteenth-century Enlightenment feminists, religious *and* sec-ular, tended toward an androgynous vision of the fundamental hu-manity of men and women; that is, they emphasized the artificial imposition of femininity upon women as part of a system subordi-nating, constricting, and controlling them, with the result that "women," as a historically created category, had had their capacities as well as their aspirations reduced. By contrast, the later-nineteenth-century feminists tended toward a female moral superiority view. They applauded what was different in women, and while they were not always biologistic in their assumptions about how we became different, the process of differentiation was less interesting to them than the result: a world divided between a male principle of aggression and a female one of nurturance. Motherhood was for them the fundamental defining experience of womanhood.

In our second wave of feminism, a similar movement from androgyny to female uniqueness occurred. The early women's liberation movement, both radical and liberal, emphasized equal rights and equal access for women to previously male privilege. In the past decade, we have seen again a celebration of women's unique and superior qualities with, again, an emphasis on mothering as both source and ultimate expression of these qualities. But it is not as if an acute shift occurred from one perspective to another; rather, this duality persists continuously within feminism. Moreover, it can be described and evaluated according to one's point of view: one historian might see a conflict between libertarian opposition to gender and sentimental acceptance of a separate sphere for women; another might see it as male-stream abstract egalitarianism vs. the assertion of an alternate female value system. The implications of each perspective are also contextual. Denial of difference can mean inauthenticity, while assertion of difference can mean retreat from supporting women's transcendent aspirations. Put another way, love of difference can mean a retreat from anger at the limitation of possibility, while hatred of difference can mean self-hatred for women.

One of the worst things about the emphasis on difference is that it allows the development of new "fields" and the adoption of new styles of critique that do not fundamentally challenge the structure of the disciplines. It does not force the reinterpretation of all existing interpretation on the basis of new evidence but instead creates, potentially, pockets of women's literature, women's psychology, women's morality, and so forth. That is not an argument against separate women's studies programs; it is an argument about what should be the content of our women's studies.

Science, perhaps because it excludes women most determinedly, and perhaps also because it is the most violent and destructive of disciplines, has evoked the most radical critiques of its basic assumptions. I am skeptical about whether such critiques can be applied directly to history. Neither do I like the segregation of women's history, its establishment, so to speak, as the description of a parallel course on which women ran through time. One main reason women do not, did not, keep to a separate track is, of course, the institution of heterosexuality. Institutionalized heterosexuality simultaneously helps to create gender and thus difference, and set limits on that difference. Lesbians and straight women alike, we are members and participants in all sorts of heterosexual institutions—economic, educational, cultural, and commercial—which construct our identity, willy-nilly.

Women's history is not just different, it is critical; it is against men's history. One reason the discourse about difference matters so much is that through it, feminists debate the conceptions of domination and resistance. Both seem to me drained of their experience, of the ways in which they *matter* so much, when they are rephrased in terms of difference.

Another meaning of difference, which equally results from feminist debates about oppression and resistance, points to differences among women. It is directly related, and negatively so, to the first meaning of difference, for the emphasis on a *unique* female voice almost always becomes an assumption of a *homogeneous* female voice. Naturally, people get angry at arrogant uses of "we." The women's movement becomes several women's movements, both because new movements are stimulated by older ones and out of rage at the pretensions of some to speak for all—worse, at the replication of elitist patterns within our work and society. Thus, if the multiplicity and variety of feminist perspectives are a strength and a richness, they are also a reflection of inequality among women.

One response to this disunity has been a flowering of narratives of varieties of femaleness. Historians do that to some extent through the documentation of individual lives and collective conditions, visible particularly in the publication of many oral-history "biographies" and autobiographies. These works are supplying sources that other historians may incorporate into larger studies. But too often these narratives do not criticize the generalizations we have made about femaleness, and instead confine themselves to the assertion, in a liberal relativist way, of variety. Indeed, by implication, they sometimes deny the legitimacy of generalization. Too often the response to Afro-American women's analyses, for example, is a tolerant acceptance of difference rather than an attempt to *integrate* that experience as part of our whole approach to the study of women.

Methodology

Everything I have said so far skirts the issue of whether there is a feminist methodology and epistemology. In history writing, one could look for feminist or different female methods of 1) defining what counts as evidence, 2) collecting evidence, 3) generalizing from specifics, and 4) drawing conclusions. Only in the first category do I see any unique contribution—I repeat, I am speaking only of methodology—in women's history. But the question of what counts as evidence is far more substantive than methodological, really. I consider as evidence material once thought of as outside history—gossip, menstruation, latrines; but historians once considered black people outside history, too. Critics of science have raised the question of a gendered methodology most forcefully, but when applied to the social sciences or the humanities, a critique such as, say, Evelyn Keller's critique of male science is not clearly a uniquely female method. The incorporation of the subjectivity of the object of study is a theme that has been raised by sociologists, anthropologists, and historians for decades, men as well as women. It is a method that I recognize in my own work; I listen very hard to my subjects, and operate on the assumption that their own self-interpretation is likely as good as mine, or at least worth a respectful hearing. But that does not seem to me different from the methods employed by Herbert Gutman, say, in his reconstruction of slave families, or E. P. Thompson in his interpretations of working-class religion. Good historical listening embodies a critique of the concept of false consciousness. But this critique was raised by anti-Leninist socialists before we second-wave feminists argued it; and feminists have also been involved in branding disagreements as inauthentic.

3

I would like to clarify what I take to be the political import of what I am saying. In order to do that, my working definition of feminism, as a historian, needs to be specified. It is clear to me that an ahistorical, unchanging definition that posits a fixed content for feminism won't do, because it cuts us off from our tradition, or, rather, narrows that tradition to a part of itself. Feminism is a critique of male supremacy, formed and offered in the light of a will to change it, which in turn assumes a conviction that it is changeable. What counts as feminist is markedly different today from what was considered so two hundred years ago. Moreover, as I have argued, there is today a great variety within feminism, and we should expect, each of us, to disagree with much that is feminist. If every feminist scholar knew something of the history of the feminist tradition, that might serve as a corrective to dogmatism, if nothing else.

If there are contradictions within feminism, it should be understood that there are traditions of female thought, women's culture, and female consciousness that are not feminist. Female and feminist consciousness stand in complex relation to each other: clearly they overlap, for the female is the basis of the feminist, yet the feminist arises also out of a desire to escape the female. That seems to me an inescapable tension.

I have wanted to raise here a troubling question. Throughout various parts of feminist scholarship today, historical and otherwise, there is an attempt to reach a false resolution of the tension I have just defined, a resolution that would obliterate the distinction between the female and the feminist. It seems to me important to claim both. The female is ourselves, our bodies and our socially constructed experience. It is not the same as feminism, which is not a "natural" excretion of that experience but a controversial political interpretation and struggle, by no means universal to women. I find a tendency to celebrate the female and to distinguish ourselves as sharply as possible from the male, in method as well as substance. This tendency is then mixed with, and sometimes supported by, the inadequate integration of women's experience as victims of oppression with our own voluntary, responsible activity against it. I cannot evade the question whether a scholarship focused on liberation must not also criticize, and even reject, part of what is constituted female. If it does not, then we may be sacrificing the understanding of gender, reverting to an operating assumption that some eternal female principle defines our destiny beyond our control.

Writing History: Language, Class, and Gender

Carroll Smith-Rosenberg

Can one write about "Writing History" and not deal with the inter-action of writing and history, an interaction so methodologically and philosophically problematic? Writing presumes words, history the world that speaks them. Seemingly distinct, they form a seamless web, for how can we know the world except through the words it constructs? History offers us no exit from this circle of mutual referents, for history itself is part of the circle, a composite of words about words, a narrative of narratives.

Historians' growing sensitivity to the power of words, the product of an active interchange between historians and literary theorists, has greatly enhanced the subtlety with which we explore the past. But it has also encouraged historical nihilism, especially among creative and sophisticated historians. Medievalist Nancy Partner, for example, in a brilliant essay argues that "the whole of historical discourse is cal-culated to induce a sense of referential reality in a conceptual field with no external reference at all." Historical evidence, Partner sug-gests, consists of words arbitrarily imposed to make time into chro-nology, to turn the uncharted chaos of reality into a simple story complete with a beginning, a middle, and an end. It is almost always linguistic, some*one*'s story about reality. Even census returns, the basis of quantitative history, are linguistic constructs, often, Partner insists, relying on "arcane and unexplained measures and procedures" ex-pressed in terms the historian must retranslate. All historical evidence is but "the partial visibilia of an entire invisible world." For Partner, history has become "the definitive human audacity imposed on form-less time and meaningless event with the human meaning-maker lan-guage."[1]

How ironic if we historians, especially feminist historians, relinquish our grasp on the world behind the words just at the moment when feminist literary critics have begun to look beyond the words to study historical worlds. The text, they insist, can be understood only in terms of the world in which it was written, and read. They have proffered an important invitation to feminist historians, one that we cannot refuse. To do otherwise—to accept historical nihilism as posited by Nancy Partner, Hayden White, and others—would not only deny the knowability of the world, it would lose for us that aspect of the world we are most committed to knowing: women.[2] For women are more than the word *female* contained within (male) quotation marks.

How can feminist historians fascinated with words, and feminist critics intrigued by the world, collectively explore the female experience? We ourselves constitute literal nodes between words and the world. Rather than seeking to transcend the complexity of our semantic existence, let us meticulously trace it by analyzing the process by which words are formed out of experiences and experiences are shaped by words. It is by rooting our conceptual models in what we do—following words that transpose experience into meaning—rather than what we cannot know—the entirety of the invisible world— that we may best address the principal criticism of White, Partner, and others.

Our sense of our own partiality within a complex world will teach us never to read the part for the whole. And never to forget the transience of words, for the meanings we assign our words, the changing narratives we tell (no story ever exactly replicating a previous story), are themselves so transient. Indeed, as women, our own experience of words will lead us to ask two of the most fundamental questions historians can ask: How does the diversity of language suggest the structure of power? How do words, products of particular power structures, acquire sufficient autonomy to critique and challenge those structures?[3] By applying the critical techniques of close reading to deduce the relations not only of words to words within a literary text but of words in one genre and one social group to the words of quite different genres and social groups—and, lastly and most fundamentally, of words to specific social relations within the ebb and flow of a particular culture—we will begin to re-form history and to hear women's stories with fresh clarity.

To illustrate my point, let me discuss a historical project I am presently engaged in. A historian, I am concerned with the ways in which class identity is formed and maintained. Three aspects of class identity in particular interest me: first, its initial construction; second, the ways in which middle-class American women and men both maintained and altered their identity over time; and third, the diversity and inner conflict that characterize all classes, but, I would argue, the middle class in particular.

I begin in the 1790–1840 period, a time when American women and men had to re-form their senses of self in response to the radical economic and institutional transformatons that characterized that period. It was a time when classes first emerged and older social configurations died out. Only just recruited into the new middle class, these women and men had to distinguish themselves from the older mercantile, artisan, and agrarian groups to which they had belonged, from the cultural norms and institutions those groups had espoused, and from the equally new and uncertain working class.[4] They did so gradually, through the construction of elaborate etiquettes and metaphoric "discourses." Through these discourses (the composites of many genres: religious, medical, and legal literature, domestic and child-rearing advice books, political rhetoric, and popular fiction), they expressed their experiences of change and rationalized their new and troubling world. Neither "discourses" nor identities became static; they altered repeatedly as economic and institutional circumstances evolved and as middle-class power became entrenched.

Classes are not monolithic. Many factors divided the nineteenth-century American middle class—ethnicity, religion, regional and generational divisions, and, most especially, gender. Women and men, affected differently by commercialization, urbanization, and industrializaton, situated differently in the power structure, told different stories about the impact of change and developed distinctive styles to discuss their experience of class. They disagreed about which forces threatened middle-class values and, in fact, about what those values were. Gender thus became a fault line undercutting the solidity of class identity.

Class and *gender* are terms that describe social characteristics: occupation, educational levels, consumption patterns, size of family, modes of social interaction. Simultaneously, they constitute conceptual systems, organizing principles, that impose a fictive order upon the complexities of economic and social development. They constitute codes of behavior by which people are expected to structure their lives—or at least their definition of the normative and the "normal."[5] The tension between the two meanings of *gender* and *class* (as sociological description and as cultural prescription) played a critical role in the construction of a middle-class identity. While the one reflected the uncertainties of a world in flux, the other constituted an attempt by new middle-class women and men to impose a sense of order on the economic and demographic disruptions of their time. The "ordered" vision women and men sought to impose differed as widely as their experiences of social change.

As will be clear by now, I have espoused a somewhat controversial definition of class. I have not defined class solely in terms of its relation to production or as a list of definitional variables. In my view, it is that and more. It is a series of relationships, of culturally constructed identities. Only if one accepts such an expanded definition of class can one call "middling" nineteenth-century Americans a class. Many historians and theorists do not. They argue that consensus, not class, characterized nineteenth-century America: that ethnic and religious, not class, identities divided Americans; that the varied and often tenuous relation of its different members to the means of production made the American middle class an "intermediate," not a true, class. Yet some—Anthony Giddens, Mary Ryan, and, most recently, Stuart Blumen—accept its class designation, because, like me, they think of class as a complex exchange between economic forces and cultural identity. To study class, Giddens argues, requires that we examine *"the modes in which* 'economic' relationships become translated into 'non-economic' social structures."[6]

Yet to quote Blumen, a "critical problem" remains. Many nineteenth-century middle-class Americans, especially men, denied that they constituted a class. Can we talk of an American middle-class identity in the face of this denial? I think we can if we keep two points clearly in mind: first, Roland Barthes's suggestion that the bourgeoisie seeks to deny its own existence, by asserting that what is economically and politically specific to it as a class is, in fact, universal and "natural"; and second, nineteenth-century middle-class men's radical polarization of gender.[7] If Barthes is right, and middle-class men sought consciously and unconsciously to deny their own class identity at the same time that they made class distinctions central to social arrangements and the structure of power, they could do so by displacing the acknowledgment and enactment of class onto middle-class women. Middle-class men used two radically different myths to rationalize middle-class identity in early-nineteenth-century America: "the Myth of the Common Man" and "the Cult of True Womanhood."[8] The one denied class, the other constructed its elaborate etiquette. These apparently opposed yet actually interdependent myths illustrate the ways in which difference, even contradiction, lies at the heart of class identity. They also constitute a paradigm for analyzing the ways in which

nineteenth-century American middle-class men simultaneously constructed and denied their class identity.

"Discourse," that is, words are central to my analysis not because
they convey "facts" but because, as Michel Foucault argues in *Les
Mots et les choses,* they constitute the point of intersection between
the world of tangible "things" and the minds that respond to those
"things."[9] Words are mental constructs, yet we cannot understand
their meanings unless we understand their interaction with "things"
such as technology, cities, wealth, work, leisure, and unless we accept
that words are themselves in some respects "things." Like the notion
of social class itself, words are cultural constructs, imaginative mediations of social experiences. We construct our sense of self out of
words.

Words, even more than clothes, make the woman and the man. A
nice conceit, but how precisely do they do so? As I have written
elsewhere, I am convinced that the varied forms that "words" and
"language" take—whether we refer to grammar, dialect, high literary
tradition, folk narrative, unconscious metaphor, or sexual or political
discourse—reflect the social location and relative power of the speakers. Take black or cockney English, for example, or Scots dialect. Their
alternative grammars, the meanings they assign words, their accents
and speech patterns deviate from standard American or English in ways
that precisely mirror both their speakers' marginality within the American or British political and economic power structure, and the social
diversity of those societies. Since "language" affects as well as reflects,
the grammatical and accentual deviance of these three dialects reinforces the dominant culture's easy condemnation of each as irregular
or anachronistic and, hence, the valuation of its speakers as disorderly
or marginal—in either case inferior. While marking their speakers as
"Other," they also give expression to "other" experiences, permit
coded discourse, and the expression of anger and protest.[10]

If "language" reflects experience, then a multiplicity of "languages"
will coexist within any heterogeneous society, reflecting the diversity
of experiences across and within gender and class. Radical special
transformations and new class formations exacerbate such semantic
diversity, producing a profusion both of new social experiences and
of resulting social dialects. Divergent, at times conflicting, narratives
and imagery will proliferate as marginal social groups, speaking the
"language" of their experiences, challenge their culture's "traditional"
discourse. At such times, the meaning of words will become problematic. However, disorder is the most transient of social states. A
new class, as it assumes political and economic dominance, will inev-

itably impose a new cultural and linguistic hegemony, seeking to silence voices it can now define as deviant. But the dominant will never
completely silence the words of the marginal and the less powerful,
within as well as without class. Cacophony, though muted, will persist.

I have just suggested a diachronic view of the interaction of class
and "language." A synchronic analysis is also crucial. This time, "language" not only provides the analytic tools, it offers itself as an analytic
model. Language construction, like class construction, is dialectical.
The need of any group of people for a body of commonly agreed-
upon meanings and grammatical constructions wars against the linguistic diversity that characterizes any heterogeneous society. The
struggle is ongoing.

"Language," like class, is never static.

As should be clear by now, my ideas are shaped to a significant
extent by Bakhtin's literary theories, and in particular by the dialectic
he posits between the forces of linguistic diversity (what he calls "heteroglossia") and the need every society and social group feels for a
commonly understood grammar and vocabulary (a "unitary language,"
in Bakhtin's metalinguistic system). Heteroglossia give voice to social
differences. Within the term, Bakhtin includes "languages that are
socioideological, languages of social groups, professional and 'generic'
languages, languages of generations and so forth." The thrust for a
unitary language seeks to confine, indeed to outlaw, such linguistic
diversity. Linguistic unification thus serves as the handmaiden of ideological unification. It is never politically innocent. It forms, Bakhtin
insists, a critical part of the "process of socio-political and cultural
centralization."[11]

Bakhtin has provided a linguistic model well suited to the needs of
the cultural historian, suggesting the ways in which language both
serves and wars against the unifying forces of class cohesion. Language
so conceived becomes a synecdochic representation of class itself. It
permits us to use the development of language competency as a metaphor for the formation of class identity. The following questions then
suggest themselves: Which specific social and gender groups originated the "unitary language" of class identity? Who taught it to whom
(that is, to which other social, gender, and generational groups)? What
techniques and technologies did they use to disseminate their words?
Did those groups who learned the language (rather than originate it)
transpose it in the process of learning, so that it more accurately reflected their sociostructural location, their anxieties, and their angers?
Did they speak a second language altogether, one that either directly
confronted or less overtly subverted the unitary language of class

cohesion? If so, were they able to maintain their social dialects against the forces of uniformity? How did the next generation of speakers alter the varied languages they inherited?

Women's popular writing in America during the first half of the nineteenth century offers an ideal body of literature for testing the usefulness of Bakhtin's thesis and of my questons. Since Foucault's early work in *Madness and Civilization*, cultural historians have examined the emergence of a restraining bourgeois "discourse" and have pondered the effect gender had upon that "discourse."[12] Jacques Donzelot, a leading student of Foucault, has insisted that bourgeois women, coopted by the offer of domestic sovereignty, collaborated actively in the dissemination of the new bourgeois ideology (to use Foucault's formulation, they became "enmeshed" in the "new technologies of power").[13] Bonnie Smith, a feminist student of the *bourgeoise,* demurs. Women resisted the new unitary bourgeois discourse, Smith argues; using religious enthusiasm and sexual purity, they constructed a counter "language."[14] Mary Ryan concurs. Demonstrating the initial appeal that male-articulated evangelical enthusiasm held for women just entering the uncertain and rapidly changing world of Utica, she explores the ways in which that appeal, and the women's responses to it, altered as the class structure of Utica became firmly entrenched. Women, she argues, took a male religious "discourse" and transformed it into a female "discourse" that both imposed fictive order on the uncertain world of commercial and industrializing Utica, and demanded their active participation in that world.[15]

Ryan's and Smith's analyses exemplify the contribution historians can make to the analysis of "discourse"—and to historians' exchange with literary critics. Their studies add a contextual richness to the analysis of texts; they demonstrate the dynamic interchange between words and the world that spoke those words. They challenge Foucault's understanding of the constraining force of "discourse" by demonstrating the political and social complexity of "discourse," even of official "discourse." That "discourse," they argue, spoken by those not at the center of power (women in Utica or Rouen, for example), will mean something quite different, socially and politically, because it is spoken by those women rather than by men at the center of power. Ryan's and Smith's studies lay the groundwork for further collaboration.

By positing "language" (and, by extension, class) as the product of an unstable balance between the forces of cohesion and of diversity, Bakhtin may have suggested a next step for our analysis both of "discourse" as a social construction and of the interaction of class and gender. Bourgeois women have always participated in both the unitary and the disruptive aspects of "language" and of "discourse"—in "discourse" as Foucault thought of it, and "discourse" as Ryan and Smith describe it. By carefully tracing women's contributions to each, we may expand our understanding of the complexity of "discourse" and "language" as actors/reactors to social event, and of the role gender plays in class identity formation.

I will now analyze one particular form of nineteenth-century women's writing: bourgeois women's discussion of prostitution, a frequent subject matter in women's writings during the first half of the century. I will argue that it is an example of a female social dialect which, while coexisting with the "unitary language" or ideology, actually worked against that ideology. Paradoxically, this literary form was far more radical than women's fiction, as found in the popular novels and literary magazines that proliferated between the 1830s and the Civil War; there, bourgeois women recorded their more conservative voice and helped to elaborate the standard language and ideology of their class. An examination of these two genres of women's writing side by side would permit us to hear the different voices that together construct a social dialect. That, however, is not possible here, because of space limitations, and must be the subject of a future publication. This essay, therefore, is a first step toward an appreciation of the complexity of "language" and toward an understanding of the complex interaction of class and gender.

One spring evening in May 1834, a small group of women met at the revivalistic Third Presbyterian Church in New York City to found the New York Female Moral Reform Society. The Society's goals were militantly ambitious: first, to attack urban prostitution and to close the city's brothels; second, to confront the double standard and the male sexual license it condoned. Too many men, the women defiantly proclaimed, were aggressive destroyers of female innocence and happiness. Women must respond militantly, challenge man's sexual norms and undermine his sexual and social hegemony. God imperiously commanded their work. "As Christians we must view it [male promiscuity and the double standard] in the light of God's word—we must enter into His feelings on the subject, engage in its overthrow just in the manner he would have us. . . . We must look away from all worldly opinions or influences, for they are perverted and wrong; and individually act only as in the presence of God."[16]

Militant in their goals, the Society's members were equally unorthodox in their behavior. They stationed themselves outside the brothels, carefully recording the names and descriptions of the men who entered, or they marched in, exhorting inmates and clients to reform. Even more aggressively, the Society's first annual report startled respectable New York by asserting that 10,000 prostitutes plied New York City's streets and claimed among their clientele not only the transient and the uncouth but the rich and the respectable.

Who were these women who so defied bourgeois proprieties? The membership of this organization, which quickly claimed over 20,000 women, had grown up, for the most part, in the quiet agricultural communities of New England and the Middle Atlantic region. The commercial and transportation revolutions then caught them up, propelling them into the eastern seaports or the western boom cities. A small but significant number of these women remained marginal to the new bourgeois class structure. These were the mill girls of Lowell and Lawrence, and of the less-well-studied industrial towns (Whitestown, outside Utica, for instance), and self-supporting widows or spinsters, especially in the older New England communities. Poor, wage-earning women, they nevertheless continued to identify with the older agrarian social order.[17] Unlike the young "Bowery girls" described by Christine Stansell, they did not see themselves as part of a new working class.[18]

Most Society members, however, married merchants, professional men, or entrepreneurs. They were thus centrally involved in constructing a class identity and new class institutions: the nuclear and economically unproductive bourgeois family, for example, or bourgeois women's religious and reform societies. These women had experienced a radical reversal in social definitions of legitimate female space, a reversal that tabooed the once familiar space of the marketplace, at the same time as it opened the traditionally tabooed sacred space of the church. They thus felt the full force of geographic and class dislocation and relocation: the loss of the secure, precommercial ways of the multifunctional farming family nestled in a network of kin; and the responsibility for elaborating a new urban (and urbane) etiquette of class and gender. Hiring and disciplining servants, employing seamstresses (all former farm girls, and as much newcomers to the cities as their mistresses), founding orphanages and societies for the relief of poor widows, and distributing charity, these bourgeois matrons were thoroughly conversant with the wage economy and the realities of life outside the family for poor urban women. They may have had far more personal contact with the working class than their merchant or lawyer husbands had.[19]

New women with new skills, so recently incorporated into the bourgeois class structure, yet so central to it; how did they conceptualize
and legitimate their extraordinary, indeed irregular, behaviors? These
reforming women had to carve out new roles for themselves within
a world structured by two male ideologies, both concerned with defining correct female behavior. These were evangelical Protestantism
and the Cult of True Womanhood.

Evangelical Protestantism, and especially the preaching of its most
influential revival minister, Charles Grandison Finney, proved particularly popular among the new male bourgeoisie. Here Finney's message of individualism and self-determination—that salvation was the
business of men, not of God, that man could remake himself and his
world—met a receptive audience. So did his promise that the man of
wealth, tithing for God, would become the man of God. Evangelical
Protestantism held an exciting message for bourgeois women, as well,
as Finney made them copartners with their brothers and husbands in
the construction of a new and Godly world. Women, even more than
men (presumably because women had leisure time—here we can see
again the class composition of urban evangelical audiences), should
go out onto the highways and byways, seeking to save sinners and to
prepare America for Christ's Second Coming. Women, then, could
publicly rebuke men whose sins or whose conservatism impeded that
Second Coming.[20]

Evangelical Protestantism thus possessed a radical potential, which
bourgeois society sought to constrain within the Cult of True Womanhood. Insisting on the complementarity of gender rooted in reproductive differences, the cult decreed that the True Woman, Domestic,
Dependent, Pure and Pious, constituted the mirror image of the Common Man, noted for his self-reliance, talent, and competitiveness.
While the home determined the boundaries of the True Woman's
sphere, the "real world" set few restraints upon the Common Man.
The True Woman and the Common Man, twin mythic constructs of
the emerging male middle class, assured that middle class that their
newly constructed social and economic arrangements were in fact
timeless, rooted in the biology of man's competitive and woman's
nurturant natures. They simultaneously rationalized and symbolized
the fragmentation of old unities: the radical separation of home and
work, of private and public, of producer and capitalist. They embodied
identifiable norms of legitimate bourgeois behavior.

The precepts of the Cult of True Womanhood and of evangelical
piety emerge on every page of the *Advocate of Moral Reform:* the
True Woman's piety and purity, her maternal devotion, her domestic

graces. Did the Female Moral Reform Society unqualifiedly espouse evangelicalism and the Cult of True Womanhood? If it did, then we must see it as one of the most effective and aggressive agencies inculcating the unifying ideology of the new bourgeoisie. It would have played a central role, as well, in what Foucault defined as the "new technology of power."[21] For the Society preached far more than simple bourgeois manners. It espoused a highly restrictive sexual code, which it sought to enforce upon urban working women and the new young men of the city. If the Society and its members did indeed accept the male fusion of evangelical zeal with the Cult of True Womanhood, they then placed female purity in the service of bourgeois class ascendancy and social control. If instead they used the doctrines of sexual purity and women's domesticity to constrain middle-class men's power, they may well have played a quite different and potentially revolutionary role in early bourgeois America. To evaluate the role the Society and its members played in the formation of a middle-class language and identity, we must more closely examine their rhetoric, the narratives they told, and the words and the form they told them in.

The members and officers of the American Female Moral Reform Society talked with each other and to the world through the medium of their bimonthly religio-reform magazine, *the Advocate of Moral Reform.* This magazine merged epistolary style and melodrama to create a uniquely American and female composite. What do I mean by epistolary style? The format of the *Advocate's* pages differed significantly from that of contemporary male religious journals (*the New York Evangelist,* for example). Sermons and authoritative articles were largely replaced by letters. Letters from rank-and-file members covered almost all but the front page of the magazine. The reports of auxiliaries frequently took the form of letters to their "sisters," and the Society's editorials that of answering the letters of members and auxiliaries.[22]

All these letters, reports, and editorials endlessly addressed one issue: the origins of urban prostitution. Their answer took the form of a sexual melodrama. They told a tale of invasion, betrayal, and abandonment. Three archetypal figures of strikingly different character and demeanor played the leads: the innocent and vulnerable young woman; the sophisticated and powerful man; the virtuous and religious mother. Fathers and brothers played virtually no role in this melodrama, which focused on a female family of mothers and daughters, a family that was two-generational, uterine, and rural.

The Female Moral Reform Society's melodrama opened with the family farm, a world of mothers, daughters, and sisters. Devoid of crass commercial values and devoted to traditional, preindustrial ways, the farm and its female family were places of relative sexual safety. Yet they contained a problematic figure, the adolescent daughter. She would prove to be the vulnerable member of an endangered family. At first that might seem odd. The women always described the daughter as "innocent," "obedient," "meek," and "gentle." She was a "delicate flower," a "plant" rooted in the country. In true melodramatic fashion, however, she harbored a secret, one that would weaken and ultimately destroy the female family. She was "susceptible" to "enticements," "a very easy prey" to the seductions of men and the blandishments of the city.[23]

Sex differentiated women and men socially as absolutely as it did physically. A source of power and pleasure to men, it brought only misery and desolation to the young woman. Sexual activity, the women contended, made women mere "merchandise," little valued in a crowded market, dependent on the whim of men with money. For the Society's members, prostitution was synonomous with destitution and isolation. If "virtue . . . be lost," one member lamented, "oh, what a poor, forlorn, withered, wretched creature you become! Abandoned by your seducer, rejected from your place, disowned by your friends. . . ."[24]

In contrast to the impoverished and abandoned prostitute, the ruthless and sexual man appeared in this script as socially respectable and economically powerful. A "gentleman," a merchant "of high and respectable connections," he flaunted his wealth and status. "The seducer mingles among the crowd," the Society warned,

> laughs at the opera, shouts in the tavern, rolls in his chariot, appears upon the 'Change, roars over his bottle, reels from the public-house . . . or settles down as a married man, neither ashamed nor reproached that he had defiled and ruined a confiding young female and qualified her to become . . . the heir to endless "weeping and wailing."[25]

The new, male, urban world, the women warned, "encouraged" and "approved" his behavior.

Such male aggression and female vulnerability were new and unexpected. At earlier times, the arm of a male protector and the self-control of the honorable man had stretched over the home and its women. Now this arm, the Society reported, "had been shorn of its strength." Men, who had been women's protectors, had become their assailants. The young woman was suddenly exposed and endangered.

The Female Moral Reform Society's members worried not only about the young woman. They feared even more for the safety of her family. A family-centered vision determined their discussion of prostitution. Both the women writers and their characters were defined in terms of their relation to the family. Women members described themselves as "mothers," the seduced women as "daughters." Men, existing outside the family, were brutal and dangerous. A typical editorial chastized a figurative seducer not so much for despoiling the young woman as for breaking into her family and wronging all its women:

> You have cooly selected your victim in the bosom of some quiet happy family . . . and then, when you have accomplished her ruin, you have abandoned her to shame and wretchedness. . . . See at what expense to our sex you purchase your gratification. Your course is strewed with the sighs and tears and groans of widowed mothers who regret that their daughters had not died in their infancy. . . . Your victim . . . but for you, might have been the pride of the family. . . . Count the sum total of all the shame, and infamy, and ruin, and woe, which your licentious indulgences occasion to our sex. . . . This may be sport to your sex, but it is death, and worse than death, to ours.[26]

Mothers without their daughters could not survive. Their families, torn asunder, fragmented.

Not only was the young woman's family of origin bereft, but her own hopes to form a reproductive family were dashed. If she had a child, it would be illegitimate, outside of all families. The female life cycle, as portrayed in the pages of the *Advocate,* took place within two families—the family of origin and the reproductive family. Ideally, the adolescent woman moved from one to the other. Illicit sex, defined as sex outside the family, removed her from both families. It cast her into a familyless world, into the city, onto the streets.

The system that transformed the seduced woman into a familial outcast was the double standard, a system of family organization that imposed a highly restrictive sexual regimen on bourgeois women. The double standard, enforced by British common-law rulings respecting divorce, required women to confine their sexuality within the narrow boundaries of their reproductive family. It permitted men to escape those restrictions. Man's sexuality could thrive within and without the family. He could even invade the family and carry off the innocent daughter—all without social penalties. Women's sexuality was controlled, men's uncontrolled and unbounded. To live beyond boundaries gave man power; it destroyed woman. Outside family boundaries, woman had no legitimate sphere.

The double standard, women moral reformers argued, not only confined women within and freed men from the family; it also established
men's absolute control over the family. It permitted men to determine
who could remain within the family and who must be expelled. In
this double sense, it deprived the mother of her daughter. Moreover,
the Society complained, it made women complicitous in their own
oppression. Bound to silence during the act of sexual invasion by rules
of sexual and social propriety, women were required by these same
rules to cooperate in the act of social expulsion. Sadly, the Society
reported, many women did collaborate. "She will drive the female
from her door . . . while the vile wretch who lured her to ruin will be
received into the family . . . to wait on the virtuous daughters."[27] Having tempted woman and driven her out of the Garden, the seductive
man could then return to Eden.

Women must resist, Society members and officers insisted time and
again. "Can *mothers,* upon whom such an awful responsibility de-
volved, continue slumbering at their posts, when an enemy so subtle
in his character, is in all our borders endeavoring to allure into captivity
and destruction the delight of our hearts?" the Society asked. "Oh!
that we who are mothers, may become doubly diligent!—watch over
the precious plants entrusted to our care, and endeavor to secure
them 'from the wild beasts of the desert' of this world." "The ladies
of Boston must take hold of the work heart and hand," a New England
contributor wrote. "Mothers, we dare no longer remain inactive . . .
lift up your warning voice. . . ." The seducer sought entrance to the
female circle. Female gate keepers must guard the boundaries.

Boundaries divide the insider from the outcast. The roles of insider
(or inmate?) and of outcast were critically important to these middle-
class women. They challenged traditional male definitions for the sexual woman as familial outcast, and in this way they challenged the
more fundamental male prerogative of naming and defining. Men, they
pointed out, by defining the outcast, had been able to set the rules
and establish the boundaries of the family. By superimposing a female
single moral standard upon the male double sexual standard, the Female Moral Reform Society's women asserted their own right to define
the rules of family membership and assert female power over the
family.

To define the sexually promiscuous male as the outcast became an
essential act in this Jacksonian war between the sexes. Through their
organization of thousands of women, they sought to assert real social
power and literally to ostracize sexually aggressive men. If female
sexuality must be confined to the reproductive family, the male sexual

athlete must be excluded from it. All members of the Female Moral
Reform Society pledged to bar the known or suspected seducer from
their own family circles and their genteel networks. They worked collectively, as well, to pressure merchants to fire clerks accused of se-
ducing young women.

The Society sought to exclude the male seducer on a conceptual
and semantic, as well as literal, plane. They defined him as outside
of human society. By defying family order, beyond female control,
they argued, the seducer had crossed the boundary between the human and the inhuman. From this perspective, the women's extravagant sexual rhetoric assumes social significance. They described him
as an "animal," a "wild beast," "a serpent's coil." He was "brutal,"
a "hideous monster," a "master demon." He existed between states,
outside of categories and boundaries. He was alien to woman's world,
beyond her control—and dangerous.

> Thousands and tens of thousands, and hundreds of thousands of dogs
> in human shape, have not only run mad with lust, but are biting and
> seizing from our own sex, victims, time and again, until the numbers
> of the victims will outnumber even the multitudes of their destroyers.[28]

"All we want is to bring public sentiment stripped of its false delicacy
to bear upon the licentious," the Society proclaimed. "They will be
driven from all society . . . and the mark of Cain will be put on them
wherever they go."

Challenging the double standard, women had begun to assume the
attributes and powers of men. Organization, knowledge, and determination, the Society urged time and again, must replace dependence,
docility, and silence. "Young ladies in the present age cannot remain
silent, inactive and ignorant," the Female Moral Reform Society of
Angelica, Allegheny County, warned. "Take a decided stand in virtue's
cause; fear not the startling cry of 'indelicate,' which is echoed and
reechoed through the land . . . they are harmless as the passing
breeze."[29]

It was in this light that the Society's newspaper adopted an aggressive publishing policy, printing the names or descriptons of known
lechers. Women could no longer remain in ignorance, nor men be
protected by a veil of silence. "In the publication of facts we shall . . .
strip vice of its gaudy attractive attire," they wrote. "Our doctrine is
to root out evil; we must expose it." When solely dependent upon
men, the Society argued in effect, women became passive victims and
hunted animals. United within the Female Moral Reform Society, ac-

tive women stripped and exposed men, and man, as a result, had become "a harmless breeze." Women must seize the initiative. "Females defend yourselves. Drive the male monsters from your society," a woman from East Haven, Connecticut wrote her "Sisters." "Then will . . . vile men respect your firmness and principles." The Society's editors concurred. "This Society," they reported, "has waged a war of extermination. . . . They wrestle not with flesh and blood, but against principalities and powers, against the rulers of the darkness of this world, against spiritual wickedness 'in high places' . . . concentrated action is essential to a final triumph. . . . The cause requires, and *must have* combined moral power—a holy alliance of principle—sanctified virtue moving forward in sole phalanx to the conflict."[30]

A series of binary oppositions structured the Society's melodrama. Male lust countered female innocence; male power, female vulnerability; male wealth, female poverty; male aggression, female nurturance; and the male city, the female country, until male and female emerged as condensed symbols. But symbols of what? The women's rhetoric was sexual, yet the binary oppositions addressed issues of power and space. What social conflicts did these binary oppositions represent? What mediation, what resolution did the women suggest through their mythic melodrama? To answer that question, we must examine their stereotypes and binary oppositions more closely.

Significantly, the women chose farm girls to symbolize innocent virtue, not city girls. Farm boys did not pose sexual danger, nor did rural men of landed wealth. Merchants and lawyers did, as did urban clerks struggling within the vicious world of the commercial city, and male college students preparing for a commercial or professional career. These men, the women claimed, willingly compromised the traditional values of home and family to achieve wealth and worldly pleasure. Habitués of the commercial city, they became its symbolic representatives.

The city, within the Society's narrative, was male and familyless. It teemed with brothels and gambling halls, counting houses, boarding houses, and hotels. These quite literally formed the new institutional nexus of men recently arrived from the country, loose for the first time from family ties and apprenticeship regulations, literally gambling on an unknown future. The women's rhetoric quickly fused male social autonomy with sexual danger. They tranposed the institutionally loose man into the sexually loose man, the man on the economic make into the man on the sexual make (the rake). Within the Society's collective imagination, the one followed the other automatically. Commercial cities were places of absolute danger.

But that is very strange imagery. Few of the women who told or responded to the stories that appeared in the *Advocate* were farming mothers who had lost their sons and daughters to the commercial cities. They were, in fact, those very daughters, married to those sons. They lived comfortable urban lives, enjoying the city's economic and cultural advantages, helping to establish its mores and etiquette, giving birth to its next generation of commercial leaders. They were the middle-class matrons, who socially ruled the new commercial cities.

It is with regard to just this point that the Society's excessive rhetoric and fantasies begin to make sense. Middle-class matrons ruled the city socially but not economically. Evidence suggests that they knew little of the commercial and industrial forces that governed the city economically and that gave birth to its new values and behavioral norms. Commerce and industry rivaled these matrons as the mothers of the new world, and as the true consorts of their husbands and sons. At the same time, they literally endangered women.

Working women fared poorly within the early wage economy. As the Society's managers pointed out time and again, the double sexual standard embodied a double economic and social standard that closed most areas of profitable employment to women. Yet the same economic pressures that pushed sons out of New England's declining agricultural villages and pushed out daughters, as well. Streams of poor farm women flocked to the city. They became domestic servants or entered what was perhaps America's first sweated industry, the garment trade. By the early 1800s, jobbing had become common in the garment industry. Seamstresses, working in their own tenement rooms, performed semiskilled piecework for putting-out merchants, or they might work in in-house shops that produced fine dresses for middle-class matrons.[31] In either case, they constituted one of America's first groups of proletarianized laborers. Their brothers' labor market was regional, as young men roamed between cities or worked on the far-flung canal system of the young nation. A local labor market constricted women's job options, just as the home theoretically constrained their social roles. Prostitution flourished during the early stages of industrialization, when low wages and frequent unemployment gave the single woman few alternatives.[32] The Society's leaders and members were fully aware of the powerlessness of women who sought to live outside the patriarchal family and within the wage economy. Their visits to their cities' slums and prisons and the frequent solicitations for domestic employment convinced them of that harsh reality.

Cities endangered bourgeois women, as well. A number of studies indicate that downward economic mobility exceeded upward mobility from the 1820s through the Civil War. With only primitive institutional and governmental supports, with an inelastic and unreliable currency, the merchant's and the entrepreneur's lot was not a stable one.[33] Middle-class matrons realized how easily bankruptcy might envelop them—and then what would they do? The fate of the seamstress and the widow spoke personally to them.

The society's sexual drama suggests a social drama. One could hypothesize that commercialized sex symbolized commercialization itself. The city metaphorically represented the wage economy, and the prostitute women's vulnerability within that economy, while the romanticized agrarian past represented the sexual and economic security woman had known in the simpler, more static agrarian-mercantile world. To insist that a sociological signified lurks behind a sexual signifier is not to deny the signifier its own sexual meaning. It is, in fact, to insist upon it.

The Society's sexual drama had a sexual content: in addition to prostitution, the courtship patterns and sexual mores of the young. While the medieval norm of consummating a marriage with the announcement of the engagement appeared common in eighteenth-century America, premarital sex became problematic in nineteenth-century communities, marked as they were by high levels of geographic transience among young men and by few institutions to monitor and constrain youthful behavior.[34] Not surprisingly, the middle class's new code of sexuality and etiquette made female purity a prerequisite for middle-class membership. Promiscuity and illegitimacy now characterized the new urban working-class *woman* and the equally alienated rural poor. *Woman's* sexual propriety became the embodiment of men's and women's social status. The Female Moral Reform Society repeatedly warned young women and their mothers that the old norms were no longer operable. Its sexual drama metaphorically depicted the dangers to which young women were exposed both within agrarian villages with high rates of out-migration and within the topsy-turvy cities—dangers that fused sexual exploitation with the loss of social status.

These sexual messages, revealing as they are, do not exhaust the rich complexity of the Society's bodily imagery and sexual dramas, especially its obsessive concern with boundaries and invasions. "Interest in [the body's] ... apertures depends on the preoccupation with social exits and entrances, escape routes and invasion," Mary Douglas suggests.[35] Anxiety over the violation of sexual boundaries suggests a highly structured system in the process of change. The process of change itself, causing, as it does, related changes in cosmological and classification systems, can evoke uncertainty about boundaries leading to symbols of bodily invasion. Definitions no longer elicit cultural consensus or reinforcement. Boundaries are no longer cleary defined. Members of societies in the process of change face contradictory demands and rewards. The culture loses a sense of secure and unquestioned order. Subgroups experiment with altering the categories of social outcast. And so we saw that while middle-class men and many middle-class women insisted on the outcast status of "the Fallen Woman," other middle-class matrons condemned the lecherous man as bestial and "Other." Righteously they cast him out of the Edenic rural family, and reclaimed the fallen daughter.

Concern over bodily boundaries can reflect actual change in the functions and structure of the family, alterations in the lines that divide the family from other social institutions, redefinitions of public and private space, and, most especially, changes in relations between the world of men and the world of women. The society melodrama presented the female body and the female family as fragile, permeable, and invaded by men associated with commercial institutions. Conversely, the Society demanded that pious mothers guard their daughters' virginity and the boundaries of the female family; indeed, that they expand those boundaries by going forth into the world to battle sin and immorality. Here again the daughter's body and the female family symbolically represent the rapid alterations bourgeois women experienced in the space society assigned them as legitimate: the shrinking size and functions of the middle-class family, compared with the eighteenth-century farm family; its vulnerability and isolation within a world of male-defined work, of rising levels of capital investment and wage labor; and women's confinement within a family shorn of its economic resources.

Images of the body and rules regulating its treatment and behavior, symbolic anthropologists have argued, correlate closely to social categories and the distribution of power. Differences in the rules governing the body (dress and sexual codes, freedom of movement, and so forth) will demarcate social differences and positions of relative power. A concern with social control will dictate a system of rigid bodily and sexual restrictions governing the group to be socially controlled. And so, social and sexual politics interact.

From this perspective, let us examine the Society's decision to challenge the double sexual standard, which formed a key but unspoken component of the Cult of True Womanhood. Two key components of the Victorian double standard—the severity of the restrictions placed upon the sexuality of middle-class women, and the freedom from sexual restraints that it granted middle-class men—expressed, through physiological and sexual rituals, men's demands that women acknowledge men's right to compel social conformity to male laws. The women who challenged those rules faced social ostracism and legal and economic punishment. The Society's demand for a single standard, in contrast, was a demand that men acquiesce to women's rules (or at least to men's rules as women interpreted them). Within the female world of home and family, men must conform to women's power and status within a sphere men had, after all, granted them.

Another way of viewing the conflict over the double standard is to place it in the perspective of class relations. On one very significant level, the debate over the double standard is a debate over who controls the right of sexual access to women: the woman herself? Older women? Older men? Men or women of the same or of a superior class?[36] If the attack upon the double standard is carried on by young women in the name of sexual autonomy, then the entire social hierarchy, that is, men's sexual and economic hegemony, is challenged. These young women would be asserting the rights of women over men, of youth over age and status, of the individual over social and familial demands. If the challenge is brought not by young women in their own name but by older women, then a less thorough challenge to the social system is involved. Then mothers battle with fathers for the control of daughters. The idea of a hierarchy of age, and the subordination of the individual to the demands of family and community, are reinforced. Rules of sexual restraint and purity are not questioned. This battle is not about ultimate social power, but, more narrowly, about who should rule at home.

It is highly significant that the Society depicted the prostitute—and hence the poor farming women, the seamstresses, and the domestic servants whom the prostitute symbolically represented—as daughters, not as sisters. The category sister implies equality, an absolute identification. Daughter implies a hierarchy of power, the right of mothers to criticize and restrain, and of bourgeois women to control the sexual and nonsexual behavior of working-class women. Middle-class matrons identified sufficiently with both the prostitute and the working-class woman to adopt her sexual and economic exploitation as an expression of their own sense of powerlessness in the new commercial system and in relation to the men of their same class. But, they did not take the further and more radical step of transforming their criticism of man's power to exploit women sexually and economically into a fundamental critique of class relations. They strove instead to teach both the prostitute and the working-class woman a sexual language and etiquette adapted to the social and psychological needs of middle-class women. What is truly remarkable is that their educational efforts among the working classes proved as successful as they did.

Word by word, character trait by character trait, the Female Moral Reform Society had redefined the Cult of True Womanhood and evangelical Protestantism, constructing, if not a radical new utopian language (as Shaker women or Oneidian Perfectionists had done), at least a sexual and social vocabulary that offered a clear alternative within the dominant bourgeois discourse. Where male legal and religious languages had defined "the Family" as an endless chain of fathers and sons existing to pass on salvation, land, and capital, the Female Moral Reform Society's "Family" was female, two-generational, uterine, emotional, and free from commercial considerations. Within male Jacksonian myths, "the Common Man," powerful, self-determined, and loosed from family ties, was the central heroic figure. In women's words, he emerged as "loose" and "common" indeed. The habitué of brothels, the deceiver of innocent women, he fell below class, outside of the human race. In contrast, "the Fallen Woman" (in male literature, the monstrous polluter of young men) emerged in the female text as a much-loved Persephone, rescued by modern Demeters from an urban underground. Indeed, following the suggestions of Sandra Gilbert and Susan Gubar, one could argue that the Female Moral Reform Society's officers and members had inverted the male identification of active woman as monster.[37] Neither the sexually active daughter (the Fallen Angel) nor the religiously active and reforming mother (the authorial and authoritative woman) appears within these women's narratives as monster. Only commercially powerful and authoritative middle-class men do.

These transpositions depended upon a fundamental shift in the meaning of the terms *Piety* and *Purity*. Within the official Cult of True Womanhood, the Society's leaders and members argued, "Purity" had translated into sexual ignorance and vulnerability. It rendered the True Woman blind and dumb to men's sexual aggressions. The cult's "Piety" had led the True Woman to accept not only the pains and disappointments of life and the authority of her male spiritual leaders, but also the sexual violation of other women. Women, the Society insisted, must redefine those "virtues." For the Society's members, revival converts for the most part, "Piety" meant not the quiet ways of Christian nurture but millennial zeal, the drive to free America from every sin.

To defend "the Home," "Religion," and "Purity," the truly "Pious Woman," the truly "Domestic Woman" must extend her domestic rule to public places, cast out fallen men, reclaim lost daughters. In their narratives, "the Home" no longer symbolized the prison or the grave. Its boundaries had become flexible. Women-controlled, they expanded to envelop the world.

The Society's melodrama ended with one more radical transformation. Asserting women's right to act, the Society's members had turned the "True Woman" into an amazonian St. George charging a male dragon. They had inverted not only the distinctions between "public" and "private" but also those between "male" and "female." When the Society's members spoke the words of True Womanhood, those words no longer rationalized a male-constructed class sytem, but became a condemnation of that system.

For a few brief years, it looked as if bourgeois women had a chance of substituting women's stories for men's in the official ideology of their class. By the late 1840's, however, they had lost their battle for both words and power. Male middle-class economic and ideological hegemony had coalesced. White middle-class women themselves had become more firmly established within the new systems of class power. The old moments of dislocation and of religious disorder (empowering moments for the marginal and powerless) were forgotten or, in fact, were never known by the daughters of the Female Moral Reform Society members. Bourgeois matrons increasingly spoke with male-defined words. But still the match between female and male words never became exact.

N O T E S

1. Nancy Partner, unpublished paper presented at the 1984 American Historical Association Convention, Chicago.

2. Hayden White, *Metahistory* (Baltimore: Johns Hopkins University Press, 1973) and *Tropics of Discourse* (Baltimore: Johns Hopkins University Press, 1978).

3. I am particularly indebted to the members of the University of Pennsylvania Mellon Seminar on the Diversity of Language and the Structure of Power for stimulating my thinking on these issues and for their criticism of this paper.

4. A number of superb studies of class formation in America, 1790–1850, have appeared recently. See, for example: Mary Ryan, *Cradle of the Middle Class* (New York: Cambridge University Press, 1981); Sean Wilentz, *Chants, Democratic* (New York: Oxford University Press, 1985); Bruce Laurie, *The*

Working People of Philadelphia (Philadelphia: Temple University Press, 1980); Susan Hirsch, *The Roots of the American Working Class: The Industrialization of Crafts in Newark, 1800-1860* (Pennsylvania: University of Pennsylvania Press, 1978); Anthony Wallace, *Rockdale* (New York: Knopf, 1978); and Stuart Blumin's recent article "The Hypothesis of Middle-Class Formation in Nineteenth-Century America: A Critique and Some Proposals," *American Historical Review* 90(1985):299-338.

5. See Blumin's discussion of the controversy surrounding definitions of *class* in his "The Hypothesis of Middle-Class Formation."

6. Anthony Giddons, *The Class Structure of the Advanced Societies* (New York, 1975), p. 132 and especially pp. 177-97, as cited by Blumin in "The Hypothesis of Middle-Class Formation," p. 307.

7. Roland Barthes, *Mythologies*, trans. Annette Lavers (New York: Hill and Wang, 1972), pp. 137-44. For the pathbreaking and definitive analysis of the Cult of True Womanhood, see Barbara Welter, "The Cult of True Womanhood, 1820-1860," *American Quarterly* (Summer 1966):151-74.

8. For the classic study of the Myth of the Common Man, see John Ward, *Andrew Jackson, Symbol of an Age* (New York: Oxford University Press, 1981).

9. Michel Foucault, *Les Mots et les choses* (Paris: Gallimard, 1966), trans. as *The Order of Things* (New York: Pantheon, 1971). See as well Foucault, *Archeology of Knowledge*, trans. A. M. Sheridan Smith (New York: Pantheon, 1972).

10. Carroll Smith-Rosenberg, *Disorderly Conduct* (New York: Knopf, 1985), chap. 1, "Hearing Women's Words."

11. M. M. Bakhtin, *The Dialogic Imagination: Four Essays,* ed. Michael Holquist (Austin: University of Texas Press, 1981), p. xix; see also "Discourse in the Novel," pp. 259-422.

12. Michel Foucault, *Madness and Civilization* (New York: Pantheon, 1973).

13. Jacques Donzelot, *Policing the Family* (New York: Pantheon, 1979).

14. Bonnie Smith, *The Ladies of the Leisure Class* (Princeton: Princeton University Press, 1981).

15. Ryan, *Cradle*, especially chap. 2 and 3.

16. *The Advocate of Moral Reform* (hereafter *Advocate*), vol. 1 (1835), p. 6. For institutional studies of the American Female Moral Reform Society, see Carroll Smith-Rosenberg, *Religion and the Rise of the American City* (Ithaca: Cornell University Press, 1971); Barbara Berg, *The Remembered Gate: Origins of American Feminism* (New York: Oxford University Press, 1978). For two conflicting analyses of its feminist rhetoric, see Mary Ryan, "The Power of Women's Networks: A Case Study of Female Moral Reform in Antebellum America," *Feminist Studies* 5 (1979): 66-96, and Carroll Smith-Rosenberg, "Beauty, the Beast, and the Militant Woman," in her *Disorderly Conduct.*

17. See *Advocate*, vol. 1, p. 6; also Ryan, "The Power"; and Marlou Belyea, "Hesitant Reformers: The Women of the New England Female Moral Reform Society, 1837-1850," unpublished paper, 1975.

18. Christine Stansell, *City of Women: Sex and Class in New York, 1789-1860*, in press.

19. Ryan, *Cradle*, chap. 3.

20. William G. McLoughlin, *Modern Revivalism* (New York: Ronald Press, 1959) and *Revivals, Awakenings, and Reform* (Chicago: University of Chicago Press, 1978); Charles G. Finney, *Lectures on Revivals of Religion*, ed. William G. McLoughlin (Cambridge: Harvard University Press, 1960).

21. Michel Foucault, *History of Sexuality*, trans. Robert Hurley (New York: Pantheon, 1978).

22. The most extensive holdings of *the Advocate* can be found at the American Antiquarian Society, Worcester, Massachusetts, and at the New York

Historical Society, New York City. I am indebted to the staffs of both institutions. I am indebted, as well, to Maureen Quilligan for pointing out to me
the significance of the *Advocate's* epistolary form.

23. *Advocate,* 1835–37, passim.
24. *Advocate,* vol. 1, p. 15.
25. *Advocate,* vol. 1, p. 3.
26. *Advocate,* vol. 2, p. 12.
27. *Advocate,* vol. 1, p. 2.
28. *Advocate,* vol. 3, p. 10.
29. *Advocate,* vol. 2, p. 3.
30. *Advocate,* vol. 3, p. 266.
31. Willentz, *Chants.*
32. For an analysis of the role economic motivation played in the complex
construction of prostitution in early-nineteenth-century America, see Christine
Stansell, "Women and Sexual Bargaining: The Case of Prostitution," in her
forthcoming book *City of Women.*
33. Wallace, *Rockdale,* presents a number of examples of such downward
mobility among the new entrepreneur class. See also Stuart Blumin, "Resi-
dential Mobility within the Nineteenth-Century City," in Allen Davis and Mark
Haller, *The Peoples of Philadelphia* (Philadelphia: Temple University Press,
1973).
34. For an analysis of this shift from sexual latitudinarianism to absolute
sexual purity, see Ryan, *Cradle* chap. 1–3.
35. Mary Douglas, *Natural Symbols* (New York: Pantheon, 1973).
36. This perspective was suggested by Gayle Rubin's highly influential essay
"Traffic in Women," in Rayna Reiter, ed., *Toward an Anthropology of Women*
(New York: Monthly Review Press, 1975).
37. Sandra Gilbert and Susan Gubar, *The Mad Woman in the Attic* (New
Haven: Yale University Press, 1979).

FOUR

Lab Coat: Robe of Innocence or Klansman's Sheet?

Ruth Bleier

> Finally, an ideological bias can lead a critical reader to make a given text say more than it apparently says, that is, to find out what in that text is ideologically presupposed, untold. In this movement from the ideological subcodes of the interpreter to the ideological subcodes tentatively attributed to the author . . . even the most closed texts are surgically "opened": fiction is transformed into document and the innocence of fancy is translated into the disturbing evidence of a political statement.
>
> —UMBERTO ECO, *The Role of the Reader*

Lest anyone believe that science has begun to falter under the increasingly public examination by feminist scholars, let us hear the words of James Watson, the wonder boy from Harvard, a man of ebullient stupidity and callousness, who nonetheless won the Nobel Prize with Crick and Wilkens for describing the double helical structure of DNA. This smug triumvirate, admittedly racing to win a Nobel Prize for their work, had their inspiration, coincidentally enough, after illicitly viewing the unpublished crystallographic pictures produced by Rosalind Franklin, whom Watson patronized as "Rosy" in his gossipy book, in which she was worthy of mention only because of her "dowdy" appearance and "difficult" personality.[1]

Watson, it seems, is now unhappy with the Reagan administration for its regulations governing genetic engineering, and through a press release he remarked:

> One might have hoped that the Republicans would have been more sensible about regulations, but they were just as silly as the others, who know something about physics or chemistry. The person in charge of

biology is either a woman or unimportant. They had to put a woman some place. They only had three or four opportunities, so they got someone in here. It's lunacy.[2]

The woman at issue, Bernadine Healy, a Harvard Medical School graduate on leave as a professor at Johns Hopkins, is the White House science advisor's deputy for biomedical affairs. We might have hoped that Watson's statement would catapult her into high feminist consciousness. But, alas, she responded with statesmanlike equanimity: "Watson's remarks are an offense to both men and women" (p. 160). Would that it were so.

This exchange may serve as an eloquent reminder
—of the implacable misogyny that characterizes science and some of its most prominent spokesmen;
—of the relative imperviousness of the natural sciences, unlike other disciplines, to its critics who are feminists or Marxists or other radical political commentators;
—of the enormity of our feminist task, to reconstitute knowledge in the sciences.

Science is truly a bull elephant being buzzed by a gnat, surefooted, ponderous, and impregnable. And for good reason. I need not review all the reasons why that is so—as an informed segment of the non-scientific public, feminists know them well: the esoteric nature of what scientists do and the mystique of science as an objective and true account of the world. But more than that, and in a way that is not true for any other field of knowledge, it has a powerful grip on the mind of every person in this country. Every person experiences the power of science through her or his own body and through medicine, in the workplace and in the household. In addition, for each of us, the depletion of the earth's resources and the immediate threat to our survival as a species are inextricably linked with scientific "progress." And, from the point of view of our government, science is synonymous with power and dominance, industrial and military, domestic and international.

Science is not just an approach to knowledge or a body of knowledge in the same fragile sense that the fields of history and literature are, though science is that, too. It is, in addition, something that can *work for* people. Thus, the feminist discourse on science, already hampered in its progress by the fact that there have been so few of us publicly engaged in the project, is immensely complicated by a variety of contradictions.

One is that science cannot be simply reduced to politics, to arbitrary power as opposed to rational knowledge. As Donna Haraway has written, these are not the stakes; rather, they constitute the mystifying dichotomy.[3] Then there is another important dichotomy. Science is an integral part, expression, and product of a culture's complex set of ideologies, and it has ideological commitments to certain social beliefs, values, and goals. These commitments are, on the one hand, a source of its great strength and value and, on the other, the source of its oppressive power. That is one of the many dilemmas facing us in our efforts to understand and transform that power. It was, after all, in response to our society's social beliefs, values, and urgent needs that scientists, for example, worked to develop antibiotics before and during the Second World War, at the same time that other scientists worked to develop the atom bomb, a weapon designed not to save lives by bringing a quick end to the war with Japan but to announce the ultimate phallic power and hegemony of United States capitalism in the leadership of the coming war against the Soviet Union. And whatever the scientific lure that walking in space holds for the individual astronaut (what *was* a nice girl like Sally Ride doing up there?), we know that the billions of dollars that are making that possible express a commitment to dominating nothing less than the universe.

Science has always had serious ideological commitments, and they account in large part for the very rapid developments of science in the Western world over the past three hundred years. Carolyn Merchant and others have written of the relationship between developing capitalism and the mechanistic views of the body, nature, and the cosmos that developed in science.[4] During the period of the Industrial Revolution, laissez faire political theories of the marketplace and theories of evolution shared concepts and language, as in ideas of the "survival of the fittest." In Western Europe and the United States during the periods of colonization, imperial expansion, and slavery, there was an ideological commitment to demonstrating the biological inferiority of nonwhites, a commitment that reemerged as an IQ and race controversy during the civil rights struggles of the 1960s. And over the past one hundred years we have seen the growing commitment to *proving* the biological inferiority of women, the biological innateness of gender differences, ideas previously taken for granted and, indeed, as Evelyn Fox Keller shows in her book, ideas that provided complex metaphors of gender and sexuality, domination and power, by which science defined and described itself from the time of Francis Bacon.[5]

Scientific theories about race and gender difference have always been put forward not by cranks but by recognized and distinguished scientists of their day, including Nobel Prize winners, and each theory becomes discredited only to be supplanted by new ones. Yet in a culture such as ours, stratified by gender, race, and class, questions of race and gender differences are scientifically unresolvable and are always raised for political reasons. The commitment to gender differences has become a scientific industry since about 1970 and provides what I consider to be a ruling paradigm of the 1980s. That paradigm is the notion that significant cognitive sex differences exist and that explanations for them may be found by looking for biological sex differences in the development, structure, and functioning of the brain. This paradigm is legitimized by an elaborate network of interdependent hypotheses, as I shall demonstrate. Standing alone, few of the hypotheses and assumptions have any independent scientific support, but together, supported by each other, they create the illusion of a structure of weight, consistency, conviction, and reason. In support of this paradigm, scientists make increasing numbers of unsubstantiated conjectures that are then taken up by other scientists as confirming evidence for their own unsubstantiated conjectures.

The profound and troublesome truth is that no single part of the paradigm is known to be descriptive of reality. In fact, I can say that so little is known about the biological processes in the brain underlying cognitive functioning or skills in general—that is, about how the brain actually processes visuospatial information, what brain processes account for verbal fluency or mathematical skill, for intelligence or even consciousness—that it is not possible at this time to formulate meaningful hypotheses about *sex differences* in those processes. And yet a vast literature exists that formulates hypotheses *and* provides answers.

The focus has been mainly on the question of hemispheric lateralization in cognitive processing. The predominant theory is that women tend to use both hemispheres in the processing of visuospatial information, whereas men rely more exclusively on the right hemisphere in visuospatial processing. Thus, women are said to be less lateralized or less specialized (with regard to the hemispheres) than men in processing visuospatial information. Yet women are said to be more lateralized to the left hemisphere in the processing of verbal information.

It is, first of all, noteworthy that the majority of studies in this area are flawed for one reason or another, and that there is no agreement among them on the question of sex differences in lateralization of visuospatial processing, as three exhaustive reviews of the literature have documented.[6] Just as many published studies find no sex differences in lateralization of cognitive processing as do find them, and probably the majority that find no sex differences are not published, because they are of no interest. Variability within each sex is greater than variability between them.

But the other serious interpretive problem is that even if sex differences in hemispheric lateralization of visuospatial function *were* clearly demonstrated, there is still no evidence that there is any correlation between hemispheric lateralization and visuospatial *ability.* One would never know that from the literature, however. That correlation is instead a product of semantic tricks and circular reasoning: men are superior in visuospatial skills because their right hemispheres are "specialized" for visuospatial cognitive processing; we know that right-hemispheric specialization provides superior visuospatial skills because men are better at visuospatial skills than women, who use both hemispheres for visuospatial processing. The semantic trick is substituting the word *specialized* for *lateralized,* since to be specialized is, clearly, to be better. But if we were just being intuitive about it, as are the proponents of the dominant theory, it is just as obvious a hypothesis that processing visuospatial information with both hemispheres makes for *superior* visuospatial skills. The only reason for believing that using both hemispheres symmetrically in cognitive processing is inferior is, presumably, that women do it and men do not.

Some recent well-publicized studies purport to add evidence for this dominant belief in sex differences in lateralization and cognitive processing. One study by Norman Geschwind, a recognized authority in the field of lateralization, reported an association between left-handedness and developmental learning disabilities such as autism, dyslexia, or stuttering, which are more common in boys.[7] (One interest in this association lies in the fact that left-handedness presumably indicates right-hemispheric dominance, since the right hemisphere is involved with functions of the left side of the body, and vice versa.) In attempting to explain this association of left-handedness and, therefore, an assumed right-hemispheric dominance in boys, Geschwind and Behan quoted a study of human fetal brains, by Chi and his colleagues, that indicated that two convolutions of the right hemisphere (superior frontal and superior temporal) develop one to two weeks earlier during gestation (at thirty-one weeks) than their partners on the left.[8] As an explanation for this asymmetry in the timing of development, Geschwind proposed that testosterone (the sex hormone secreted by fetal testes but not by fetal ovaries) has the effect *in utero* of slowing the development of the left hemisphere. They offer this proposal, then, as an explanation for right-hemispheric dominance in males.

However, there is no evidence whatsoever for such an inhibitory effect of testerone on the cortex in general, and, furthermore, one does not have to be a scientist to wonder how it is possible that testosterone circulating in the blood stream could affect only two convolutions on the left side of the brain. Geschwind could not answer this question, but as a serious scientist he should have acknowledged it as a problem for his theory and should have offered some tentative and plausible explanations for a clearly implausible situation. Even more important to note is that in the same study quoted by Geschwind, Chi et al. had measured 507 brains from infants of ten to forty-four weeks' gestational age and had clearly stated in their paper that they found *no significant sex differences* in their measurements. If testosterone does indeed inhibit the development of the cortex on the left, there would have to be detectable sex differences in the rate of growth or development of the left-hemispheric cortex in a series of this size.

Ignoring the obviously contradictory findings by Chi et al. on normal *human* brains, Geschwind went to experimental findings in a study by Marion Diamond and her colleagues on *rats'* brains to find supporting evidence for his hypothesis. It is interesting to examine this study, since it also fits into the paradigm I am discussing. The study found that in male rats, two areas of the cortex (the layers of nerve cells covering the hemispheres) that are believed to process visual information are 3 percent thicker on the right side than on the left. This difference was not found in female rats. The authors interpret their findings to suggest that "in the male rat it is necessary to have greater spatial orientation to interact with a female rat during estrus and to integrate that input into a meaningful output."[9] We see in this interpretation an unsupported conceptual leap from the finding of a thicker right cortex in the male (in two areas) to the assumption of "greater spatial orientation" in male rats. Yet there is no evidence that "spatial orientation" is related to any asymmetry of the cortex or that female rats have a "lesser" or somehow deficient orientation. I am aware of no studies showing that female rats get lost or fall off cliffs.

One suspects that beliefs in the superior visuospatial abilities of human males, and in their reported functional lateralization to the right hemisphere, became hidden premises for the interpretation of the findings in this study on rats. The results of the study, including its unsupported conjectures, are then used by others (e.g., Geschwind) as evidence for their own otherwise unsupported conjectures that testosterone enhances right-hemispheric development and, therefore, superior mathematical ability in boys and men. Whatever the significance of a thicker right cortex may be for the male rat's behaviors (a significance that is presently unknown), it surely is even more obscure what significance the rat's thicker right cortex has for *human* brains or behaviors.

Though Geschwind and Behan did not study (or report) the incidence of giftedness in their population, it is part of what I am talking about that the study, and in particular its wilder speculations, would be used to support the dominant popular belief in cognitive sex differences. And, indeed, in news reports of his work in *Science,* Geschwind suggested that testosterone effects on the fetal brain can produce "superior right hemisphere talents, such as artistic, musical, or mathematical talent."[10] The *Science* news article was titled "Math Genius May Have Hormonal Basis," a headline designed for consumption by the mass media, and indeed this completely unfounded claim has entered the scientific canon with fanfare.

Scientists believe that the language they use is simply a vehicle for the transmission of information about the objects of their research, another part of the scientist's tool kit, separate from the scientist's subjectivity, values, and beliefs. They do not recognize or acknowledge the degree to which their scientific writing itself participates in *producing* the reality they wish to present; nor would scientists acknowledge the multiplicity of meanings of their text. The writers and readers of scientific texts need to pay heed to literary theorists. Contemporary literary textual criticism explodes the "comfortable relationship" between the word and what it represents; it disturbs the apparent "harmony of form and content."[11] As literary criticism has "debunked the myth of linguistic neutrality" in the literary text, it is time to debunk the myth of the neutrality of the scientific text. The façade of neutrality and the techniques of scientific language (e.g., the required passive voice) create the illusion of objectivity and anonymity, which, as critic Terry Eagleton has pointed out, contributes to the authority of the text.[12]

But in addition, as Nelly Furman has written, "not only is the literary text a transmitter of explicit and implied cultural values, but the reader as well is a carrier of perceptual prejudices. It is the reader's acumen, expectations, and unconsciousness which invest the text with meaning" (p. 49). That is no less true of the scientific text. The place where the full meaning of the text is made, where the ambiguities are resolved, is in the reader; that is where the multiplicities of interpretations, significances, and assumptions act and are resolved in some particular meaning. In Roland Barthes's words, "A text's unity lies not in its origin but in its destination."[13]

The meaning of the words of Geschwind and Diamond that I quoted, for example, is not fixed; it does not reside simply in the words as they lie on the page or as they represent authorial intentions or thought (conscious or unconscious), but in the *reading* of it by other scientists, science writers, and the public who reads scientific reporting. Today that reading public is large, and it, including the scientists, is in some important respects a cultural unit. However unreflective the process may be, scientists, such as those I quoted, are able to stop just short of making the kinds of assertions that their own and others' data cannot defensibly support, yet they can remain secure in the knowledge that their readers will supply the relevant cultural meaning to their text; for example, that women *are* innately inferior in the visuospatial and (therefore) the mathematical skills, and that no amount of education or social change can abolish this biological gap. It is disingenuous for scientists to pretend ignorance of their readers' beliefs and expectations and unethical to disclaim responsibility for the effects of their work and for presumed misinterpretations of their "pure" texts. Scientists are responsible, since they themselves build ambiguities and misinterpretations into the writing itself.

It is the lab coat, literally and symbolically, that wraps the scientist in the robe of innocence—of a pristine and aseptic neutrality—and gives him, like the klansman, a faceless authority that his audience can't challenge. From that sheeted figure comes a powerful, mysterious, impenetrable, coercive, anonymous male voice. How do we counter that voice?

Because of all that I have said (and much that I have not), I have begun to think about the task in terms of disruption and subversion, with open conflict at key points of greatest interest to us. I do not believe we can think in terms of taking over the field, as feminist field primatologists have almost accomplished in theirs, and as cultural anthropologists are on the way to doing in theirs. The scientific establishment is too large, too powerful, and its system of rewards too compelling. But we can, and have begun to, bring about important changes within the sciences, as feminists have done in the field of women's health care, and others have done in the field of ecology. I can only skim over a possible agenda.

First, we *have* demonstrated, at least to women—and must continue to do so—the gendered and sexualized structure, the ideologies, and the symbolism that characterize the institution, the practices, the methodologies, and the theories of science. Second, I hope that we have begun to show that this subject is accessible to other feminist scholars, and that to some degree it can be dismantled by familiar means; for example, that the scientific text is part of the territory of the feminist literary-textual critic. Third, so long as science is in and of culture, a set of social practices engaging individuals who are specifically located within cultural categories, each person having a history, beliefs, and a world view, science cannot be seen as the objective pursuit of a body of knowledge that is itself free of cultural values and social commitments. Nor can the scientific method itself be seen as free of human values, subjective factors, and needs. As is the case for everyone else, scientists bring their beliefs, values, and world views to their work. These affect what scientists believe needs explaining, what questions they ask, what assumptions they make, the language they use, what they consider valid evidence to be, what they actually can see with their eyes, how they interpret their data, and what they hope, want, need, and believe to be true. That is not necessarily good or bad, but a condition of being human; scientists cannot simply hang their subjectivities up on a hook outside the laboratory door.

Thus, so far as science goes, it is not a matter of just tidying up a sturdy structure that happens to be cluttered with androcentric and ethnocentric biases. Rather, it seems to me, we can first of all insist that scientists recognize and acknowledge the values and beliefs that affect their particular work, and we can insist that they come to understand in what ways those beliefs may limit or enhance their perspectives. Second, and more important, I wonder if we can claim a feminist epistemology of scientific knowledge that in its language, approaches, interpretations, and goals acknowledges its commitments to particular human values and goals, instead of denying their existence, as is the case in mainstream scientific practice. (I do not mean to insist that all biological research be committed to certain social values; rather, that whatever relevant values exist be made explicit. I believe it is legitimate to do research that has no apparent or immediate social applicability outside of the desire to understand more about the natural world.)

In some fields, as in primatology, an explicit female and feminist commitment to studying the behaviors of female primates did more than just provide balance to a field previously devoted exclusively to the study of male primates and their presumably universal dominance hierarchies. It actually redirected the field, its methodologies, basic assumptions and principles, interpretations, and conclusions.[14] Furthermore, in so doing, feminists undermined the most influential theories of human cultural evolution, which grounded present-day gender asymmetries in skewed notions of social relationships among living primates that served as models of our ancient hominid ancestors.

In examining the practices of women primatologists in the late-twentieth-century United States, Donna Haraway argues that "feminist contests for authoritative accounts of evolution and behavioral biology work by phase shifts and field disruptions in narrative patterns, and not by paradigm replacement."[15] We may consider her argument about the history of primatology in relation to the feminist enterprise in science in general, as she may well intend. She claims that "redistributing the narrative field by telling another version of a crucial myth is a major process in crafting new meanings." One version never *replaces* another; it is not a question of substituting "true versions for false, feminist for masculinist, scientific for ideological accounts." I do believe, however, that in science, as Linda Gordon has claimed for history, though there may be no objective truths possible, there *are* objective lies: "There are degrees of accuracy, there are better and worse pieces of history," states Gordon in her essay in this volume; and, I would add, there are better and worse pieces of science.

Both Haraway and Gordon describe the processes of constructing and understanding our origins, history, meanings, and consciousness in terms of tensions: necessary tensions between myth making and fact seeking (Gordon), between new or different versions of the narratives and myths that are crucial to our "crafting new meanings" (Haraway). We may wish to consider that the feminist contest for meanings in the sciences lies, at least for the moment, in the destabilizing and restructuring of the narrative fields that constitute the natural sciences.

Finally, one of the great and indestructible myths of all time is that of the dichotomy between biology and learning, the ultimate site of contention over the meaning of gender differences. Implicit in the efforts to measure and define gender differences, and to distinguish biological from cultural forces in the shaping of behaviors and characteristics, is a commitment to—a belief in—the ability of science to isolate and reduce, and to find linear causality amidst complexity. On the other hand, some of us who do science are committed to an appreciation of the irreducible complexity of human characteristics and behaviors and of our nearly infinite potential for change and flexibility. For ideological commitment, that, it seems to me, is a place to begin.

At every stage of fetal development from the time of conception, genes, cells, the fetal organism as a whole, its maternal environment, and the external environment are in continuous interaction with each other, and each of these elements—including genes and their effects—undergoes continual change in response to these interactions. That is no less true of the brain, the organ of mind and behavior. The major growth and development of the human brain occurs after birth, with a fourfold increase by the age of four years. This growth occurs precisely during the period of a massive new input of sensory information from the external world. The growth that occurs is in the 100 billion or so nerve cells (neurons) that make up the brain, in their tremendously intricate, treelike processes that receive and transmit information from the external world and make connections each with 1,000 to 5,000 other neurons. The nerve cells themselves *require* sensory input for normal structural and functional development. When deprived of sensory input, neurons in the relevant sensory system are abnormal in number, size, shape, and functioning.[16] Thus, the biology of the brain itself is shaped by the individual's environment and experiences.

The endlessly recurring efforts to separate and measure biological and cultural effects on brain functioning, intelligence, behaviors, and characteristics represent a dichotomy that is scientifically meaningless. It recurs not because it has value as a scientific question that can possibly be solved, but because it has great value in the political and social world. A more useful view of human life and social relationships assumes that, rather than biology posing constraints, it is the cultures that our brains have created that most severely limit our visions and the potentialities for the development of each individual.

N O T E S

I am grateful to Elaine Marks for first bringing the work of contemporary literary theorists to my attention.

1. James D. Watson, *The Double Helix* (New York: Atheneum, 1968).

2. Barbara J. Culliton, "Watson Fights Back," *Science* 228 (1985):160.

3. Donna Haraway, "Primatology Is Politics by Other Means," in *Feminist Approaches to Science,* ed. Ruth Bleier (New York: Pergamon, forthcoming).

4. Carolyn Merchant, *The Death of Nature: Women, Ecology, and the Scientific Revolution* (New York: Harper and Row, 1980), pp. 216–35.

5. Evelyn Fox Keller, *Reflections on Gender and Science* (New Haven: Yale University Press, 1985), pp. 33–42.

6. Joseph S. Alper, "Sex Differences in Brain Asymmetry: A Critical Analysis," *Feminist Studies* 11 (1985):7–37; Meredith M. Kimball, "Women and Science: A Critique of Biological Theories," *International Journal of Women's Studies* 4 (1981):318–38; and Jeannette McGlone, "Sex Differences in Human Brain Asymmetry: A Critical Survey," *Behavioral and Brain Sciences* 3 (1980):215–63.

7. Norman Geschwind and Peter Behan, "Left-handedness: Association with Immune Disease, Migraine, and Developmental Learning Disorder," *Proceedings of National Academy of Sciences* 79 (1982):pp. 5097–5100.

8. Je G. Chi, Elizabeth C. Dooling, and Floyd H. Gilles, "Gyral Development of the Human Brain," *Annals of Neurology* 1 (1977):86–93.

9. Marian C. Diamond, Glenna A. Dowling, and Ruth E. Johnson, "Morphological Cerebral Cortical Asymmetry in Male and Female Rats," *Experimental Neurology* 71 (1981):266.

10. Gina Kolata, "Math Genius May Have Hormonal Basis," *Science* 222 (1983):1312.

11. Nelly Furman, "Textual Feminism," in *Women and Language in Literature and Society,* ed. Sally McConnell-Ginet, Ruth Borker, and Nelly Furman (New York: Praeger, 1980), p. 48.

12. Terry Eagleton, *Literary Theory* (Minneapolis: University of Minnesota Press, 1983), p. 170.

13. Roland Barthes, *Image, Music, Text,* trans. Stephen Heath (New York: Hill and Wang, 1977), p. 148.

14. Meredith F. Small, *Female Primates: Studies by Women Primatologists* (New York: Alan R. Liss, 1984).

15. Haraway, "Primatology."

16. D. Webster and M. Webster, "Effects of Neonatal Conductive Hearing Loss on Brain Stem Auditory Nuclei," *Annals of Otolaryngology* 88 (1979):684–88; Torsten N. Weisel and David H. Hubel, "Effects of Visual Deprivation on Morphology and Physiology of Cells in the Cat's Lateral Geniculate Body," *Journal of Neurophysiology* 26 (1963):978–93.

Making Gender Visible in the Pursuit of Nature's Secrets

Evelyn Fox Keller

In teaching us to see gender as a socially constructed and culturally transmitted organizer of our inner and outer worlds, in, as it were, making gender visible, feminist theory has provided us with an instrument of immense subversive power. And along with this provision comes a commitment: nothing less, as the title of this conference suggests, than the deconstruction and reconstitution of conventional knowledge. Necessarily, such a venture requires close textual reading of all attributions of gender, wherever they occur. My own work, for example, has focused on the implications for science and, accordingly, for all of us, of the uses of gender in modern constructions of mind, nature, and the relation between the two.[1] Ultimately, what we are most interested in is clarification of the space of alternative possibilities. If meaning depends on gender, we want to know what changes in meaning, in science as elsewhere, would accrue from shifting meanings or uses of gender—even from abandoning gender altogether—in our construction and de(con)struction of nature.

This method of feminist analysis is unquestionably powerful, but it is not always unproblematic. Two difficulties come to mind immediately: one arises from the obvious fact that images of male and female evoke different responses in different people, and the second arises from the fact that people are not necessarily consistent. Although labels of masculine and feminine are almost always used to designate polarities (or dichotomies), sometimes the two poles are distinguished in one way, sometimes in another. Consider, for example, discussions of brain lateralization: sometimes the right brain is said to be feminine, sometimes the left brain.[2] True, whichever is assumed to be better is sure to be seen as masculine. But my point is that however eager we seem to be to divide the world of personal attributes into categories of male and female, we are not always sure which is which.

So it is, as well, when we try to explore the function of gender in the world of archetypal myths and abstract categories. Sometimes the ambiguity of gender can itself be functional and indeed can be read as a map of another kind of structure. Nature, for instance, although almost always female in Western prescientific and scientific traditions, is not always so. As I have tried to show in examining the differences in imagery between Plato and Bacon, a great deal can be learned about the range of impulses and aims underlying the pursuit of scientific knowledge by exploring the differences of meaning that accrue as the gender of nature shifts.[3]

In this paper, I want to address—and even to take issue with—a reading of gender associations that has become familiar in recent feminist literary criticism. Christine Froula, for one, writes of "the archetypal association of maleness with invisibility, and of femaleness with visibility."[4] She cites Freud for rooting the evolution from immediate sense perception to abstract thinking (what Freud himself calls the "triumph of invisibility," "a victory of spirituality over the senses") in "the turning from the mother to the father." The basis for this presumed archetypal association, Freud tells us, is the fact that "maternity is proved by the senses whereas paternity is a surmise."[5]

For anyone who has thought about the psychology of gender, this claim must seem at least a little surprising, and to someone like myself, used to thinking about the function of gender metaphors in science, it is deeply startling. More reasonably, it might seem, the rise of modern science could be called the "triumph of the visible," its principal goal being clarity, elucidation, enlightenment, the elimination of opacity, and the vanquishing of darkness. The scientific text is, ideally, an open book, and the scientific society an open community—both constructed on a principled intolerance of secrets. Does that suggest that science should be seen as a returning from the father to the mother? Clearly not. Rather, it reminds us of how necessary to our understanding of these archetypal associations it is that we ask: visibility of what, and to whom? An absence of which secrets, and from whom? Even a superficial inspection of scientific discourse, and indeed of much of ordinary language, suggests, at the very least, the need for a higher dimensional typology. At the very least, the link Froula (like Freud) intuits between masculinity and invisibility must, as I will try to show, be seen as mediated by a prior link between power and invisibility.

There is, in fact, a long historical tradition in which femaleness is most typically associated not with visibility but with obscurity: visible, to be sure, on the surface, but invisible in its (or her) interior, in her innermost and most vital parts. Prior to the advent of science, nature as female is dark, secretive, and opaque. In more immediate human experience, paternity may demand surmise from a father, but in principle, if not in practice, it can be clear enough to the mother: she remains the ultimate arbiter of doubt. Pregnancy, on the other hand, though visible to all the world in its outward signs, is—be it distressingly or miraculously—invisible in its internal dynamics. It is, in fact, the ultimate secret of life, knowable if not visible to the mother, but absolutely inaccessible to the father.

Well-kept secrets pose a predictable challenge to those who are not privy. Secrets function to articulate a boundary: an interior not visible to outsiders, the demarcation of a separate domain, a sphere of autonomous power. And indeed, the secrets of women, like the secrets of nature, are and have traditionally been seen by men as potentially threatening—or if not threatening, then alluring—in that they articulate a boundary that excludes them, and so invite exposure or require finding out. Nobel laureate Richard Feynam once said, perhaps by way of explaining the extraordinary facility for lock picking that had won him so much fame as a young physicist at Los Alamos: "One of my diseases, one of my things in life, is that anything that is secret, I try to undo."[6]

In Western culture, the threat or the allure presented by nature's secrets has met with a definitive response. Modern science has invented a strategy for dealing with this threat, for asserting power over nature's potentially autonomous sphere. That strategy is, of course, precisely a *method* for the "undoing" of nature's secrets; for the rendering of what was previously opaque, transparent, and of what was previously invisible, visible—to the mind's eye, if not to the physical eye. However, the representation of the book of nature as a transparent text is a move with consequences that are anything but transparent.

The ferreting out of nature's secrets, understood as the illumination of a female interior, or the tearing of nature's veil, may be seen as expressing one of the most unembarrassedly stereotypic impulses of the scientific project. In this interpretation, the task of scientific enlightment—the illumination of the reality behind appearances—is an inversion of surface and interior, an interchange between visible and invisible, that effectively routs the last vestiges of archaic, subterranean female power. Like the deceptive solidity of Eddington's table, the visible surface dissolves into transparent unreality. Scientific enlightenment is in this sense a drama between visibility and invisibility, light and dark, a drama in need of constant reenactment at ever-receding recesses of nature's secrets.

In the remarks that follow, I want to give two examples, or rather one example and one counterexample, which together serve to inform each other in their apparent contradiction. The example is a particularly vivid reenactment of that "drama" which can be seen in the story of the rise of molecular biology—a drama that was, in fact, quite explicitly cast in the language of "light and life,"[7] the quest for the secret of life, and then, once that secret was claimed to have been found, ended with the ultimate banishment of the very language of secrets, mystery, and darkness from biological discourse.

As it is usually told, in its classical format, the story of the rise of molecular biology is a drama between science and nature. It begins with the claim of a few physicists—most notably Erwin Schroedinger, Max Delbruck, and Leo Szilard—that the time was ripe to extend the promise of physics for clear and precise knowledge to the last frontier: the problem of life. Emboldened by their example, two especially brave young scientific adventurers, namely, James Watson and Francis Crick, took up the challenge and did, in fact, succeed in vanquishing nature's ultimate and definitive stronghold. As if in direct refutation of the earlier, more circumspect suggestion of Niels Bohr that what quantum mechanics taught us was that "the minimal freedom we must allow the organism will be just large enough to permit it, so to say, to hide its ultimate secrets from us,"[8] Watson and Crick succeeded in showing "that areas apparently too mysterious to be explained by physics and chemistry could in fact be so explained."[9] In short, they found the secret of life.

There is another story here, however, one that takes place in the realm of science itself—a drama not between science and nature but between competing motifs in science, indeed among competing visions of what a biological science should look like. When Watson and Crick embarked on a quest that they themselves described as a "calculated assault on the secret of life," they were employing a language that was, at the time, not only grandiose and provocatively unfashionable but, as Donald Fleming has pointed out, "in total defiance of contemporary standards of good taste in biological discourse."[10] The story of real interest to historians of science, I suggest, is in the redefinition of what a scientific biology meant; the story of the transformation of biology from a science in which the language of mystery had a place not only legitimate but highly functional, to a science that tolerated no secrets, a science more like physics, predicated on the conviction that the mysteries of life were there to be unraveled. In this retelling, our focus inevitably shifts from the accomplishments of molecular biology to the representation of those accomplishments.

The subplot is in effect a story of cognitive politics. It is a story of the growing authority of physics, and physicists; of an authority that drew directly from the momentous achievements of quantum mechanics early in the century and indirectly from the very fresh acclaim accruing to physicists for their role in winning World War II. Told in this way, we can begin to make sense of the puzzle that has long plagued historians of contemporary biology. Despite initial claims and hopes, molecular biology gave no new laws of physics and revealed no paradoxes. What, then, did the physicists, described as having led the revolution of molecular biology, actually provide?

Leo Szilard said it quite clearly: it was "not any skills acquired in physics, but rather an attitude: the conviction which few biologists had at the time, that mysteries can be solved."[11] He went on to say, "If secrets exist, they must be explainable. You see, this is something which modern biologists brought into biology, something which the classical biologists did not have. . . . They lacked the faith that things are explainable—and it is this faith . . . which leads to major advances in biology."

And indeed, he was right. This attitude, this conviction that life's secrets could be found, this view of themselves (especially Watson and Crick) as conquistadores who could and would find it—a stance that drew directly and vigorously on the authority of physicists for its license—proved to be extraordinarily productive. It permitted the conviction, and just a few years later the sharing of that conviction, that life's secret *had* been found. As Max Delbruck said in his Nobel address in 1970:

> Molecular genetics has taught us to spell out the connectivity of life in such palpable detail that we may say in plain words, "the riddle of life has been solved."[12]

In shifting our focus from the successes of molecular biology to the representation of those successes, this retelling inevitably raises the question, What difference does such a representation make?

Much has been written about the race to the double helix—about why Rosalind Franklin, or even Erwin Chargaff, did not see it, about how long it would have taken Franklin if Watson and Crick had not beaten her to it, etc. And I've always thought that that was an essentially boring discussion. It was relevant, of course, to matters of credit, but it had no bearing, I thought, on the course of science. I now think differently. If Rosalind Franklin *had* found the structure of DNA, as she surely would have, she would also, almost equally surely, have seen in that structure a mechanism for genetic replication. *What she would not in all likelihood have seen in it was the secret of life.* Or, as Chargaff himself has written:

> If Rosalind Franklin and I could have collaborated, we might have come up with something of the sort in one or two years. I doubt, however, that we could ever have elevated the double helix into "the mighty symbol that has replaced the cross as the signature of the biological alphabet."[13]

The representation of the mechanism of genetic replication as the secret of life was a move that neither Rosalind Franklin, nor Chargaff, nor any number of others could have made, for the simple reason that the traditions from which they came would not have permitted such a linguistic and ideological sweep. That Watson and Crick *were* able to make it was a direct consequence of the existence of a small but significant culture of like-minded "new thinkers" in biology that had grown up around them, in response to the same forces that had influenced them.

I also want to suggest that this description of the mechanism of genetic replication as the secret of life—or, conversely, this representation of the secret of life as the mechanism of genetic replication—had decisive consequences for the future course of biology. It permitted a more complete vindication of a set of beliefs than would otherwise have been possible: beliefs in the absolute adequacy of mechanism, in the incontrovertible value of simplicity, and in the decisive power of a particular conception of biology. No doubt the triumph of the double helix would have been major no matter how it had been described, but its particular representation allowed molecular biologists an assumption of scientific hegemony theretofore unfamiliar in biology. Having solved the problem of life "in principle if not in all details," as Jacques Monod put it,[14] there was no longer room for doubt, for uncertainty, for questions unanswerable within that framework, even for data that would not fit, or for another conception of biology. A science that had historically been characterized by diversity—perhaps like the life it presumed to study—became if not quite monolithic, then very close to it. Certainly in their own minds, molecular biology had become synonymous with scientific biology.

The representation of the secret of life as the mechanism of genetic replication led, once that mechanism had been illuminated, to the conclusion that life itself was not complex, as had been thought earlier,

but simple; simple, indeed, beyond our wildest dreams. The only secret of nature was that there were no secrets, and now that secret
was out. Henceforth, the very language of biological discourse was
to be cleansed of any reference to mystery. Words such as *complexity*
and *mystery,* words with a long-standing tradition in biology, soon
became disreputable and manifestly unscientific.

Barbara McClintock, finally rewarded in 1983 with the Nobel Prize,
was for many years discounted, in part because of her blatant indifference to the new credo. If she continues to be described as "unscientific," it is for the same reason: mystery, for her, remained, and
continues to remain, a positive value.[15] And if McClintock is revealed
as a relic of a bygone era by her regard for mystery, Erwin Chargaff is
revealed as not only old but also bitter and jealous. *Only* a bitter old
man would say, in 1978, as he did,

> It would seem that man cannot live without mysteries. One could say,
> the great biologists worked in the very light of darkness. We have been
> deprived of this fertile light. . . . What will have to go next?[16]

Finally, it was not only language that changed. The very conception
of what counted as a legitimate question also changed. Questions
without clear and definitive answers not only were not worth asking,
they were not asked. Similarly, the meaning of explanation was correspondingly circumscribed. Biological explanations were now limited
to "how things worked." The proof of understanding was to be provided by a mechanism. That which mechanism failed to illuminate,
rapidly fell from consciousness.

It is important to note, at this juncture, the great irony of the fact
that in the end, it was the very pursuit of molecular mechanisms that
ultimately created the conditions enabling the retelling of its own story.
That is, the story of the representation of the successes of molecular
biology can be told today precisely because of all the research that
has emerged, from molecular biology itself, to challenge that representation.[17] Because of this work, we are granted *scientific* authority
to look at the underside of the successes of molecular biology, to look
at some of the costs that were incurred by embracing the metaphoric
quest of nature as an open book or a transparent text harboring no
secrets, having no interior, and science as a clear and apparent (although not transparent) reflection of that text. This quest is one in
which both science and nature are collapsed into two-dimensional
surfaces, both are self-evident texts in which nothing is hidden; there
is, apparently, nothing behind the text. But while it may or may not
be true that nothing lies behind the book of nature, it is certainly the

case that behind the scientific text lies its author—his invisibility and unassailability now secured by the very self-evidence of his text. Science thus becomes less of a mirror and more of a one-way glass, transparent to the scientist, but impenetrable to anyone or anything outside.

To return to my opening remarks, I think Freud was right when he argued that the invisibility of Moses' divine patriarch permitted believers "a much more grandiose idea of their God" (p. 143). But I suggest that Freud's crucial insight has more to do with the relationship between invisibility and power than with the relationship between invisibility and masculinity. That is to say, the invisibility of nature's interiority, like the invisibility of women's interiority, is threatening precisely because it threatens the balance of power between man and nature, and between men and women. To this problem, the culture of modern science has found a truly effective solution, indeed a far more effective solution than those that had gone before. Instead of banishing the Furies underground, out of sight, as did the Greeks, modern science has sought to expose female interiority, to bring it into the light, and thus to dissolve its threat entirely.

In a parallel assertion of power, the secrets of God are also put to the light: where the secrets of nature are *visible,* the laws of nature are *knowable,* that is to say, visible to the mind's eye. In this new ontology, invisibility is sanctioned in only one place: ideally, the scientific text has no signature. The author of the modern scientific text, or the authority of modern science, is simultaneously everywhere and nowhere; on the one hand, it is manifest, self-evident, the arch-enemy of secrets and secrecy, and on the other, anonymous, uninterpretable, and unidentifiable. There for all to see, eschewing all constraints, barriers, and walls, the scientific text denies the very possibility of decoding by its insistent visibility, and all the while remains, in its own interior, as invisible as Moses' patriarch.

That is the predominant mythology in its normal form. Powerful, formative, it shapes the very meaning of science. But before concluding, I want to put before you an apparent counterexample; in fact, an example illustrating what can happen to this mythic structure when its fundamental condition of openness is not met. As it happens, perhaps not accidentally, this example is drawn from the very events which served so conspicuously to bolster the authority of science in our own time, and, more specifically, to bolster the authority of physics at just the time when molecular biology was coming into existence.

Many people have written about the severe problems that the demands of military secrecy posed for the physicists of the Manhattan Project. The very nature of their enterprise, Oppenheimer claimed, demanded the free and open exchange of ideas and information—free and open amongst the physicists themselves, that is. Oppenheimer won enough concessions from General Groves to permit the physicists to proceed, but the larger demand for secrecy was, of course, never relaxed. The making of the bomb was perhaps the biggest and best-kept secret that science has ever harbored. It was a secret kept from the Germans and the Japanese, from the American public, and indeed from the wives of the very men who produced the bomb. Several of the Los Alamos wives have remarked that Alamogordo was the first they knew of what their husbands were doing, and indeed of what their entire community—a community fully dependent on intimacy and mutual dependency for its survival—was working toward.

The Manhattan Project was a project in which the most privileged secret belonged not to the women but to the men. It was a scientific venture predicated not on openness but on its opposite, on absolute secrecy. Hardly an open book that anyone could read, Los Alamos had an interior. And what was produced out of this interiority was (shall we say, with pregnant irony?) "Oppenheimer's baby." As Brian Easlea has amply documented, the metaphor of pregnancy and birth in fact became the prevailing metaphor surrounding the production and the testing of first the atomic bomb and later the hydrogen bomb.[18] It was used not only as a precautionary code but as a mode of description that was fully embraced by the physicists at Los Alamos, by the government, and ultimately by the public at large.

As early as December 1942, physicists at Chicago received acknowledgment for their work on plutonium with a telegram from Ernest Lawrence that read, "Congratulations to the parents. Can hardly wait to see the new arrival."[19] In point of fact, they had to wait another two and a half years. Finally, in July 1945, Richard Feynman was summoned back to Los Alamos with a wire announcing the day on which the birth of the "baby" was expected. Robert Oppenheimer may have been the father of the A-bomb, but Kistiakowsky tells us that "the bomb, after all, was the baby of the Laboratory, and there was little the Security Office could do to dampen parental interests."[20]

Two days after the Alamogordo test, Secretary of War Henry *Stimpson* received a cable in Potsdam which read:

> Doctor has just returned most enthusiastic and confident that the little boy is as husky as his big brother. The light in his eyes discernible from

here to Highhold and I could have heard his screams from here to my farm.[21]

And, as the whole world was to learn just three weeks later, the "little boy" was indeed as husky as his brother.

In this inversion of the traditional metaphor, this veritable backfiring, more monstrous in its reality than any fantasies of anal birth explored by psychoanalysts, nature's veil is rent, maternal procreativity is effectively coopted, but the secret of life has become the secret of death. When the bomb exploded, Oppenheimer was reminded of the lines from the Bhagavad-Gita:

> If the radiance of a thousand suns
> were to burst into the sky,
> that would be like
> the splendor of the Mighty One.

But as the cloud rose up in the distance, he also recalled,

I am become Death, the shatterer of worlds.[22]

It is perhaps not surprising if, after that, some physicists sought to retreat to the safer ground of biology. Here they could reassert a more traditional quest, now (merely!) the secret of life. But in this turn, or return, they brought them a new authority, grounded in a vastly more terrible prowess.

N O T E S

1. Evelyn Fox Keller, "Feminism and Science," *Signs: Journal of Women in Culture and Society* 7, no. 3 (1982): 589–602; and *Reflections on Gender and Science* (New Haven: Yale University Press, 1985). For other work dedicated to the same venture, see Brian Easlea, *Science and Sexual Oppression* (London: Weidenfeld and Nicolson, 1981); Elizabeth Fee, "Is Feminism a Threat to Scientific Objectivity?" *International Journal of Women's Studies* 4 (1981):378–92; Sandra Harding, "Is Gender a Variable in Conceptions of Rationality?" *Dialectica* 36, no. 2–3 (1982): 225–42; Carolyn Merchant, *The Death of Nature* (San Francisco: Harper and Row, 1980); Hilary Rose, "Hand, Brain, and Heart: A Feminist Epistemology for the Natural Sciences," *Signs* 9, no. 1 (1983): 73– 90.
2. For an excellent review of this subject, see Ruth Bleier, *Science and Gender* (New York: Pergamon, 1984), and her essay in this volume.
3. See Keller, *Reflections*, chaps. 1, 2, and 3.
4. Christine Froula, "When Eve Reads Milton: Undoing the Canonical Economy," *Critical Inquiry* 10 (December 1983): 321–47.

5. Sigmund Freud, *Moses and Monotheism,* trans. Katherine Jones (New York, 1967), pp. 145–46, quoted by Froula, p. 133.

6. Richard Feynman, "Los Alamos from Below," *Engineering and Science* 39, no. 2 (1976):19.

7. See Niels Bohr, "Light and Life," in *Atomic Physics and Human Knowledge* (New York: John Wiley and Sons, 1958).

8. Ibid., p. 9.

9. Letter from Crick to Olby, in Robert Olby, "Francis Crick, DNA, and the Central Dogma," *Daedalus* (Fall 1970), pp. 938–87.

10. Donald Fleming, "Emigré Physicists and the Biological Revolution," *Perspectives in American History,* vol. 2 (Cambridge, Mass.: Harvard University Press, 1960), p. 155.

11. Ibid., p. 161.

12. Max Delbruck, "A Physicist's Renewed Look at Biology: Twenty Years Later," *Science* 168 (1970): 1312.

13. Erwin Chargaff, *Heraclitean Fire* (New York: Rockefeller University Press, 1978), p. 103.

14. Quoted in Horace Freeland Judson, *The Eighth Day of Creation* (New York: Simon and Schuster, 1979), p. 216.

15. See Evelyn Fox Keller, *A Feeling for the Organism: The Life and Work of Barbara McClintock* (New York: W. H. Freeman, 1983).

16. Chargaff, *Heraclitean Fire,* p. 109.

17. See, e.g., Keller, *A Feeling.*

18. Brian Easlea, *Fathering the Unthinkable: Masculinity, Scientists, and the Nuclear Arms Race* (London: Pluto Press, 1983).

19. Ibid., p. 107.

20. Ibid., p. 203.

21. Ibid., p. 90.

22. Robert Jungk, *Brighter Than a Thousand Suns* (New York: Grove Press, 1958), p. 201.

A Desire of One's Own: Psychoanalytic Feminism and Intersubjective Space

Jessica Benjamin

The question of woman's desire actually runs parallel to the question of power. We have often had cause to wonder whether the feminist focus on personal life, and for that matter the preoccupation with inner life that characterizes psychoanalysis, is fated to surrender the great issues of power. That would mean that the revaluation of things feminine in fact perpetuates the split between transcendence and immanence that Simone de Beauvoir saw as the great divide between the sexes. And yet, the challenge to this kind of split may be the greatest theoretical insight that feminism has to offer. Feminist thought is caught between three tasks: to redeem what has been devalued in women's domain, to conquer the territory that has been reserved to men, and to resolve and transcend the opposition between these spheres by reformulating the relationship between them. The structural tension between male and female categories and the difficulty of reformulating it are as pertinent to the problems of sexuality as to those of politics.

Consider again the origins of the idea that "the personal is political." It grew and flourished from within the high-flown rhetoric of revolutionary idealism as a critique of the ideal of sacrifice for the greater good that is intimately connected with the vision of individual transcendence through social struggle. As Carol Gilligan has pointed out in a discussion of the *Aeneid,* the notion of social responsibility conceived as duty or obligation has gone hand in hand with the representation of the self as separate, bounded, and autonomous.[1] This notion of sacrifice is inextricably associated with the idea that one is responsible only for one's self and that one can consider the web of immediate personal connections as less important than, for example, the abstract, universal cause of humanity, the founding of Rome, or the liberation of the oppressed.

It should be obvious that the reason women began to question this conception of struggle and sacrifice, to claim that the personal was also political, came from their very inability to detach themselves from such personal ties, especially from their responsibilities to children. They were not as able to devalue such attachments as were men. In de Beauvoir's terms, that could be seen only in the negative: women were trapped in immanence while men could heroically struggle for transcendence, for the personal glory that comes with sacrifice and valor. Indeed, what has always seemed curious about de Beauvoir's feminism is her agreement with the male idealization of individual transcendence and sacrifice over personal connection and responsibility. The doctrine of "the personal is political" not only meant the affirmation of personal responsibilities as equal to abstract ones; it also meant the rejection of this idealization, the awareness that it had fostered submission and passivity and hero worship on the part of women.

With the emergence of women's liberation, women began to reflect on the contradictory position in which they found themselves; more skeptical about detachment, less committed to idealizing absolute separation, women were yet ready to idealize the man who represented and gave them vicarious access to transcendence. Women's defense of personal attachment had been double-edged—at once a critique of heroism and a reflection of woman's need to be close to her hero and to his project, thus compliance with, as well as a challenge to, male idealized independence. Suddenly, in a kind of euphoric moment of demystification, this contradiction became visible and unsupportable.

De Beauvoir herself did much to analyze and demystify the wish for vicarious transcendence, woman's hope that the idealized other will give "her possession of herself and of the universe he represents."[2] Here she quotes a patient of Janet's, who expresses with un-self-conscious ardor the yearning for what I call ideal love:

> All my foolish acts and all the good things I have done have the same cause: an aspiration for a perfect and ideal love in which I can give myself completely, entrust my being to another, God, man, or woman, so superior to me that I will no longer need to think what to do in life. ... Someone to obey blindly and with confidence ... who will bear me up and lead me gently and lovingly toward perfection. How I envy the ideal love of Mary Magdalene and Jesus: to be the ardent disciple of an adored and worthy master; to live and die for him, my idol. (pp. 716–19)

The subject of this paper is woman's propensity toward ideal love. Ideal love typifies the curious role of women in both criticizing and complying with the elevation of masculine individuality and the devaluation of femininity. I shall argue that ideal love is the key to understanding the intricate relationship between woman's desire and woman's submission. I will try to show how the critique of individualism that has been developing within psychoanalytic feminism leads us to explore another level of an old problem, the problem of woman's desire. Today we may consider this problem with the greater clarity that derives from an analysis of the gender split, and with the resolve to confront not only the idealization of masculinity but also the reactive revaluation of femininity—a femininity whose character has been constituted as the other, the opposite, the excluded.

According to current developments in psychoanalytic feminism, the salient feature of male individuality is that it grows out of the repudiation of the primary identification with and dependency on the mother. That leads to an individuality that stresses, as Nancy Chodorow has argued, difference as denial of commonality, separation as denial of connection; and that is made up of a series of dualisms, of mutually exclusive poles, where independence seems to exclude all dependency rather than be characterized by a balance of separation and connection.[3] The critique of this form of individualism is the contribution of the evolving integration of object relations theory with feminism that began with Chodorow's work. Central to this critique of dualism, cogently elaborated by Evelyn Fox Keller in relation to scientific thought, is the awareness that the idealization of a particular form of one-sided autonomy permeates the Western notion of the individual as thinking subject, as explorer of the world. I have argued that this idealization is profoundly embedded in all modern social acitivity and forms of knowledge; it informs the traditions of Western rationality and underlies the instrumental character that stamps that rationality.[4]

Elsewhere I have tried to show how the one-sided autonomy that denies dependency characteristically leads to domination.[5] Since the child continues to need the mother, since man continues to need woman, the absolute assertion of independence requires possessing and controlling the needed object. The intention is not to do without her but to make sure that her alien otherness is either assimilated or controlled, that her own subjectivity nowhere asserts itself in a way that could make his dependency upon her a conscious insult to his sense of freedom. In his discussion of the ideal subject in philosophical idealism, Herbert Marcuse explains:

> Self-sufficiency and independence of all that is other and alien is the
> sole guarantee of the subject's freedom. What is not dependent on any
> other person or thing, what possesses itself, is free . . . . Having excludes
> the other . . . . Relating to the other in such a way that the subject really
> reaches and is united with him counts as loss and dependence.[6]

Naturally, Marcuse identifies this form of individuality with the bourgeois era, with the possessive individualism of specific property relations. Historically, that identification—based on Marx's ideas about
the interaction of economics and ideology—has been the springboard
for the critique of the autonomous individual. In Max Weber's view,
the precondition of this individuality and its consummation in the
Protestant ethic can be located in the essential rationality of the Oc-
cident.[7] To these frameworks, feminist theory added an analysis of
psychological and social core of this individual in the domination of
woman by man. Thus, the missing piece in analyzing Western rationality and individualism is the structure of gender domination. This
structure is materialized—in a way that occludes its gender roots—in
the instrumentalism that pervades our economic and social relations.
A feminist analysis reveals this apparent gender neutrality of instrumental rationality to be a mystification, parallel, if you like, to the
mystification of commodity fetishism—an illusion created by the gender relations themselves.

In psychoanalysis, it becomes more apparent that the celebration
of individuality is a gender-related project. Indeed, the feminist critique of individualism has taken psychoanalysis itself to task both for
its tendency to make independence and separateness the goal of development (as in the view that the ego develops from oneness to
separateness) and for the idea that femininity is defined by the lack
of the penis. As Chodorow has pointed out, these two coordinates of
Freudian thought are interconnected, drawn from the plane of the
masculine experience of individuation. In fact, the idealization of separation and the idealization of the phallus go together. We see that
in Juliet Mitchell's argument that the phallus is the representative of
the principle of individuation. The father and his phallus intervene to
spring the child from the dyadic trap, the oneness with mother, forcing
the child to individuate.[8] This theme has been reiterated in myriad
forms; indeed, the relationship to the father's phallus may be the
indissoluble lump in the batter for a feminist version of psychoanalysis.[9] It presents us with the dilemma that desire and power, symbolically speaking, are one. And the consequences for the girl are, as
Mitchell put it, "no phallus, no power, except those winning ways of
getting one" (p. 96).

The logic of this position can only succumb to a massive critique of a whole set of assumptions in Freudian thought: that individuality is defined by separateness; that separation is brought about through paternal intervention (read authority); that the father's phallus, which forbids incest, is the prime mover of separation; that the girl's lack of the phallus relegates her to a passive, envious relationship to father and phallus; that this position, in which the girl is deprived of her own agency and desire, is the hallmark of femininity. Against each of these assertions, persuasive evidence has been cited and arguments have been mounted. New ways of looking at self and other emerged, in fact, before the recent wave of feminism. What psychoanalytic feminists have done is to locate the problem in the structure of gender relations, thus offering a materialist explanation for the misapprehensions in Freudian thought, and for the insistent sticky pull of orthodoxy that every critic must still confront. The critique of psychoanalysis as ideology ultimately goes beyond the idea of bias to the idea of real appearance: it shows how the sexual fallacies reflect the real appearance of gender relations.

Briefly, a critical feminist psychoanalytic theory offers the following answers. We argue that individuality is properly, ideally, a balance of separation and connectedness, of the capacities for agency and relatedness. We rely on infancy research that suggests that the self does not proceed from oneness to separateness, but evolves by simultaneously differentiating and recognizing the other, by alternating between "being with" and being distinct.[10] We say that once we shift from the oedipal perspective that Mitchell uses to the preoedipal one, it is clear that the impulse toward separation is present from the start, that no outside agitator is required. We maintain that the vital issue is whether the mother herself is able to recognize the child's subjectivity, and later whether the child can recognize the mother. Thus, we dispute the necessity of the patriarchal mode of separation.

Perhaps most important, we begin with a new position on femininity; we argue that long before the oedipal phase and the emergence of penis envy, the little girl has consolidated her feminine gender identity on the basis of her identification with her mother. Freud's argument that such identification is not truly feminine, that only the penis wish and the passive love of the father are feminine, seems simply implausible. It gives way before the explanatory power of the alternate model of gender evolution—that the girl sustains her primary identification with the mother and that the boy must break that identity and switch to the father.[11] It is this break in identification that brings about the attitude of repudiation and distance toward primary connectedness, nurturance, and intimacy that characterizes the male model of independence, the male idealization of autonomy. Thus, maternal identification theory leans toward the revaluation of the mother, whose influence Freud neglected in favor of the father, and is less likely than the theory of phallic monism to emphasize the negativity of the female condition.

Yet this position, precisely because of its emphasis on the mother, is vulnerable to the objection that it disregards the Freudian argument, not so easily explained away, that women lack a desire of their own. The problem of desire is more likely to be addressed by feminists who work in the Lacanian tradition, which begins with the phallus as the central organizer of gender.[12] The idea of desire suggests power and activity, even as, it would seem, does the image of male desire, the phallus. Freud cautioned against the easy equation of femininity with passivity and masculinity with activity, yet he found that the circuitous path to femininity culminates in the acceptance of passivity. Thus, Mitchell herself has proposed that we accept Freud's understanding of feminine passivity in representing desire. Only by acknowledging the power of the phallus, she argues, can we finally confront the negativity of our condition and understand the origins of woman's submission, the deep unconscious roots of patriarchy.

Indeed, we must admit that we are still unable to produce a female image or symbol that would counterbalance the monopoly of the phallus in representing desire. Woman's sexuality is primarily portrayed through her object status, her ability to attract. The closest we have come to an image of feminine activity is motherhood and fertility. But the mother is not culturally articulated as a sexual subject, one who actively desires something for herself—quite the contrary.[13] And once sexuality is cut loose from reproduction, once woman is no longer mother, we are at a loss for an image of woman's sexual agency. What is woman's desire?

The idea that little girls develop their gender identity through identification with the mother is persuasive. But it does not entirely solve the problem that penis envy was meant to explain.[14] The fact is, as Dinnerstein has described it, that the little girl's sexuality is muted by the fact that the woman she must identify with, her mother, is so profoundly desexualized (Dinnerstein sees the girl, like the boy, as complicit in this desexualization, because it is a way of reacting against the mother's omnipotence; thus, as mother, she must deny her own sexuality). The reasons for the desexualization of the mother—the fear of her power and the need to control her, the source of goodness— have often been discussed. But there is a reason beyond the wishes of the child in each of us, one that arises from the current practice of motherhood, that is, the frequent depression of the isolated mother, the "housewife's syndrome." To be a subject of desire, a sexual agent, implies a control over one's own destiny, a freedom to will, that mothers often lack. Their power over their children is not to be mistaken for the freedom to act on their own wishes and impulses, to be author and agent in their own lives. The mother's sexual feelings, with their threat of selfishness, passion, and uncontrollability, are a disturbing possibility that even psychoanalysts would relegate to the "unnatural."

Briefly, then, the power of the mother cannot, as in the case of the father, be described as the power of a sexual subject. Ironically, psychoanalytic thought often depicts the power the mother has over her child with the emblem of the phallus. In this view, the child does not know that the mother's power is not the power of a subject until desire, especially genital desire, begins to enter the picture. Thus, it is the "phallic" mother who is powerful in the preoedipal era and the "castrated" mother who is repudiated by the boy in the oedipal era. According to this theory, the little girl loves her phallic mother actively but turns away from her when she discovers that she can get the phallus only from her father, whom she agrees to love passively.[15] Hence, Freud argued, for woman desire is constituted by the effort to get the missing phallus, an effort that leads her irrevocably into the passive position of being the object for the father, the male subject. In this sense, woman has no active desire; instead, she is doomed to envy the embodiment of desire, which forever eludes her since only a man can possess it. Desire in women thus appears as envy, and only as envy. For Freud, what woman lacks is a desire of her own.

Let us acknowledge the real problem, the partial truth of this gloomy view.[16] So far, women do not have an equivalent image of desire; the existing equation of masculinity with desire, and femininity with object-of-desire, reflects a condition that does exist; it is not merely a biased view. It is a real appearance—real, yes, but only apparently essential, rather a manifestation of deeper causes. This condition, then, is not inevitable but has come into being through forces we intend to understand and counteract. We need not deny the contribution of anatomical reality in shaping the current condition of femininity; we only have to argue that how biological givens are psychically organized is partly the work of culture, of social arrangements, which we can change or redirect. To begin to think about such changes, we need to understand the complex unconscious forces that contribute to our current gender arrangements. In this case we are asking, What are the deeper causes to which we might attribute woman's lack of sexual subjectivity? How does woman's desire become alienated into forms of submission and dependency? How does it come about that femininity appears inextricably linked to passivity, even to masochism, or that women seek their desire in another, hope to have it recognized and recognizable through the subjectivity of an other?

The danger of the position that sees identification with the mother as the source of femininity is that we will accept, even idealize, the deprivation to which women have been subjected. We may detect in some contemporary feminist thought the incipient rejection of sexuality as a component of woman's autonomy. That would mean avoiding a confrontation with the aspects of masculinity we wish to appropriate, making sexuality and desire the right of the stronger. The idealization of motherhood, which can be traced through popular culture to both antifeminist and feminist cultural politics, can be seen as an attempt to preserve a sphere of influence and agency, the power of the apron strings. But all these tendencies are united by the tendency to naturalize woman's desexualization and lack of agency in the world. Two dangers arise from a one-sided revaluing of woman's position: freedom and desire might remain unchallenged male domain, leaving us to be righteous and deeroticized, intimate, caring, and self-sacrificing; or we might ignore the power of sexual imagery and the unconscious relationships represented by it. Then we would fail to understand the psychology of male domination, the force of desire that substantiates power, the adoration that creates it ever anew.

The theory of maternal identification does provide us with a new starting point, but it has to be further developed in order to confront the problem of woman's desire. It must struggle with the unconscious and the exclusive power of the phallus in representing desire. With what shall we represent our desire? I believe that the new theory of gender identification can yet point the way out of the dilemma of penis envy; that we do not, as Mitchell claimed in her allegiance to Freud, have to wait until some other principle of individuation and desire appears in the society of the future. Briefly, I will argue that what Freud saw as the little girl's early masculine orientation really reflects the wish of the toddler—of both sexes—to identify with the father, who is perceived as a representative of the outside world.

Psychoanalysis has accepted the importance of the boy's early love for the father in forming his sense of agency and desire; it has not assigned equal importance to the girl's early love. This early love of the father is an ideal love; that is, it is full of the idealization that such a little child forms not merely because the father is big but because the father appears to be the solution to a series of conflicts that occur at this point in development. This idealization becomes the basis for future relationships of ideal love, the submission to a powerful other who seems to embody the agency and desire one lacks in oneself, someone who can be a mirror of one's ideal image of the self.

Critics of Freud have long argued that the father and his phallus have the power they do because of their ability to stand for difference and separation from the mother. The phallus is not intrinsically the symbol of desire but becomes so because of the child's search for a pathway to individuation. As long as the traditional sexual division of labor persists, the child will turn to the father as the "knight in shining armor"[17] who represents freedom, the outside world, will, agency, and desire. But the way in which the father represents all of that is given by the interaction of the child's own internal psychological workings with social and cultural conditions. As each phase of infancy has been analyzed in terms of the infant's own contribution to interaction, the different responses of mothers and fathers can be schematized for each phase. Thus, we can see the creation of composite gender representations through accumulated experience in each phase. For example, it has been noted that in early infancy the father plays more exuberantly and wildly with the baby, jiggling and whooping, while the mother, absorbed with caretaking and responsibility, feeling less separate from the child she has borne, is less playful.[18] In the child's earliest perceptions, then, the father may stand for outsideness, novelty, stimulation, and excitement; the mother for soothing, holding, and containment.

The importance of the father as a figure of excitement becomes crucial only at the point where the child begins to experience differentiation—the process of sorting out self and other and becoming more autonomous—in a more conflictual way. This point, according to the most powerful psychoanalytic paradigm of early development, Margaret Mahler's separation-individuation theory, occurs around the second half of the second year of life.[19] The Rapprochement phase, as she has called it, might be seen as the great fall from grace. At this point, the child's awareness of its separate existence intensifies, with the child becoming conscious of its dependency. The child is confronted with this truth: mother is not an extension of myself; since we are separate, I possess only my own limited powers; everything she does for me is not under my control, not a reflection of my will. This blow to the child's narcissism has to be repaired by parental confirmation of the child's independence. Thus emerges a fundamental paradox: the need to be recognized as independent by the very person you once depended upon. The underlying question is whether the price of selfhood is going to be the loss of the mother's love, or, conversely, whether the price of love is to be the inhibition of autonomy.

What is really wanted at this point in life is recognition of one's desire, that one *is* a subject of desire, an agent who can will things and make them happen. And at this very point, early in life, where desire enters in, the first realizations of gender difference begin to take hold in the psyche. That is, coincidentally, the period of "core gender identity formation," in Robert Stoller's term. And it is the point at which the father's difference from the mother first becomes crucial. What is interesting is that little boys seem to get through this phase with more bravado and less depression than girls. If boys tend to escape the depression associated with Rapprochement, it is because they are able to deny the feeling of helplessness that comes with the realization of separateness. Mahler says they do so by virtue of their greater "motor-mindedness," which helps sustain the buoyancy of their body ego feelings, their pleasure in active aggressive strivings.[20] In light of the well-known fascination of little boys with motor vehicles, that could be called the tendency to brmm brmm brmm one's way through Rapprochement.

Feminists have argued that the mother's greater identification with the daughter and her willingness to bolster the son's independence are responsible for the differences between boy and girl toddlers' reactions to Rapprochement.[21] That may be true. But equally important is that boys seem to resolve the conflict of independence with the mother by turning to someone else. And this other is conventionally the father, or male substitute or symbol, who can be a different object of identification. At this point, when the child is discovering its own desire and agency, the father's position as the one who was outside, who was exciting, becomes crucial. The father, as Ernest Abelin has argued, becomes the subject of desire in whom the child wishes to recognize himself.[22] Importantly, in this phase of life excitement begins to be felt not as emanating from the object (she, it is so attractive) but as a property of the self, one's own inner desire. The father now becomes the symbolic figure who represents just such an owner of desire, desire for the mother (Abelin makes much of the fact that the desire is toward the mother; I am inclined to think it more diffuse, but that may vary with the mother's ability to juggle availability to the demanding husband and son). This recognition of himself in the father also enables the boy to deny the helplessness felt at this phase, to feel that he is powerful like his father. Paternal identification thus has a defensive aspect—the son denies dependency and dissociates himself from his previous tie—that later stamps this ideal image of the father.

The child is in conflict between the desire to hold on to the mother and the desire to fly away, and wants to solve this problem by becoming independent without experiencing loss. The great desire of the child is to be recognized in all its triumphant willing. The solution to this dilemma is to split—to assign the contradictory strivings to different objects. Schematically, the mother can become the object of desire, the father the subject of desire in whom one recognizes oneself. This "way out" of the internal conflict around dependency is usually realized fully only in boys, for only in boys is this identification with the father encouraged by mother and father alike. Both children have the wish to separate and experience themselves as subjects of desire, but only boys seem to have full access to a vehicle for this wish. The vehicle has both defensive and constructive aspects: on the one hand, it enables the child to separate, avoiding the Rapprochement conflict and denying feelings of helplessness; on the other, it helps consolidate a representation of desire, excitement, and the outside world with which the child can identify.

The ideal love of the child for the father reflects the child's longing to be recognized by a powerful other as being like him. Psychoanalysts have called the period preceding this one, where the child is elated about his new abilities and locomotion, a "love affair with the world." In Rapprochement, the love affair with the world becomes a love affair with the father, indeed, a homoerotic love affair. The boy's identificatory love for the father, his wish to be recognized as like him, is the erotic force behind separation. Desire is intrinsically linked, at this point, to the idea of freedom. But the separation that is presumably occurring actually takes place in the context of a powerful connection. Indeed, identification is the chief mode of connecting with others in this phase, as the well-known phenomenon of parallel play suggests. The longing for this ideal love, this identificatory love of the child for the father, is the basis of the idealization of the father and male power, as well as of the cultural construction of the autonomous individual that I referred to earlier. But it is an idealization untainted with submission as long as the wonderful, exciting father says, "Yes, you are like me."

Thus, I believe that the key to the missing desire in women is in one sense the missing father. Being the I who desires is routed through identification with him. Why has the discussion of the father-daughter relationship been so thin compared to that of the father-son relationship?[23] The psychoanalytic commonplace is that the boy has one object (the mother), and the girl has two (mother and father). But at times we are tempted to think that the boy has two and the girl has none. I believe that behind the missing phallus, the envy that has been attributed to women, is the longing for just such a homoerotic bond, just such an ideal love. That is why we find so many stories of woman's love being directed to a hero such as she herself would be, accompanied by the wish for disciplehood and submission to an ideal. We can also explain the identification with little boys that Freud found in women's masochistic fantasies ("A Child Is Being Beaten"[24]) by reference to the longing for this homoerotic, ideal love. It is the wish to be like the powerful father, and to be loved by him, that appears in this alien form. The more common variety of ideal love, a woman's adoration of heroic men who sacrifice love for freedom, can thus be traced back to this phase of life and the disappointments a girl usually suffers. When Bogart tells Bergman that in this world the troubles of a few little people don't amount to a hill of beans, and he walks off into the sunset with the French colonel to join the resistance, we have the whole story.

I will draw several conclusions from this model. Historically, the gap left in the girl's subjectivity by the missing father appeared as a lack, which the theory of penis envy emerged to fill. On the level of real life, when the desire to identify is blocked, envy takes its place. Unlike jealousy, envy is about being, not having, and should be read as a signal of thwarted identification. On the other hand, under the present gender system, the girl's wish to identify with the father, even if it is satisfied, leads to myriad problems. As long as the mother is not articulated as a sexual agent, identification with the father's agency and desire must appear illegitimate and stolen; furthermore, it conflicts with the cultural image of woman-as-sexual-object and with the girl's maternal identification. It will not correspond with what she knows about her mother's position in her father's eyes.[25]

The "real" solution to this dilemma of woman's desire is much further-reaching and has to do with the need for a mother who *is* articulated as a sexual subject, who is an agent, who does express desire. Thus, psychoanalytic feminism rejects both the idea that the mother cannot be a figure of separation and a subject of desire for her children, and the idea that the father cannot offer himself as a figure of identification for the daughter. We therefore challenge the structure of heterosexuality as it is formed through the differential meanings of mother and father, rooted in the early acquisition of gender, and shaped by the earliest splitting of the psyche.

Yet, even this early phase of gender is less rigid than the oedipal organization that comes after it. In the second and third years of life, gender is still loose, contradictory, and vague. The child is still interested in identifying with both parents, in being everything. My point is not that gender can or should be eliminated but that along with a conviction of gender identity, the individual ideally integrates and expresses male and female aspects of selfhood. This integration then allows flexibility in the expression of gender and one's own individual will. That could be called an argument for androgyny or bisexuality—not a rejection of gender but a vision of reconciling the gendered self with the self that is bi-, or supra-, or nongendered.

In making this argument for gender flexibility, I am aware that I am crossing the frontier into defending, rather than merely explicating, the early magical and narcissistic wishes against the oedipal reality principle. It is not my intention wholly to deny the critique of narcissism and early splitting made by Otto Kernberg or Christopher Lasch in particular. I am not saying that individuals should not grow up, should bask in preoedipal unreality. But this period, if all goes well, is precisely not characterized by more intense splitting of opposites, especially when it comes to gender. Rather, I believe that the magical hope of reconciling gender oppositions that children of this age possess appears wholly unrealistic only in the light of our present cultural schisms. If our interest is in gender structures rather than ego pathology, it is worth questioning the conventional psychoanalytic position that splitting is more of a problem in preoedipal than in oedipal life.

What hampers the crossing over and intermingling, the abrogation of boundaries that ideally should exist alongside gender structures? The verdict is that the derogation of the female side of these polarities in every case leads to a hardening of the opposition between aspects of male and female individuality as now constructed.[26] The taboo on maternal sexual agency, the defensive mode of separation where the father is used to deny the mother, the idealization of the male figure in identificatory love, and the confirmation that the price of freedom is the relinquishment of nurturance and dependency—each of these reflects the derogation of femininity. The oedipal sexual organization now defines the form of our parenting arrangements, our cultural imagery, and our separation of public and private spheres. In this sense, gender structures are not merely materialized or reproduced through parenting, but are embedded in social and cultural life at all levels.

At each level, the division between male and female accentuates the irreconcilability of opposites. In every case, the male side of the pole, particularly the emphatic autonomy that denies interdependence and mutuality, has been idealized.

The upshot of this analysis is that the paradigm of sexual repression now appears secondary to another overarching concept whose significance has outgrown its original position in the Freudian edifice: the idea of splitting. In splitting, two complementary elements that should be held in tension are instead set up as opposites, with one side idealized and the other devalued. Thus, at the broader level, psychoanalytic feminism does not merely challenge the splitting of nurturance and freedom in the division of parenting (as in the exciting father and the holding mother); it also points to the dualistic mentality that inheres in our culture.[27]

But still one question remains: does woman have a desire of her own, one that is distinct in its form or content from that of man? Would something different come of identifying with the mother as subject of desire instead of with the father as subject of desire? I can argue with some confidence that a great difference would result from the opportunity to identify with both parents as subjects of desire, rather than repeating the triangular pattern where one is the agent, the other is the object. But reaching further, is there an alternate mode of representing woman's desire that does not occur through the phallus?

Although I have argued against attributing primary importance to the phallus in producing the conventional organization of gender and sexuality, I should like now to return to its symbolic significance. The phallus still has the power to represent desire, to represent the idealized force of paternal liberation. While we can now see that the phallus acquires its power not only as a defensive reaction to maternal power but also as a figure of excitement that contrasts with maternal holding and containment, we must still answer the question, What alternative to the phallus is there? Is there another relationship to desire than the one represented by the idealized phallus? Even if we question the existing gender division, seeing it as the source of the unique status of the phallus in representing desire, we must consider Mitchell's argument that until that division is overcome, there is no other way to represent desire or difference or separation. Is she right, or can we discern the rudiments of another form of representing desire, woman's desire, in the here and now of patriarchal culture?

There is a line of thought that answers this question by offering a female representation of desire derived from the image of our organs. This representation would have to be formed at the same symbolic

level on which the phallus works. But the representational level, which
has been organized and dominated by the phallus, keeps the female
body in its place as object. Agency is not restored to woman by aesth-
eticizing her body—that has already been done in spades. For the
symbolic level of the psyche seems to be occupied and organized by
phallic structures. The representation of woman's sexuality does not
seem to have its own symbolic structures but rather seems to be
incorporated into the system organized by phallic structures. That is
why women appeared to Freud to be defined by their absence of
phallic or masculine structures.

Finding woman's desire, I believe, requires finding an alternative to
the phallic structures, to the symbolic mode. And that means *an alternative mode of structuring the psyche, not just a symbol to replace
the phallus.* The phallic mode includes the whole constellation of
using the father as a vehicle for separation, of internalizing the father
qua phallus as a representation of agency and desire. The problem is
to find another psychic mode rather than just a female counterpart to
the phallic symbol. I have tried to develop a notion of this other mode
using the concept of *intersubjectivity.*

Intersubjectivity refers to what happens between individuals, and
within the individual-with-others, rather than within the individual
psyche. The mode of representing intrapsychic events, the symbolic
use of the body that psychoanalysis discovered, does not distinguish
between real and imagined, inside and outside, introjective-projective
processes and interaction. It does not distinguish between you as an
independently existing subject and you as a fantasy extension of my
wishes and desires. Similarly, it does not distinguish between I as
independently existing and desiring and I as merely embodying your
wishes, agency, and desire. It does not distinguish when I am really
the subject, with a desire of my own. Thus, Mitchell can speak of the
child wishing to represent the phallus for the mother as if this fantasy
of being something for the other constituted desire in its essential
aspect.[28] The intersubjective mode assumes the possibility of a context
with others in which desire is constituted for the self. It thus assumes
the paradox that in being with the other, I may experience the most
profound sense of self.

If it is clear that the intrapsychic mode is also the phallic mode, that
it has heretofore dominated the representation of desire and activity,
then we might speculate that the intersubjective mode is distinct from
phallic organization and provides a different arena for experiencing
will, agency, and desire. The intrapsychic mode operates at the level
of subject-object experience, where the other's actual independent

subjectivity is not relevant. Alternatively, the intersubjective mode, where two subjects meet, where both woman and man can be subject, may point to a locus for woman's independent desire, a relationship to desire that is not represented by the phallus.

Since there is no elaboration of this alternative to the phallic order equal to it in conceptual clarity and richness, I can only propose an exploration. First, the intersubjective mode refers to aspects of the self that each individual brings with her from infancy—agency and receptivity toward the world. While this self needs the other's response to develop, it exists a priori, before the response. It requires response and recognition, but is not called into being by them. This capacity for connection and agency later meshes with symbolic structures, but it is not created by them. Second, the intersubjective mode acknowledges that the other person really exists in the here and now, not merely in the symbolic dimension. What he or she actually does, matters. So depending on how things go between me and you, either I can really get through to you and you to me and there can be real recognition, or we can go along each encapsulated in our subjective bubble, having fantasies about one another. According to D. W. Winnicott, this moment of really getting through, of really recognizing the other as existing outside the self and not just as a bundle of my own projections, is the decisive aspect of differentiation.[29]

This moment, which Winnicott sees as created by destruction, occurs when the other is truly placed outside the control of fantasy. That is, one destroys the object in fantasy and discovers that it still exists in reality; it survives, setting a limit to the power of fantasy and self. To me it seems that the clarity of such a moment, the heightened awareness of both self and other, the reciprocal recognition that intensifies the self's freedom of expression, is actually the goal of erotic union. That is not to say that fantasy, phallic symbolic processes, and the pleasure principle are extraneous to the goal but that in love they are organized by the self-other recognition rather than the other way around. The desire for the heightened sense of self is the central meaning of getting pleasure *with* the other. Here the desire to lose the self in the other and really to be known for oneself can coalesce. Receptivity, knowing or taking in the other, becomes a mode of activity in its own right. My point is that this set of experiences—experiences of recognition—is not adequately represented by the concepts and symbols we have used for intrapsychic life, for identificatory or instinctual relationships, for ideal or object love.

Winnicott tried to grasp this set of experiences by using spatial metaphors, by describing a space that contains and a space in which we create. This space begins between mother and baby—he calls it the holding environment—and expands into what he calls the transitional area, the child's area of play, creativity, and fantasy.[30] The transitional space is suffused with the mother's protection and one's own freedom to create and imagine and discover. The central experience to which Winnicott refers is being and playing *alone* in the presence of the other; to be truly alone with oneself paradoxically requires this sense of the other's being there.[31] Given safety without intrusion, the infant can be in a state of relaxation—that well-known inward gaze—where its own impulses or drives are experienced as coming from within and feeling real. It is in this way, through the unobtrusive mediation of the other, that drives become one's own desire.

This intermediate terrain may and even should be experienced as within one's own body self, as well, and the body may come to be such a metaphor of transitional fantasy. The interior of the body and the space between bodies form an elusive pattern, a plane whose edge is ever-shifting. Winnicott often quoted a line of poetry by Tagore—"On the seashore of endless worlds children play"—that expressed what he thought about play and the transitional area. This image suggests something that both forms a boundary and opens up into endless possibility; it evokes a particular kind of holding, similar to the first bodily holding by the mother. It refers to a presymbolic sense of self as having resources, a sense of self that evolves through relationships that validate what we can do for ourselves. The confidence in one's inner resources is also founded in the experience of the other's integrity and separateness, her ability to tolerate and create limits for our impulses, which permits us the freedom of spontaneous interaction. The awareness of one's own intentions, the ability to express them through action, and the confidence that they are one's *own*, evolve through the flow of recognition between two persons.

The self that develops and accumulates through such experiences of recognition is a different modality that sometimes works with, but sometimes is at cross-purposes to, the symbolized ego of phallic structuring. It is essential to retain this sense of the complementary, as well as the contrasting, relationship of these modes. Otherwise, one falls into the trap of choosing between them, grasping one side of a contradiction that must remain suspended to be clarifying. But even if we can sketch the idea of the intersubjective dimension, can we describe a mode of representing desire unique to intersubjectivity? And are we justified in linking this desire with women, with femininity as now constituted and known? I suggest that the intersubjective mode of desire has its counterpart in spatial rather than symbolic representation, and that this mode does have something to do with female experience. I would have to say that Erik Erikson was not all wrong in his intuitions about inner space, though he was wrong in some of the conclusions he drew from them.[32] I would also add that the idea of inner space or spatial representation of desire can be associated with subjectivity only when the interior is not merely an object to be discovered or a receptacle in which to put things. Rather, inner space should be understood as part of a continuum that includes the space between the I and the you, as well as the space within me; and, further, the space within should be understood as a receptacle only insofar as it refers to the receptivity of the subject.

Winnicott has suggested that the lines between the two psychic modes correspond to gender lines, that the classic view of oral and anal stages "arises out of consideration of the pure male element," whereas the "pure female element has nothing to do with drive." It has, rather, to do with "*being,* and this forms the basis of self-discovery . . . the capacity to develop an inside, to be a container."[33] We could read that negatively, as has often been done, equating this notion of being, of inside, of container, with passivity and lack of desire. But I think that would be wrong. Rather, I think it points to the side of the self preoccupied not with gender but with whether the drives I feel are really my own, whether they come from within me, and whether I can contain them (bear them without losing or injuring myself). In other words, it is about the *relationship* of the self to desire.

Ideally, this relationship is formed through a wide series of experiences and identifications that are not restricted by rigid gender formulas. I have argued that girls should get what boys get from their father—recognition of agency, curiosity, movement toward the outside—and that they should get it from their mothers as well as their fathers. All of that contributes to the conviction of owning one's desire. I am arguing here for simultaneity and equality, not exclusion and the privileging of either male or female sets of experiences, capacities, and relationships.

I should like to explore further the possibility that femininity has been based not only on the lack of male experience but also on access to a different kind of experiences. Furthermore, these experiences are not merely the excluded opposites to male experience, the familiar half of the dualistic equation (if male equals rational, female equals irrational). Here, I think, the key is the idea of *self-discovery* that is associated with having an inside. This experience has been less well articulated in our culture and has never achieved the rich elaboration that we have for phallic structures. We can thus only begin to evaluate what woman's capacity for developing her inside, for self-discovery, might mean. Donna Bassin has argued that woman's inner space provides a metaphor of equal importance to "phallic activity and its representations, which serve as structures of knowing and creating the world."[34] The opportunity to explore one's own inner life as a creative activity, rather than waiting to be found by the phallic explorer, is one of the possible gifts of psychoanalysis to women, particularly the form of psychoanalysis that stresses not the analyst's mutative interpretations (the analyst brings the hidden unconscious to light) but the analyst's creation of an environment in which transitional experience is possible, where play and creativity can occur (the analyst provides a crucible in which experience can be transformed in the process of self-discovery). The persisting interest women have had in psychoanalysis despite its frequent antifeminist stance testifies to that possibility, to the hope of the inward journey.

Returning to the contrasting figures of infancy, the holding mother and the exciting father, we can now see the equal importance of each: recognition in and by the exciting other, and the holding that allows the self to experience desire as truly inner. So it is not merely the recognizing response of the exuberant and excited father that ignites the child's own sense of activity and desire. An important component of women's fantasy life centers around the wish for a holding other whose presence does not violate one's space but permits the experience of one's own desire, who recognizes it when it emerges of itself. This experience of inner space is in turn associated with the space between self and other: the holding environment and transitional experience. The sense of having an inside is dependent upon a sense of the space in between inside and outside—again the paradox that we need to experience being alone in the presence of the other.

The emphasis for a woman is likely to be on finding her *own, inner* desire because of the fear of impingement, intrusion, and violation. These fears, in turn, may be seen as the counterpart to a wish, the wish to submit to or to incorporate the phallus, the instrument of penetration, in order finally to be found. Woman's desire to be found and known can be symbolically apprehended as the reception of the penis. But the wish to be found and known, the desire for access to one's own interior that has found no external representation, also implies the dimension of the self's experience with the holding other. Here the spatial metaphor comes into play. A woman who had experienced incestuous violation in early puberty dreamed often of rooms. Her need to use the therapeutic environment as a space in which she could experience aloneness without fear of intrusion, control, or responsibility for the other, was an important theme. Once when she was looking forward to an overseas business trip, she announced that the best part would be to be alone in her hotel room where no one could call her. Here she would be held, safe, and alone with her thoughts; in this room of her own, this full rather than empty aloneness, she could look into herself.

I was interested to find that Carol Gilligan has made a similar point about women's desire in her analysis of the Psyche myth. The myth, as told by Apulius, contains a description of women's sexual awakening occurring in a state of benign aloneness. Gilligan points to the image of female self-discovery: Psyche is carried by the wind and laid in a bed of flowers, there left to herself. She contrasts this self-discovery with Psyche's previous state, when, adulated for her beauty, she was the idealized object: "You ought to have wept for me then," Psyche told her father, "for it was as though I had become dead."[35]

The women I have seen in clinical practice who present such images of spatial containment and inner space also have masochistic fantasies in which surrender is called forth by the other's power to penetrate, to know, and to control their desire. Yet in these fantasies we gradually discern a strand of seeking recognition for a force that originates within, a force imbued with the authenticity of *inner* desire. It seems to me that what is experientially female is the association of desire with a space, a place within the self, from which this force can emerge. This space is in turn connected to the space between self and the other. Ideally, in the psychoanalytic process the analysand gains access to transitional experience. As play in this transitional space develops, spatial metaphors may articulate the search for a desire of one's own. In them, a union or balance of holding and excitement is finally achieved. Within this space one's own desire can emerge, not as borrowed but as authentically one's own. It is thus not a different desire but a difference relation of self to other that is at stake.

The fantasy of submission in ideal love is that of being released into abandon by another who remains in control. Here I would argue that the freedom and abandon called forth by this powerful, controlling other represent an alienated version of the safe space that permits self-discovery, aloneness in the presence of the other.[36] Too often woman's desire has been known through these alien offshoots of idealization: submission and envy.

No doubt what we see in early ideal love reveals another profound truth: the pathway to desire leads through freedom. Woman's desire,

I believe, can be found not through the current emphasis on *freedom from*: as autonomy or separation from a powerful other, guaranteed by identification with an opposing power. Rather, we are seeking a relationship to desire in the *freedom to*: freedom to be both with and distinct from the other. This relationship can be grasped in terms of intersubjective reality, where subject meets subject. The phallus as emblem of desire has represented the one-sided individuality of subject meeting object, a complementarity that idealizes one side and devalues the other. The discovery of our own desire will proceed, I believe, through the mode of thought that can suspend and reconcile such opposition, the dimension of recognition between self and other.

N O T E S

1. Carol Gilligan, "Remapping the Moral Domain: New Images of Self in Relationship," paper presented at the Conference on Reconstructing Individualism, Stanford Humanities Center, February 1984, forthcoming in *Reconstructing Individualism: Autonomy, Individuality, and the Self in Western Thought,* ed. Thomas C. Heller, Morton Sosna, and David Willberry (Stanford University Press).

2. Simone de Beauvoir, *The Second Sex,* trans. H. M. Parshley (New York: Vintage, 1974), p. 717.

3. These and other illuminating distinctions are laid out in Nancy Chodorow's "Gender, Relation and Difference in Psychoanalytic Perspective," in *The Future of Difference,* ed. Hester Eisenstein and Alice Jardine (Boston: G. K. Hall, 1980), pp. 3-19.

4. See Nancy Chodorow, *The Reproduction of Mothering: Psychoanalysis and the Sociology of Gender* (Berkeley: University of California Press, 1978), and Evelyn Fox Keller, *Reflections on Gender and Science* (New Haven: Yale University Press, 1985). See also Carol Gilligan, *In a Different Voice: Psychological Theory and Women's Development* (Cambridge: Harvard University Press, 1982). Although quite different in emphasis, these books share a common intention, and I have benefited from reading and discussing with each of these authors. The decisive perspective is the idea of a necessary balance between individuation and sociability as mutually interdependent experiences, as first formulated by Chodorow: "Differentiation is not distinctness and separateness, but a particular way of being connected to others" ("Gender, Relation and Difference," p. 11); Chodorow has amplified this perspective in "Toward a Relational Individualism: The Mediation of Self through Psychoanalysis," paper presented at the Conference on Reconstructing Individualism, Stanford Humanities Center, February 1984. Dorothy Dinnerstein's critique of female mothering in *The Mermaid and the Minotaur: Sexual and Human Malaise* (New York: Harper and Row, 1976) has been very influential, although less explicitly critical of psychoanalytic theory or the concept of the individual. See also Jane Flax, "Political Philosophy and the Patriarchal Unconscious," in *Discovering Reality: Feminist Perspectives on Epistemology, Metaphysics, Methodology, and the Philosophy of Science,* ed. Sandra Hard-

ing and Merrill E. Hintikka (Boston: Reidel, 1983), and Seyla Benhabib, "The Generalized and the Concrete Other: Visions of the Autonomous Self," paper presented at the Conference on Women and Morality, SUNY-Stonybrook, March 1985. I have explored the theme of individualism and instrumental rationality in "Authority and the Family Revisited; or A World without Fathers?" *New German Critique,* no. 13 (Winter 1978), pp. 35-57, and the psychoanalytic perspective on development in "The Oedipal Riddle: Authority, Autonomy, and the New Narcissism," in *The Problem of Authority in America,* ed. John P. Diggins and Mark E. Kann (Philadelphia: Temple University Press, 1981), pp. 195-224.

5. Jessica Benjamin, "Master and Slave: The Fantasy of Erotic Domination," in *Powers of Desire: The Politics of Sexuality,* ed. Ann Snitow, Christine Stansell, and Sharon Thompson (New York: Monthly Review Press, 1983), pp. 280-99.

6. Herbert Marcuse, "Philosophy and Critical Theory," in his *Negations: Essays in Critical Theory,* trans. Jeremy J. Shapiro (Boston: Beacon, 1968), pp. 134-58.

7. Max Weber's thesis is elucidated in his *The Protestant Ethic and the Spirit of Capitalism,* trans. T. Parsons (New York: Charles Scribner, 1958).

8. Juliet Mitchell, *Psychoanalysis and Feminism: Freud, Reich, Laing, and Women* (New York: Pantheon, 1974), pp. 392-93.

9. For example, Janine Chassequet-Smirgel refers to it as "the patriarchal law of separation" in "Perversion and the Universal Law," *International Journal of Psycho-Analysis* 10 (1983):293-301, and explains that the phallus, by reminding the boy of his insufficiency and the father's exclusive possession of the mother, affirms that law.

10. This complex issue cannot be elaborated here. The most interesting summary and innovative perspective on the meaning of the new infancy research is Daniel Stern's "The Early Development of Schemas of Self, of Other, and of Various Experiences of 'Self with Other,' " in *Reflections on Self Psychology,* ed. Joseph Lichtenberg and Samuel Kaplan (Hillsdale, N. J.: Analytic Press, 1983), pp. 49-84.

11. This perspective originated with Robert Stoller's research and theorizing; see his *Sex and Gender* (New York: Science House, 1968), and "The Sense of Femaleness" (1968), in *Psychoanalysis and Women,* ed. Jean Baker Miller (Baltimore: Penguin, 1973). Its consequences were elaborated in feminist terms by Chodorow in *The Reproduction of Mothering.*

12. See Mitchell's *Psychoanalysis and Feminism,* and more recently her introduction to *Feminine Sexuality: Jacques Lacan and the "Ecole Freudienne,"* ed. Juliet Mitchell and Jacqueline Rose, trans. Jacqueline Rose (New York: Norton, 1982), pp. 1-26. See also Jane Gallop's *The Daughter's Seduction: Feminism and Psychoanalysis* (Ithaca: Cornell University Press, 1982).

13. Nancy Chodorow and Susan Contratto in "The Fantasy of the Perfect Mother" (in *Rethinking the Family: Some Feminist Questions,* ed. Barrie Thorne with Marilyn Yalom [New York: Longman, 1982], pp. 54-76) explicate clearly the relationship between the fantasy that the mother is all-powerful and the denial of her sexuality, both dependent on viewing the mother from the perspective of the child. Contratto also critiques current views of asexual motherhood in "Maternal Sexuality and Asexual Motherhood," in *Women, Sex, and Sexuality,* ed. Catharine R. Stimpson and Ethel Spector Person (Chicago: University of Chicago Press, 1980), pp. 224-40.

14. Jacqueline Rose, in her introduction to *Feminine Sexuality,* argues that gender identity theory as used by Chodorow "displaces" the concepts of the unconscious and of bisexuality. This dismissal of object relations theory ap-

pears to contain a misapprehension of the process of identification, which proceeds through the unconscious fantasies of the child, but is associated with specific phases of cognitive and affective development that have been empirically documented. Thus, it misses the qualitatively distinct aspect of sexual experience and identification in the preoedipal phase that is not captured by oedipal categories. Moreover, it assumes that only the structuralist version of the unconscious—an abstract category in which representation of the world subsumes experience in the world—deserves the dignity of the term. This level of abstraction may have its own uses. But the global rejection of maternal identification theory by Rose and other feminist Lacanians only hinders the analysis of the specific difficulty that confronts the girl in the effort to reconcile gender identity and sexuality.

15. Sigmund Freud, "Some Psychical Consequences of the Anatomical Distinction between the Sexes" (1926), *Standard Edition*, vol. 19, pp. 248-60, and "Female Sexuality" (1931), *Standard Edition*, vol. 21, pp. 225-46.

16. A discussion of the differing meanings of sexual inhibition and identity for men and women can be found in Ethel Spector Person's "Sexuality as the Mainstay of Identity: Psychoanalytic Perspectives," in Stimpson and Person, *Women, Sex, and Sexuality*, pp. 36-61.

17. This phrase is apparently Margaret Mahler's, quoted in Ernest L. Abelin, "Triangulation, the Role of the Father and the Origins of Core Gender Identity during the Rapprochement Subphase," in *Rapprochement: The Critical Subphase of Separation-Individuation*, ed. Ruth F. Lax, Sheldon Bach, and J. Alexis Burland (New York: Jason Aronson, 1980), p. 152. The most persuasive discussions of father and phallus as ways of defending against maternal power can be found in Janine Chassequet-Smirgel's anthology, *Female Sexuality: New Psychoanalytic Views* (Ann Arbor: Michigan University Press, 1970) and her "Freud and Female Sexuality," *International Journal of Psychoanalysis*, 57, pp. 275-286.

18. For a number of articles on this difference, see *Father and Child: Developmental and Clinical Perspectives*, ed. Stanley H. Cath, Alan R. Gurwitt, and John Munder Ross (Boston: Little, Brown, 1982).

19. Margaret S. Mahler, Fred Pine, and Anni Bergman, *The Psychological Birth of the Human Infant: Symbiosis and Individuation* (New York: Basic Books, 1975).

20. Ibid., pp. 213-14.

21. See Jane Flax, "Mother-Daughter Relationships: Psychodynamics, Politics, and Philosophy," in Eisenstein and Jardine, *The Future of Difference*, pp. 20-40. More generally, Chodorow argues in *The Reproduction of Mothering* that mothers bind their daughters by virtue of greater identification, and separate from boys by conferring the status of heterosexual love object upon them.

22. This thesis was developed and elaborated by Ernest Abelin in several notable articles, including "Triangulation," see note 17 above. Freud also noted the intensity of the preoedipal boy's identification with the father, whom he takes as his ideal, and indeed Freud states that identification is the earliest form of love ("Group Psychology and the Analysis of the Ego" [1921], *Standard Edition*, vol. 18, pp. 67-143).

23. This point has also been made by Doris Bernstein. Her work is a notable exception; see "The Female Superego: A Different Perspective," *International Journal of Psycho-analysis* 64, pt. 2 (1983):187-201. For a similarly exceptional account, see also Ricki Levenson, "Intimacy, Autonomy, and Gender: Developmental Differences and Their Reflection in Adult Relationships," *Journal of the American Academy of Psychoanalysis* 12 (1984):529-44.

24. Sigmund Freud, "A Child Is Being Beaten" (1919), *Standard Edition,* vol. 17, pp. 159–72.

25. The conflict between paternal identification and paternal object love becomes infinitely more complicated in the oedipal period than I can here describe. It would seem that the more the idealization of the father is sustained, the less likely is the daughter's persuasion of a right to her own desire. For example, if the oedipal father of adolescence, a period when the issues become more explicit, discourages or forbids manifest sexuality in his daughter, that blocks both separation from and identification with him and encourages submission and idealization. As Miriam Johnson ("Fathers and 'Femininity' in Daughters: A Review of the Research," *Sociology and Social Research* 67 [1983]:1-17) notes, the daughter's tie to the father, if sexualized, is more likely to discourage autonomy.

26. See Chodorow, "Gender, Relation and Difference," and Keller, *Reflections.*

27. Keller's *Reflections* has contributed a great deal to the theme of sustaining a tension rather than splitting opposites. See also Gilligan's remarks on the essential tension in "Remapping the Moral Domain," Linda Gordon's comments in this volume on sustaining the tension of opposing tendencies in historical research, and my elucidation of the balance of differentiation and its breakdown in "Master and Slave" (see note 5 above).

28. See Mitchell, *Psychoanalysis and Feminism,* pp. 396-97, and her introduction to *Feminine Sexuality.* Desire is thus by its very nature "insoluble," Mitchell argues. Lacanian desire—always a desire for what is not—would seem to be the impediment to ever reaching the other, and thus finally at odds with love, with the meeting of two minds, two bodies. Desire is then a kind of addiction to the ideal.

29. This analysis proceeds from the principal text of D. W. Winnicott on differentiation, in which he makes a similar distinction between the self as isolated and the intersubjective self; see "The Use of an Object and Relating through Identifications," in *Playing and Reality* (London: Penguin, 1974), pp. 101-111. An excellent interpretation of Winnicott's theory, to which I am indebted, is Michael Eigen's "The Area of Faith in Winnicott, Lacan, and Bion," *International Journal of Psycho-analysis* 62 (1981):413-33.

30. See D. W. Winnicott's "Transitional Objects and Transitional Phenomena," and the other essays in *Playing and Reality.*

31. D. W. Winnicott, "The Capacity to Be Alone" (1958), in his *The Maturational Processes and the Facilitating Environment: Studies in the Theory of Emotional Development* (New York: International Universities Press , 1965). Elsa First provided a very helpful account of the significance of this text in her paper at the *New York Freudian Society,* March 1985.

32. Erik Erikson, "Womanhood and the Inner Space," in *Identity, Youth, and Crisis* (New York: W. W. Norton, 1968), pp. 261-94.

33. D. W. Winnicott, "Creativity and Its Origins," in his *Playing and Reality,* p. 97.

34. Donna Bassin, "Woman's Images of Inner Space: Data towards Expanded Interpretive Categories," *International Review of Psycho-analysis* 9 (1982):200.

35. Carol Gilligan, "The Psychology of Love," Seminar on Sex and Consumerism, New York Institute for the Humanities, March 1985.

36. This idea has been developed by Emmanuel Ghent in "Masochism, Submission, Surrender," Colloquium, New York University Postdoctoral Psychology Program, December 1983.

SEVEN

Changing the Subject: Authorship, Writing, and the Reader

Nancy K. Miller

I want to begin with a brief account of the circumstances involved in the construction and destination of this paper. For the past few years, I have been putting together a book about women's writing; more specifically, about the act of reading women's writing, and what might be at stake—critically, politically, historically—in such a project. Since I work "in French," and since I am well aware that there is not a women's writing, my examples (my corpus, as we used to say in the days of high structuralism) come primarily from what I think I can show is a tradition of female authorship in France. To situate my project within the field of French studies, rather than the more heterogeneous world of feminist studies, has meant locating my "problematic" within the discussion of writing and sexual difference that has been taking place on both sides of the Atlantic, in French and English departments, though with the usual jet (and intracontinental) lag, over the past fifteen years.

This spring I had on my calendar two conferences that provided me with an occasion to think and write more explicitly about the woman writer and her feminist reader in relation to that continental context and at the same time in relation to questions to feminist theory: one held at the Pembroke Center of Brown University in March 1985, entitled "Feminism/Theory/Politics"; the other, the one we have been attending now for three days in Milwaukee, "Feminist Studies: Reconstituting Knowledge."

The session in which I presented an earlier version of this paper, at the Pembroke conference, was called "The Feminist Politics of Interpretation," and the panelists were asked to reflect upon an agenda of issues not radically different from the questions animating this conference as Teresa de Lauretis described it in her opening statement. I can locate the overlap for you in one key formulation: "What is

specifically feminist *about the varieties of feminist critical practice?*
Are feminist strategies of reading written and visual texts transferable
to the study of such things as social and political institutions?" (Pem-
broke conference, emphasis added) In de Lauretis's letter to partici-
pants: "There are a general uncertainty, and, among feminists, serious
differences as to what the specific concerns, values and methods of
feminist critical work are, or ought to be. . . . Speakers will seek to
identify the specificity of feminism *as a critical theory." (Milwaukee*
conference, emphasis added)

   These are very hard questions, and I have not attempted to describe
the specificity of feminist theory and practice directly. Instead, I have
chosen to rehearse a certain number of positions against, from, and
through which feminist critical theory might define itself as it emerges
within the discourse of literary studies (I wish to make no wider claims
for this work). This rehearsal identifies two chronologies, poststruc-
turalist and feminist; two rhetorics, dilatory and hortatory; and, to re-
turn to the figure of the "exquisite dance of textual priorities"—named
by Hortense Spillers and evoked by de Lauretis at the opening of the
conference, two moves, or perhaps a hesitation between the calls of
a square dance and the ritual of a minuet, as the dance searches for
the right steps and rhythm—perhaps the waltz satirized by Dorothy
Parker, or, as one of the participants suggested to me after the con-
ference, the fox trot?[1]

   Though I may be looking for a third tropology, in the feminist spirit
of modeling a future perspective, I want to say clearly here that I wish
to leave the hesitation in place, and refuse the temptation of a syn-
thesis, because the question forming before us is no other than the
question of female subjectivity, the formation of a female critical sub-
ject. And that, in the current trend toward the massive deconstitution
of subjectivity, is finally the figure I'm looking for.

Authorship, Writing, and the Reader

   The question of authorship has been on the agenda of intellectuals
and literary critics in France since at least 1968, a date that also marks

*With the exception of the introductory remarks, which I in fact read at Milwaukee,
the material that appears in italics was written after the events of the paper in performance as discursive endnotes; not so much as side issues but as asides the essay could
not recontain within the limits of its own rhetorical space. Its place here in dialogic
relation to the main body of the text is the result of an experiment brought about by
the always imaginative critical judgment of the editor of this volume, Teresa de Lauretis.

a certain theoretical repositioning in political and social chronologies. In 1968, for example, Roland Barthes contended in "The Death of the Author" that the author, as we have known him, has lost what was thought to be a "natural" authority over his work. The author gives way to *writing*, a theory and practice of textuality which, Barthes argued then, "substitutes language itself for the person who until then had been supposed to be its owner."[2] From such a perspective, the emergence of this disembodied and ownerless *écriture* in fact requires the author's suppression. In the structuralist and poststructuralist debates about subjectivity and the status of the text that continue to occupy and preoccupy the contemporary critical marketplace, the story of the Author's disappearance has remained the standard currency.

Now, to the extent that the Author, in this discourse, stands as a kind of shorthand for a whole series of beliefs about the function of the work of art as (paternally authorized) monument in our culture, feminist criticism, in its own negotiations with mainstream hegemonies, should have found a supporting (if not supportive) argument in the language of its claims. It is, after all, the Author, canonized, anthologized, and institutionalized, who excludes the less-known works of women and minority writers from the canon, and who by his authority justifies the exclusion. By the same token, feminist criticism's insistence on the importance of the reader—on positing the hypothesis of her existence—should have found affinities with a position that understands the birth of the reader as the necessary counterpoint to the death of the Author. (Barthes actually puts it a good deal more apocalyptically: "the birth of the reader must be at the cost of the death of the Author" [p. 148].)

The critical potential of such an alliance, however, has by now proved to be extremely vulnerable. The removal of the Author has not so much made room for a revision of the concept of authorship as it has, through a variety of rhetorical moves, repressed and inhibited discussion of any writing identity in favor of the (new) monolith of anonymous textuality, or "transcendental anonymity," in Michel Foucault's phrase.[3] If "writing," then, as Barthes describes it, "is that neutral, composite, oblique space where our subject slips away, the negative where all identity is lost, starting with the very identity of the body writing" (p.142), then it matters not *who* writes. In the same way, the shift that moves the critical emphasis from author to reader, from the text's origin to its destination, far from producing a multiplicity of addressees, seems to have reduced the possibility of differentiating among readers in their subjective identity altogether: "The reader,"

Barthes declares, "is without history, biography, psychology" (148). What matters who reads? The reader is a space and a process. The reader is only "*someone*" written *on*.

In part, but this deserves a discussion of its own, the failure of a critical alliance between feminism and (speaking reductively) "deconstruction" is due to the fact that their relationship has never been one of complicity—of being on the same side. Nonetheless, I want to make a distinction that should modify this picture of cognitive dissonance, a distinction between the asymmetrical demands generated by different writing identities, male and female, or, perhaps more usefully, canonical or hegemonic and noncanonical or marginal. It is inarguable that the destabilization of the paternal (patriarchal, really) authority of authorship (Milton's, for example) brought about through deconstruction has been an enabling move for feminist critics. But it does not, as I will argue, address the problem of his "bogey" at the level of subjectivity formation: the effect of his identity and authority on a female writing identity remains another matter. The stress of that negotiation for the nineteenth-century woman writer has been formulated centrally by Sandra Gilbert and Susan Gubar in the opening section of The Madwoman in the Attic. *In this paper I am trying to pose the question at the level of theory itself, or rather of theory's discourse about its project.*

So why remember Barthes, if this model of reading and writing by definition excludes the question of an identity crucial to feminist critical theory? Well, for one thing, because Barthes's interest in the semiotics of literary and cultural activity—its pleasures, dangers, zones, and codes of reference—intersects thematically with a feminist emphasis on the need to situate socially and symbolically the practices of reading and writing. Like the feminist critic, Barthes explores and exploits the complex and tricky relations between the personal and the political; the personal and the critical; the interpersonal and the institutional (his seminar, for example). Finally, for those of us in literary studies, Barthes translates (seductively) from within French thought the more arduous writings of Derrida, Lacan, Kristeva for (or into) literature; and in the same gesture represents metonymically outside the Parisian scene (or in North American literature departments) most of the concepts that animate those feminist (and other) literary critics not hostile to Theory's stories: currently, the poststructuralist epistemologies of the subject and the text; the linguistic construction of sexual identity.

In the preface of *Sade/Fourier/Loyola* (1971), Barthes returns to the problem of authorship: "For if," he writes, "through a twisted dialectic, the Text, destroyer of all subject, contains a subject to love [*un sujet à aimer*] that subject is dispersed, somewhat like the ashes we strew into the wind after death." And he continues famously, "Were I a writer, and dead [*si j'étais écrivain, et mort*] how I would love it if my life, through the pains of some friendly and detached biographer, were to reduce itself to a few details, a few preferences, a few inflections, let us say: to 'biographemes'. . . ."[4] What interests me here, more than yet another nomination, another code, is Barthes's acknowledgment of the persistence of the subject as the presence in the text of perhaps not some*one* to love in person, but the mark of the need to be loved, the persistence of a peculiarly human(ist?) desire for connection. It is as though to think of a writer's life—a "life" of Sade, a "life" of Fourier, appended to a reading of their writings—generated a thinking of self: for Barthes then imagines himself "a writer."[5] But we have just seen that the writer is already dead, his ashes scattered to the winds; and the self/subject fatally dispersed. Thus, no sooner is the subject restored metaphorically to a body through love than he is dispersed figuratively through death. If one is to find the subject, he will not be in one place, but modernly multiple and atopic.

Will *she*?

I will argue, in this paper, that the postmodernist decision that the Author is dead, and subjective agency along with him, does not necessarily work for women and prematurely forecloses the question of identity for them. Because women have not had the same historical relation of identity to origin, institution, production, that men have had, women have not, I think, (collectively) felt burdened by too much Self, Ego, Cogito, etc. Because the female subject has juridically been excluded from the polis, and hence decentered, "disoriginated," deinstitutionalized, etc., her relation to integrity and textuality, desire and authority, is structurally different.

In Breaking the Chain, *Naomi Schor takes up Barthes's analysis in* S/Z *of what he sees as a disoriginated discourse on "femininity," which he locates for the sake of argument in a passage from* Sarrasine.[6] *Curiously, it is also the passage that serves as the opening citation of "The Death of the Author": "This was woman herself. . . ." Following Schor's lead, it is interesting to puzzle the connections that, for Barthes, join* écriture *and "woman" in a definition of textuality that refuses a coherent subjectivity.*

In "Mapping the Postmodern," Andreas Huyssen asks: "Isn't the 'death of the subject/author' position tied by mere reversal to the very ideology that invariably glorifies the artist as genius, whether for

marketing purposes or out of conviction and habit? . . . doesn't post-
structuralism, where it simply denies the subject altogether, jettison
the chance of challenging the ideology of the subject *(as male, white,*
and middle-class) by developing alternative and different notions of
subjectivity?"[7]

In *"Women Who Write Are Women,"* Elaine Showalter argues
against Cynthia Ozick's belief *(recently reaffirmed by Gail Godwin)*
that "writing transcends sexual identity, that it takes place outside of
the social order," and underlines the important point that "the female
witness, sensitive or not, is still not accepted as first-person universal."[8]

It seems to me, therefore, that when the question of identity—the
so-called crisis of the subject—is posed, as it generally is, within a
textual model, that question is irreducibly complicated by the historical, political, and figurative body of the woman writer. That is, of
course, if we accept as a working hypothesis, as a working metaphor,
really, the location of female subjectivity in female authorship. Because the discourse of the universal seems historically neither to include the female nor to emerge from its testimony, it is imperative for
the feminist critic to bring the question of her subjectivity forward on
these grounds.

Feminist critics in the United States have on the whole resisted the
fable of the author's demise on the grounds that stories of textuality
which trade in universals—the Author or the Reader—in fact articulate
marked and differentiated structures of what Gayatri Spivak has called
masculine "regulative psychobiography." They have looked to the
material of the female authorial project as the location of perhaps a
different staging of the drama of the writing subject. But what does it
mean to read (for) the woman writer when the Author is dead? Or,
how can "reading as a woman"—a deconstructionist phrasing of a
reconstructionist feminist project—help us rethink the act of reading
as a politics? I'd like to see a more self-conscious and deliberate move
away from what I think remains, in the dominant critical modes, a
perhaps unconscious) *metaphysics* of reading. As Foucault asked in
"What Is an Author": "In granting a primordial status to writing (*écriture*), do we not, in effect, simply reinscribe in transcendental terms
the theological affirmation of its sacred origin?" (p. 120)

In her presentations at both the Pembroke and the Milwaukee con-
ferences, Spivak contrasted the psychobiography of a male subjectivity
based on naturalized access to dominant forms of power with that of
the "postmodern female subject" created under postmodern impe-

rialism (emblematized by the hegemony of the computer chip): women of color constructed as a permanent casual labor force doing high-tech work for the multinationals. Her relation to networks of power is best understood through the concept of "women in the integrated circuit," which Donna Haraway describes as "the situation of women in a world . . . intimately restructured through the social relations of science and technology."⁹ It is not self-evident what form testimony would take in such an economy.

Speaking from within a certain new French feminism, Hélène Cixous makes a homologous argument for the need to recognize a deuniversalized subjectivity: "Until now, far more extensively and repressively than is ever suspected or admitted, writing has been run by a libidinal and cultural—hence political, typically masculine—economy."¹⁰ This definition of a sexually "marked writing" that expresses and valorizes masculine access to power emerges from the analysis of phallocentrism, but because of its place in the network of Derridean concepts, it necessarily does not support the reconstructive impulses of much feminist literary criticism in the United States: the analysis of canon formation and reformation through the study of women's writing.

Thus, in his concluding remarks to the section of On Deconstruction *that he devotes to feminist criticism, Jonathan Culler builds on Peggy Kamuf's analysis of female signature and identity, "Writing as a Woman": "For a woman to read as a woman is not to repeat an identity or an experience that is given but to play a role she constructs with reference to her identity as a woman, which is also a construct, so that the series can continue: a woman reading as a woman reading as a woman."¹¹ The question for feminist critical theory today is how to imagine a relation between this logic and ethics of deferral and the assumption of immediacy and transparence that animates a critic such as Barbara Smith.*

I want to offer one kind of political reading with a passage from a famous account of a female "psychobiography." I take it as an example of what has been characterized as the "first moment" or first stage of feminist criticism, a criticism Culler describes as "based on the presumption of continuity between the reader's experience and a woman's experience" (p. 46). The account is Adrienne Rich's "When We Dead Awaken: Writing as Re-vision," which was originally given as a talk on "The Woman Writer in the Twentieth Century" in a forum sponsored by the Commission on the Status of Women in the Profession at the MLA in 1971. I mention these dates by way of suggesting that we try to look at the history of these issues both in "women's time" and in men's—the Eastern Standard time of traditional or mainstream events.[12]

> A lot is being said today about the influence that the myths and images of women have on all of us who are products of culture. I think it has been a peculiar confusion to the girl or woman who tries to write because she is peculiarly susceptible to language. She goes to poetry or fiction looking for *her* way of being in the world, since she too has been putting words and images together; she is looking eagerly for guides, maps, possibilities; and over and over . . . she comes up against something that negates everything she is about: she meets the image of Woman in books written by men. She finds a terror and a dream, she finds a beautiful pale face, she finds La Belle Dame Sans Merci, she finds Juliet or Tess or Salomé, but precisely what she does not find is that absorbed, drudging, puzzled, sometimes inspired creature, herself, who sits at a desk trying to put words together.[13]

Rich's woman "susceptible to language," like Roland Barthes, goes to literature as a *writing subject*: she does not, however, find there *"un sujet à aimer."* She finds, instead, a terror and a dream. To find "somebody to love," as the song goes, Rich, like Barthes, would have to find someone somehow *like her* in her desire for a place, in the discourse of art and identity, from which to imagine and image a writing self: "absorbed, drudging, puzzled"; at a desk, not before a mirror. For the girl "susceptible to language," the words have established a split she cannot overcome: Woman, whose image, whose "beautiful pale face," has installed in her place a regime of the specular and excluded her from production. Woman leaves the woman poet in exile.

In her 1983 essay "Blood, Bread, and Poetry: The Location of the Poet" (where she outlines the borders of scenes of writing in North America and in Central America), Rich returns to the biography of her reading, or the history of its subject, to develop in more explicitly political terms the implications of the "split" between the girl and the poet, "the girl who wrote poems, who defined herself in writing poems, and the girl who was to define herself by her relationships with men."[14] To close "the gap between poet and woman," Rich argues here, the fragmentation within the writing subject requires the context of a "political community."[15] For Rich, on *this* side of identity, the condition of dispersal and fragmentation that Barthes valorizes (and fetishizes) is not to be achieved but to be overcome:

> I write for the still-fragmented parts in me, trying to bring them together. Whoever can read and use any of this, I write for them as well. I write

in full knowledge that the majority of the world's illiterates are women, that I live in a technologically advanced country where forty per cent of the people can barely read and twenty per cent are functionally illiterate. I believe that these facts are directly connected to the fragmentations I suffer in myself, that we are all in this together. (p. 540)

In "Blood, Bread, and Poetry," Rich maps the geopolitics of a poetics of gender. This vision of a global context for women's writing emerges from a program of text production as a collective project. In the sixties, under the logic of "the personal is the political," the communication with the community involved writing "directly and overtly as a woman, out of a woman's experience," taking "women's existence seriously as theme and source for art" (p. 535). In "When We Dead Awaken," Rich had contrasted this euphoric turn to feminocentric production (a more prosaic, or rather less lyrical, account of the agenda valorized by Cixous in "The Laugh of the Medusa") with the anxieties of the fifties: "I began to feel that my fragments and scraps had a common consciousness and a common theme, one which I would have been very unwilling to put on paper at an earlier time because I had been taught that poetry should be 'universal', which meant, of course, nonfemale" (p. 44). Now, in the eighties, the formula "the personal is the political" requires a redefinition of the personal to include most immediately an interrogation of ethnocentrism; a poetics of identity that engages with the "other woman."[16]

If for Rich, in 1971, the act of women's reading as a critique of the dominant literature was not merely "a chapter in cultural history" but "an act of survival," in 1983 the act of women's writing becomes inseparable from an expanded definition of, and expanded attention to, the social field in which the practices of reading and writing are located and grounded. Now the question arises, If the ethics of feminist cultural production involve writing for the woman who doesn't read (to push this model to its limits), then what would be required of a responsive, responsible feminist reading?

The question will remain open and generate other questions: Does the specificity of feminist theory entail reading for the other woman? Would that mean reading *as* the other woman? In her place? Wouldn't this assumption reinstate the interchangeability of women under the name of woman and thereby "collapse," as Denise Riley put it to me at the Pembroke conference, "the different temporalities of 'women' from the side of politics"? In more strictly literary terms, we must think carefully about the reading effects and implications of a poetics of transparence—writing directly from one's own experience—especially when conjoined with an ethics of wholeness.

Rich speaks of her discovery of the work of contemporary Cuban women poets in a book edited by Margaret Randall, Breaking Silences. *And it is in part because of reading this book (her* tolle e lege*) that she decides to go to Nicaragua (a decision that provides the occasion for the essay). To what extent does this active/activist model of reading establish the grounds for a prescriptive esthetics—a "politically correct" program of representation—of the sort that shaped the arguments of Barbara Smith and Sondra O'Neale at the Milwaukee conference?*

Against the necessarily utopian rhetoric of an unalienated art that Rich reads in Cuban women poets ("the affirmation of an organic relation between poetry and social transformation," p. 537), I want now to juxtapose the discourse with which I began this discussion of critical strategies. On the back jacket to *Sade/Fourier/Loyola,* Barthes states the "theoretical intention" of his project. It is a kind of self-referential challenge: to discover "how far one can go with a text speaking only of its writing (*écriture*); how to suspend its signified in order to liberate its materialist deployment." "Isn't the social intervention achieved by a text," he asks rhetorically, located in the "transport" of its writing, rather than in the "message of its content"? In the pages of the preface, Barthes addresses the problem of the "social responsibility of the text," maintaining that since there is "today no language site outside bourgeois ideology," "the only possible rejoinder" to, say, the establishment is "neither confrontation, nor destruction, but only theft: fragment the old text of culture, science, literature, and change its features according to formulae of disguise, as one disguises ("*maquille*") stolen goods" (p. 10). We see here the double move we saw earlier in "The Death of the Author": on the one hand, disperse the subject; on the other, fragment the text and repackage it for another mode of circulation and reception.

Dispersion and fragmentation, the theft of language and the subversion of the stereotype, attract Barthes as critical styles of desire and deconstruction, rupture and protest. Certain women writers in France, such as Hélène Cixous, Luce Irigaray, and, I would argue, paradoxically, Monique Wittig, have also been attracted to this model of relation: placing oneself at a deliberately oblique (or textual) angle to intervention. Troped as a subversion—a political intertextuality—this positionality remains necessarily a form of negotiation within the dominant social text, and ultimately a local operation; by *some* of us, institutionally based. But *could* we be, all of us, together in that?

Because it is also my sense that the reappropriation of culture from within its own arenas of dissemination is still a political urgency, I will recast my earlier question about the female subject and retreat from its broadest implications for feminist theory, to ask more narrowly now: What does it mean to read and write as a woman within the institution that authorizes and regulates most reading and writing?

"Oubliez les professeurs"

In Charlotte Brontë's *Villette*, acute attention is paid to the construction of female subjectivity, and in particular to the way in which female desire as quest aligns itself uneasily with the question of mastery (including, importantly, mastery of the French language), mastery and knowledge within an academy, and necessarily, in 1853, a female one. In the scene I will review here, the heroine, Lucy Snowe, is dragged off to be examined by two professors, "Messieurs Boissec and Rochemorte" (the etymology is, of course, motivated). This examination—perceived by Lucy as a "show-trial" set up to prove that she indeed was the author of a remarkable essay the men suspected their colleague, M. Emmanuel, Lucy's professor/friend, of having written for her, forging her signature in order to document his pedagogical agency—provides us with a vivid account of the institutional power arrangements that historically have constructed female experience. The two specimens of "deadwood" interrogate Lucy:

> They began with classics. A dead blank. They went on to French history. I hardly knew Mérovée from Pharamond. They tried me in various 'ologies, and still only got a shake of the head, and an unchanging "Je n'en sais rien."[17]

Unwilling or unable to reply, Lucy asks permission to leave the room.

> They would not let me go: I must sit down and write before them. As I dipped my pen in the ink with a shaking hand, and surveyed the white paper with eyes half-blinded and overflowing, one of my judges began mincingly to apologize for the pain he caused. (p.494)

They name their theme: "Human Justice."

> Human Justice! What was I to make of it? Blank, cold abstraction, unsuggestive to me of one inspiring idea. . . . (p. 495)

Lucy remains blocked until she remembers that these two men were in fact known to her; "the very heroes" who had "half frightened [her] to death" on the night of her arrival in Villette. And suddenly, thinking how little these men deserved their current status as judges and enforcers of the law, Lucy falls, as she puts it, "to work."

"Human Justice" rushed before me in novel guise, a red, random beldame with arms akimbo. I saw her in her house, the den of confusion: servants called to her for orders or help which she did not give; beggars stood at her door waiting and starving unnoticed; a swarm of children, sick and quarrelsome, crawled round her feet and yelled in her ears appeals for notice, sympathy, cure, redress. The honest woman cared for none of these things. She had a warm seat of her own by the fire, she had her own solace in a short black pipe, and a bottle of Mrs Sweeny's soothing syrup; she smoked and she sipped and she enjoyed her paradise, and whenever a cry of the suffering souls about her pierced her ears too keenly—my jolly dame seized the poker or the hearthbrush. (pp.495-96)

Writing "as a woman," Lucy Snowe domesticates the public allegories of Human Justice. Her justice is not blind (hence serenely fair), but it is deaf to the pathetic cries that invade her private space: arbitrary and visibly self-interested, marked not by the sword and scales of neoclassical iconography, Lucy's "red, random beldame" smokes her pipe and sips her syrup.

However perversely, I am tempted to take this scene, in which a woman is brought forcibly to writing, as a parable—which is not to say a recommendation—of the conditions of production for female authorship (or for the practice of feminist criticism). Because she reappropriates the allegory of timeless indifference, particularized and ironized first through the identification of the men, then privatized and fictionalized through the imagined body of an aging woman, Lucy both overcomes the daunting terror of the blank page and undermines the universal claims of humanism's transparent self-reference.

I should perhaps have mentioned that the chapter in which this writing out takes place begins with a line rich in implications for the conclusion of my argument: "*Oubliez les professeurs.*" Now, in context, this imperative is a warning issued by Mme Beck that Lucy not think of M. Paul for herself. But clearly, in this collegial psychodrama, the relation to *him* is not only a question of female rivalry and the love plot. As I have just suggested, the scene also asks more generally the question of women's relation to the arbitrariness of male authority, to the grounds of their power and their laws.

Lucy, we know, can't forget her particular professor, for she is moved more than she will say by his offer of friendship. But in her apprenticeship to the world of work, she has learned to make distinctions. To accept M. Paul does not mean that she accepts the system of institutional authorization in which their relation is inscribed. Nor is the point of her essay, its style, lost on M. Paul, who, having read the exam paper, calls her "*une petite moqueuse et sans coeur*" (p. 496).

Lucy's mockery, which is the flip side of her pathos, could also be figured as irony, which is, I think, a trope that by its status as the marker of a certain distance to the truth, suits the rhetorical strategies of the feminist critic.[18]

The chapter in which the scene of writing is staged is called "Fraternity," for it is here that M. Paul asks Lucy to be the "sister of a very poor, fettered, burdened, encumbered man." His offer of "true friendship" (p. 501), of a "fraternal alliance" (p. 503), while not exempt of its own ironies, nonetheless may be a more promising model of future relations between women and institutional authorities than that of the "daughter's seduction" diagnosed by Jane Gallop, for it at least poses a ground of parity and reversibility; the phrase, moreover, despite its linguistic familiality, also has the advantage of avoiding the metaphorics of the maternal fix, a currently invoked feminist alternative. My hope for the fraternal (as opposed to sororal) model is that its oddness in feminist discourse saves it—if only rhetorically, but rhetoric is of course key—from the *automatic* solidarities of sisterhood that have recently come under attack in so many quarters as being repressive of the differences between and among women. In the end, through the enabling alliance of a "feminine" fraternity—if we can allow the term its apparent self-contradiction for the time being—Lucy Snowe has not only her own seat by the fire but also her own house and school for girls.[19] Within her space, she makes Paul a "little library"; Paul, whose mind, she had said earlier, was her library, through which she "entered bliss" (p. 472). And, of course, in his absence and in his place, she writes the narrative of *Villette*.

Subject to Change

In 1973, in an essay called "Toward a Woman-Centered University," Adrienne Rich described her vision of a future for feminist studies. In it we read: "The university I have been trying to imagine does not seem to me utopian, though the problems and contradictions to be faced in its actual transformation are of course real and severe."[20] Yet, looking back over the past ten to fifteen years of women's studies, can we say that "masculine resistance to women's claims for full humanity" (as Rich defines the project) has been overcome in any serious way? Nothing could be less sure.

In fact, I think that though we may have our women's studies programs, our centers, journals, and conferences, feminist scholars have not succeeded in instituting the transformative claims we articulated in the heady days of the mid-seventies. Supported by the likes of William Bennett, Rochemorte and Boissec are going strong: they continue to resist, massively, feminism's fundamental understanding that the deployment of the universal is inherently, if paradoxically, partial and political. And the M. Paul's, who, like Terry Eagleton *et al.*, offer friendship and the promise of "fraternal alliance," seem to be saying at the same time: "feminism is theoretically thin, or separatist. Girls, shape up!"[21] More serious, perhaps, because it is supported by the prestige of philosophy, the ultimate purveyor of universals, is the general failure on the part of most male theorists, even those most interested in "feminine identity," to articulate sufficiently in their own enunciation what Rosi Braidotti calls "the radical consciousness of one's own complicity with the very power one is trying to deconstruct."[22] Like the humanists, they have not begun to question the grounds on which they stand, their own relation to the "sexual differential" that inhabits "*every* voice":[23] their own difference from the universal, from the institution that houses them, and from which they speak.

But we have, of course, participated in our own failure to challenge the "'ologies" and their authorities in a significant way. Our greatest strength in the seventies, I think, was our experience, through consciousness raising, of the possibility of a collective identity resistant to, but intimately bound up with, Woman; in fact, our account, analysis, and valorization of experience itself, as Teresa de Lauretis points out at the end of her brilliant book *Alice Doesn't*.[24] For reasons I don't fully understand, but which I think have to do, on the one hand, with an anxiety about claiming theoretically what we know experientially (by which I mean our life in discourse), because of the feminist bugaboo about essentialism; and, on the other, particularly for those of us working in things French, with an anxiety about accounts of postgendered subjectivities, we seem to have gotten stuck between two varieties of self-censorship.

In the face of a prevailing institutional indifference to the question of women, conjoined with a prevailing critical ideology of the subject that celebrates or longs for a mode beyond difference, it is difficult to know where and how to move. On what grounds can we remodel the relations of a female subject to the social text? In a recent issue of *Tulsa Studies* devoted to the current state of feminist criticism, there is at least one pressing call to forget the professors, theorists masculine and feminine, to "reject male formalist models for criticism" in the belief, Jane Marcus writes, that "the practice of formalism professionalizes the feminist critic and makes her safe for academe."[25] We must, I think, see that as too simple—not only because, as Nina Auerbach argues in the same issue, "whether we like it or not, we live in one world, one country . . . one university department with men" (p. 155), but because we don't. If women's studies is to effect institutional change, we cannot afford to proceed by the unequivocal rejection of "male" models. Rather, like Lucy in the school play (another forced performance), who refuses to play a man's part dressed in men's clothes, and instead assumes the signifiers of masculinity *"in addition"* to her "woman's garb" (p. 209, emphasis added), the possibility of future feminist intervention requires an ironic manipulation of the semiotics of performance and production.[26]

Earlier in *Villette*, Ginevra pressed Lucy to explain herself, to reveal some real identity that seems to escape her penetration: "Who *are* you, Miss Snowe?" And Lucy, "amused at her mystification," replies: "Who am I indeed? Perhaps a personage in disguise. Pity I don't look the character" (pp. 392-93). But Ginevra is not satisfied with this flip account of identity: "But *are* you anybody?" This time Lucy is slightly more forthcoming, supplying information, at least, about her social insertion: "Yes . . . I am a rising character: once an old lady's companion, then a nursery-governess, now a school-teacher" (p. 394). Ginevra persists in thinking there is more to Lucy than Lucy will say, but Lucy will offer nothing more. If we take Lucy Snowe's account of herself at face value, not persisting like Ginevra in a hermeneutics of revelation that is structured, Barthes has taught us, on oedipal narratologies, then we begin to take the measure of Brontë's radical achievement in this novel: creating a heroine whose identity is modulated through the cadences of work; even to an institution. I do not, of course, mean to suggest that her subjectivity is recontained by a job description. On the contrary, we have seen Ginevra's conviction that despite the institutional inscription, Lucy somehow continues to escape her—not only because Ginevra is looking for a social language she can relate to ("a name, a pedigree") but because, in some palpable way, Lucy, like the Lacanian subject she anticipates, also resides elsewhere, in "the field of language" that constitutes her otherness to herself.[27]

I want to float the suggestion, nevertheless, that any definition of the female writing subject, not universalized as Woman, that we may try to theorize today must include Lucy Snowe's ambiguities. That is a process that recognizes what Elizabeth Weed describes as the "impossible relation of women to Woman," and that acknowledges our ongoing contradictions, the gap, and the (perhaps permanent) internal split that makes a collective identity or integrity only a horizon, but a necessary one.[28] It is a fragmentation we can, however, as feminist readers, work with and through. That is the move of resistance and production that allows Lucy to find language "as a woman" despite the power of the " 'ologies," despite the allegory of *human* justice.

At the end of "Femininity, Narrative, and Psychoanalysis," an essay in which she takes as her example Emily Brontë's Wuthering Heights, *Juliet Mitchell outlines a question, "What are we in the process of becoming?" by way of providing herself with an ending to her discussion of the female subject and her critique of Kristeva's valorization of the semiotic, the so-called heterogeneity of the subject-in-process. To the implications of the apparent alternative of female carnival, Mitchell responds: "I do not think that we can live as human subjects without in some sense taking on a history; for us, it is mainly the history of being men or women under bourgeois capitalism. In deconstructing that history, we can only construct other histories. What are we in the process of becoming?"[29]*

Mitchell shrewdly leaves the question open, but since this is my essay and not hers, I have felt it important to risk a reply. At Pembroke I answered the question "What are we in the process of becoming?" by saying: "I hope we are becoming women." Because such a reply proved to be too ironic to occupy the privileged place of the last word, I will now say: "I hope we are becoming feminists." In both phrases, however, the hope I express is for all that we don't know about what it might mean to be women beyond the always already provided identity of Woman, with which we can only struggle; the hope for a negotiation that would produce through feminism the constitution of a new "social subject," as de Lauretis puts it in Alice Doesn't *(p. 186), and that I figure as a female critical subject.*

N O T E S

1. The foxtrot is defined in Webster's Third as "a ballroom dance in duple time that includes slow walking steps, quick running steps, and two steps." What appeals to me here is the change of pace, the doubleness of moves within the shape of the dance, and the collaborative requirement. The latter will reemerge at the end of this paper, but really runs through the argument: the dead-endedness of the one-way street that bears the traffic (to mix a few metaphors) between feminist and dominant critics. I realize that this figuration of the problem bears a certain resemblance to my earlier discussion of shoes and tropes, in "The Text's Heroine: A Feminist Critic and the Fictions," *Dia-*

critics 12, no. 2 (Summer 1982): 48-53. I think my current position was formulated for me at the Milwaukee conference by Biddy Martin, who said (approximately) that indeterminacy (what I am thematizing as the denegation and denigration of identity) is no excuse for not acting; that we must find a way to ground indeterminacy so that we can make political interventions. The question before us then becomes how to locate and allow for particularities within the collective.

2. Roland Barthes, "The Death of the Author," in *Image-Music-Text*, trans. Stephen Heath (New York: Hill and Wang, 1977), p. 143. Barthes's essay should be situated within the discussion of changing definitions of art in conjunction with the laws governing authorship in France, in particular a 1957 law that attempted to account for new kinds of artistic and authorial production not covered by the copyright law (*droits d'auteur*) of 1793. I am indebted to Molly Nesbit's "What Was an Author," in a forthcoming special issue of *Yale French Studies* edited by Alice Kaplan and Kristin Ross, for an illuminating explanation of this material. Nesbit points out that the death of the author for Barthes seems to have meant "really the imprinting author of 1793"; she also supplies what I think is little-known information about the original destination of the piece: "In 1967 in America for *Aspen* magazine, nos. 5+6 . . . dedicated to Stéphane Mallarmé." It is boxed (literally) along with all kinds of "authorial work, much of it technologically based." See also "Le droit d'auteur s'adapte à la nouvelle économie de la création," in *Le Monde*, August 3, 1985 on the latest copyright law, July 3, 1985. We clearly need a more contextual history of criticism.

3. Michel Foucault, "What Is an Author?" in *Language, Counter-memory, Practice: Selected Essays and Interviews by Michel Foucault*, ed. Donald F. Bouchard (Ithaca, N.Y.: Cornell University Press, 1980), p. 120.

4. Roland Barthes, *Sade/Fourier/Loyola*, trans. Richard Miller (New York: Hill and Wang, 1976), pp. 8-9.

5. At the Cerisy colloquium of which he was the "prétexte," this phrase drew a certain amount of attention. See Hubert Damisch's presentation "La 'prise de langue' et le 'faire signe'" and the discussion that followed (*Prétexte: Roland Barthes, Colloque de Cerisy* [Paris: UGE, 10/18, 1978], pp. 394-418). In his comments on the meaning of the phrase, Barthes situates his own relation to the historical context of writing *Sade/Fourier/Loyola*: "It was the heyday of modernity and the text; we talked about the death of the author (I talked about it myself). We didn't use the word writer [*écrivain*]: writers were slightly ridiculous people like Gide, Claudel, Valéry, Malraux" (pp. 412-13).

6. Naomi Schor, *Breaking the Chain: Women, Theory, and French Realist Fiction* (New York: Columbia University Press, 1985), p. 127.

7. Andreas Huyssen, "Mapping the Postmodern," *New German Critique*, no. 33 (Fall 1984), p. 44.

8. Elaine Showalter, "Women Who Write Are Women," *New York Times Book Review*, December 16, 1984, p. 33.

9. Donna Haraway, "A Manifesto for Cyborgs: Science, Technology, and Socialist Feminism in the 1980s," *Socialist Review*, no. 80 (May-April 1985), pp. 84-85.

10. Hélène Cixous, "The Laugh of the Medusa," *Signs: A Journal of Women in Culture and Society* 1, no. 4 (Summer 1976):879.

11. Jonathan Culler, *On Deconstruction* (Ithaca, N.Y.: Cornell University Press, 1982), p. 64.

12. In "Women's Time, Women's Space: Writing the History of Feminist Criticism" (*Tulsa Studies in Women's Literature* 3, no. 1-2 [Spring-Fall 1984]:29-

44), Elaine Showalter adopts Julia Kristeva's attempt at a "genealogy" of subjectivity, of a *space* of generation that is both "European *and* trans-European." In writing the history of American feminist criticism, she wants "to emphasize its specificity by narrating its development in terms of the internal relationships, continuities, friendships, and institutions that shaped the thinking and writing of the last fifteen years" (p. 30). As examples of asymmetrical events in these nonparallel chronologies, Showalter contrasts the 1966 conference on "The Structuralist Controversy and the Sciences of Man" at Johns Hopkins University with "the first feminist literary session at the Chicago MLA in 1970" (p. 32), neither of which I attended. In 1971 I was reading Barthes, not Rich. The discovery of Rich, for me a recent one, comes from being involved with a women's studies program; this trajectory, I think, figures an inverse relation to the reading habits of mainstream American feminist criticism, while remaining outside the classical reading patterns of women in French—which may or may not explain the feeling people have had that I am mixing things that don't belong together. What is worrisome to me is the way in which conferences on literary studies continue to follow their separate paths: though women are invited to, say, the English Institute (for which Showalter wrote this essay), and men to Pembroke and Milwaukee, there is no evidence yet that feminist critical theory has affected dominant organizations and theorizations.

13. Adrienne Rich, *On Lies, Secrets, and Silence; Selected Prose, 1966-1979* (New York: Norton, 1979), p. 39.

14. Ibid., p. 40.

15. Adrienne Rich, "Blood, Bread, and Poetry: The Location of the Poet," *Massachusetts Review* (1984), p. 536.

16. This move corresponds to Gayatri Spivak's insistence on "a simultaneous other focus; not merely who am I? but who is the other woman? How am I naming her? How does she name me?" "French Feminism in an International Frame," *Yale French Studies* 62 (1981):179.

17. Charlotte Brontë, *Villette* [1853] (New York: Penguin, 1983), pp. 493-95.

18. In "A Manifesto for Cyborgs" (see above), Donna Haraway, calling for a greater use of irony "within socialist feminism," argues: "Irony is about contradictions that do not resolve into larger wholes, even dialectically, about the tension of holding incompatible things together because both or all are necessary and true" (p. 65). At the Milwaukee conference, Jane Gallop, knowing that I have had trouble with the reception of this paper, asked about the implicit risk one runs that irony can misfire. In *A Handlist of Rhetorical Terms*, Richard Lanham describes this problem under the rubric of "rhetorical irony" (p. 61). He points out that the "relationship of persuader and persuaded is almost always self-conscious to some degree," and goes on to make the claim that "every rhetorical posture except the most naive involves an ironical coloration, of some kind or another, of the speaker's *Ethos*." To the extent that the ethos (character, disposition) of feminism historically has refused the doubleness of "saying one thing while it tries to do another" (the mark of classical femininity, one might argue), it may be that an ironic feminist discourse finds itself at odds both with itself (its identity to itself) and with the expectations its audience has of its position. If that is true, then irony, in the final analysis, may be a figure of limited effectiveness. On the other hand, since nonironic, single, sincere, hortatory feminism is becoming ineffectual, it may be worth the risk of trying out this kind of duplicity on the road.

19. In other words, the task of "dephallicizing the father," as Jane Gallop puts it (*The Daughter's Seduction: Feminism and Psychoanalysis* [Ithaca, N.Y.:

Cornell University Press, 1982], p. xv), must break out of the limits of the family circle to succeed.

20. Rich, *Lies, Secrets, and Silence*, p. 153.

21. Gayatri Chakravorti Spivak, "The Politics of Interpretations," *Critical Inquiry* 9 (September 1982):277.

22. Rosi Braidotti, "Patterns of Dissonance: Women and/in Philosophy," manuscript, p. 12.

23. Spivak, "Politics of Interpretations," p. 277.

24. See Teresa de Lauretis, *Alice Doesn't: Feminism, Semiotics, Cinema* (Bloomington: Indiana University Press, 1984).

25. Jane Marcus, "Still Practice, A/Wrested Alphabet: Toward a Feminist Aesthetic," *Tulsa Studies* 3, no. 1/2 (Spring/Fall 1984):90 and 91; see also Nina Auerbach, "Why Communities of Women Aren't Enough," pp. 153-37.

26. If Lucy writes her way out of humiliation and into subjective agency, on stage the use of language becomes a question of performance as voice. The difficulty Lucy discovers, once she begins to speak, lies not in the audience but in the mastery over her own voice *as* representation: "When my tongue got free, and my voice took its true pitch, and found its natural tone, I thought of nothing but the personage I represented" (p. 210). In other words, identity also depends on displacement and translation: Lucy speaks through a text, in another language. That is also another way of arguing for theory's place, and for "dancing shoes" even if (or precisely because) after the play, off stage, Lucy won't dance. (For another view on the subject of shoes and discourse, see Jane Marcus, "Storming the Toolshed," *Signs* 7, no. 3 [Spring 1982]:623.

27. Juliet Mitchell, "Psychoanalysis: A Humanist Humanity or a Linguistic Science?" in *Women: The Longest Revolution* (New York: Pantheon, 1984), p. 241.

28. In "A Man's Place," a talk she gave at the 1984 MLA session on "Men in Feminism," Elizabeth Weed brilliantly outlined many of the issues with which I struggle here.

29. Mitchell, "Psychoanalysis," p. 294.

EIGHT

Feminism and the Power of Interpretation: Some Critical Readings

Tania Modleski

Recognizing that women have long been held prisoners of male texts, genres, and canons, many feminist critics have argued for the necessity of constructing a theory of the female reader and have offered a variety of strategies by which she may elude her captors. Thus, Judith Fetterley urges women to become "resisting readers" of men's texts so that they "will lose their power to bind us knowingly to their designs."[1] And in an article on women's autobiographies, Nancy Miller argues that we should develop a way of reading women's writings that deliberately transgresses generic boundaries, since "not to perform an expanded reading is to remain prisoner of a canon that bars women from their own texts."[2] For Fetterley and Miller, the issue of power seems to be a crucial stake in developing a feminist reader-centered theory: hitherto men have had the power to direct and control women's literary response, and it now becomes imperative for female prisoners of male texts to refuse to exhibit the good behavior that has rendered them docile and model readers.

Unfortunately, it seems to me that for a variety of complex reasons, feminist criticism is in danger of losing some of its political edge and of forgetting the important stakes of a feminist theory of the reader. In this essay, I want to examine some readings that have been proposed as models for the process of "reading as a woman" to show how the force of the feminist critique has been weakened, as well as how women are being negated once again by a new universalizing practice that denies the specificity of their encounters with literary texts. My choice of essays to critique on these pages was determined by their being in some way representative of certain widespread tendencies in feminist criticism and by my desire to show how these tendencies inform some of the most influential kinds of "feminisms": American pluralist feminism, French feminism, and "male feminism." Thus, I do not want so much to quarrel with any particular "school" of criticism or theory as to engage with certain problems common to them all.

Perhaps the most articulate advocacy of a feminist-pluralist kind of criticism can be found in the work of Annette Kolodny. Now, as Kolodny admits, pluralism and feminism would seem to be somewhat antagonistic, since pluralism rests on what Gayatri Spivak has called "an ideology of free enterprise at work."[3] This ideology insists on the sovereignty of the individual subject and on his right and ability to choose from among any number of viable alternatives. Whereas the pluralist tends to ignore or minimize the constraints on the individual's freedom, feminism, of course, stresses the way in which women's freedom has been curtailed, their right to choose severely restricted.

Aware of a potential incompatibility, Kolodny nevertheless counsels feminists to adopt "a playful pluralism" in interpretation. In her prize-winning and controversial essay "Dancing through the Minefield: Some Observations on the Theory, Practice, and Politics of a Feminist Literary Criticism," she writes that such a pluralism would be "responsive to the possibilities of multiple critical schools and methods, but captive of none"—a salutary objective at a time when much feminism seems indeed to be captive of various methods generated by male theorists.[4] Kolodny emphasizes at the end of her essay that her pluralism does not reject "ideological commitment" or pretend to critical objectivity (p. 20). Quite the contrary, she says, the feminist critique inevitably calls into question the "dog-eared myth of intellectual neutrality" and "exposes the minefield for what it is . . . the male fear of sharing power and significance with women" (p. 21-22).

These are very large and important claims, but I believe that they are not altogether consistent with Kolodny's main argument and with her own critical practice. Kolodny's model of canon formation stresses the role of the reader, who favors those texts which speak most directly to his own experience and whose competence in analyzing these texts is acquired through continued exposure to them. Works that are alien to the reader's milieu are rejected from the canon as being of inferior literary quality—a fact that explains how the canon has been formed so as to "bar women from their own texts," to recall Miller's words. Kolodny proceeds to attribute men's "incapacity . . . to properly interpret and appreciate women's texts" to a "lack of prior acquaintance" (p. 12). But, we are told, men will be "better readers or appreciators of women's texts when they have read more of them," just as "women have always been taught to become astute readers of men's texts" (p. 14-15).

Kolodny discusses the difficulty that a story such as Charlotte Perkins Gilman's "The Yellow Wallpaper" is likely to present for the male reader who is "unacquainted with the ways in which women traditionally inhabited a household" (p.14). She fails, however, to address the question of why men are unfamiliar with the manner in which half the population has inhabited the world. Moreover, her use of the past tense is deceptive: many of our male colleagues live with women who continue to inhabit their households in ways not entirely dissimilar to that of Gilman's heroine (that is, they devote much of their time to their homes and children). If most of these men have not bothered to learn the activities and feelings of such women, it is unlikely that they will bother to attempt to understand the literary messages sent them by their sisters.

In her desire prematurely to include men in the feminist reading process, Kolodny underestimates the most crucial factor in men's traditional disregard and contempt for women's writings and women's modes of existence: the reality of male power. This fact of power renders asymmetrical the process by which men and women acquire competency to read each other's texts and guarantees that the majority of men will not gradually become "appreciators" of women's texts, since there is no compelling reason for them to begin to be interested in what women have to say (unless, as we shall see, they want to appropriate woman's discourse). Let me suggest an analogy that I believe to be apt given the current critical emphasis on the erotics of the reader's response to the text (Roland Barthes's "bliss" or "jouissance"). Speaking of men's putative physiological inability to fake orgasm, Catharine MacKinnon once remarked that if women had men's power, men would find a way to fake it.[5] Because of their economic and emotional dependence on men, women have historically been forced to find ways to enjoy or pretend to enjoy even the most virulently misogynistic texts. But until there is an appreciable change in the power structure, it is unlikely that women's fictional accounts of their lives in "the lying-in room, the parlor, the nursery, the kitchen, the laundry" (p. 13) will have the force to induce masculine jouissance.[6]

In her essay "Turning the Lens on 'The Panther Captivity': A Feminist Exercise in Practical Criticism," written for the influential issue of *Critical Inquiry* entitled *Writing and Sexual Difference*, Kolodny provides us with an extremely interesting reading of an early American captivity narrative in order to show how a woman reading a literary text from a feminist perspective can expand upon traditional interpretations of that text. In her introductory remarks, she is careful to forestall any potential charges of feminist criticism's castrating powers: "Because feminist criticism essentially adds a vital new perspective to all that has gone before, rather than taking anything away, it enjoys at least the possibility of enhancing and enlarging our appreciation of what is comprised by any specific literary text."[7]

"The Panther Captivity" tells of two men traveling deep into the wilderness and encountering a white woman who had eloped from her father with a man later killed by the Indians. The woman escaped, and after slaying a giant who menaced her, she took up residence in the giant's cave, where she has been dwelling in peace for nine years when the men discover her. Brilliantly, Kolodny demonstrates that "The Panther Captivity" makes use of a variety of discourses—the male adventure narrative, the captivity narrative, the sentimental romance, and Indian fertility myths—in order to quell the anxiety of its readers about women's ability to survive in the wilderness with their gentility intact.

In doing so, she corrects one interpretation of the narrative advanced by Richard Slotkin, who ignores the question of gender and sees only a variant of the oedipal myth: "the dilemma of all men coming of age, inheriting their parents' world, and replacing their sires as the shapers of that world" (p. 169). And in response to a hypothetical Fiedlerian reading of the narrative that would focus on the white woman as the intruder into the masculine preserve of the wilderness, Kolodny proceeds to view the story from the lady's perspective, claiming that it is "*she* who has suffered recurrent intrusions" (p. 193): from the father, the father's hired men, the Indians, the giant, and, finally, the two white men who persuade her to return to civilization and the father's house, thus ensuring at the end of the narrative that the wilderness once more becomes "the exclusive precinct of the white male hunter" (p. 175). Kolodny ends her essay with further assurances that she has not "changed cameras" (i.e., methodologies) and that her reading has not displaced those of male interpreters such as Slotkin (p. 175).

But suppose for a moment that we turn the lens on Kolodny's reading of this text and propose it as an allegory of feminist criticism in the wilderness, to borrow a phrase from Elaine Showalter, who borrows it from Geoffrey Hartman.[8] Hitherto, as we know, criticism has been largely an all-male preserve, jealously guarded from the possible intrusions of the feminist critic. Given the courage that it has taken for women to encroach on this terrain, it is understandable that many of us will want to persuade male critics that we retain our ladylike qualities and have no intention of changing the character of the wilderness itself, asking only that we be granted a small piece of the territory to cohabit peaceably.

But, as Kolodny's reading of "The Panther Captivity" indicates, even that may be asking too much. For, it must be remembered, at the same time that the story assuages male fears about women's existence in the wilderness, it takes pains to eradicate that existence, so that men once more retain sole possession of both women and the wilderness. As Kolodny writes of the tale's heroine, "what she has introduced into the wilderness is not only the fleshly symbolization of the male fantasy projection but, as well, a way of relating to that wilderness which is altogether different from the men's—and potentially, a threat to it" (p. 172). Similarly, Kolodny's reading exposes the male fantasy projection of critics such as Slotkin, who project onto the text an interpretation at odds with the protagonist's gender; and it introduces a way of relating to the story altogether different from the men's, in that it presents the female point of view. As such, Kolodny's interpretation is indeed a potential threat to masculine theory and criticism.

For it is impossible that two such opposed interpretations can coexist: one which sees woman as the intruder in the masculine wilderness idyll, and another which exposes the interest men have in controlling and subduing autonomous woman. If patriarchy entails male dominance, and if Kolodny is correct about the male critic's "fear of sharing power and significance with women," then a reading of a text that reveals the significance of the woman's point of view will certainly not alleviate this fear. The heroine of "The Panther Captivity" may be considered a monitory figure for the feminist critic, who, despite her protestations to the contrary, remains "captive,"— if not of a particular male methodology, then of masculine criticism in general. Rather than returning to the "fathers," as Kolodny does at the end of her essay, insisting that she has not displaced the interpretations of the male critics, feminist criticism might want to acknowledge the full extent of masculine resistance to female autonomy, as well as to understand its own power to disturb masculine authority.[9] Only then will we be in a position to assess what we must do and what we can do to survive and prosper in the critical wilderness.

If a pluralist critic such as Kolodny claims too little for feminist criticism, and tends to downplay the issue of male power, such would seem not to be the case with the criticism influenced by French feminism. Whereas Kolodny, for example, never questions the fact that the aim of criticism is to produce interpretations of literary texts, French feminism often goes as far as to consider the act of interpretation itself to be a patriarchal enterprise, the goal of which is to achieve power and mastery over a given text. In this theoretical schema, the text—writing in general—is identified with femininity, and interpretation becomes a means of arresting the free play of meaning analogous to the way patriarchy continually attempts to contain women and women's sexuality.

For example, Caren Greenberg says of oedipal literary criticism, "Woman is the text in the Oedipus myth, and if we pursue the analogy, the fate of the text (and therefore of language) in the Oedipal reading process parallels the fate of women in the patriarchy: both are without intrinsic value and gain importance only to the extent that they signify something other than themselves."[10] Greenberg's essay "Reading Reading: Echo's Abduction of Language" proposes an alternate myth meant to rescue simultaneously the text and the female from the male reader's will to dominance. Greenberg offers the Echo myth as a kind of allegory for a nonoedipal way of relating to texts, one that ultimately makes space for a female reader and allows for the possibility of the expression of *her* desires.

Here are the salient features of the Echo and Narcissus version of the myth outlined by Greenberg: Echo's speech problem is a result of her punishment at the hands of Juno, whose wrath she incurs because, by entertaining her with chatter, Echo keeps the goddess from discovering Jove's sexual infidelity. Juno condemns Echo to eternal repetition, so that when Echo falls in love with Narcissus, she cannot "initiate a conversation with him" in order to declare her love. She tries to embrace him, but he pulls away, "saying that he would rather die than give her power over him, and Echo responds by saying that she gives him power over her" (p. 304). After being rejected, Echo pines away for Narcissus, and soon nothing is left of her but her voice.

Greenberg observes that if we treat Echo as text and Narcissus as reader, we must pronounce him a poor one, since, like the oedipal critic, he disregards her and prefers to search only for his reflection. When, however, Echo repeats Narcissus's words of rejection in such a way as to express her love for Narcissus, she produces a *reading,* according to Greenberg, one that transforms the negation of passion into the expression of passion. "In short, repetition by a different-sex speaker is a creative act of reading involving a new locus of desire and a non-Oedipal act of identification. Identification in this case does not render the identifier identical to the text, it changes the desires." Repetition here is paradoxically a transformation of the meaning of language: "Where once there was no desire, the words come to express desire. Where once the first person subject was male, it is now female" (p. 307-308).

As ingenious as this reading of the myth certainly is, Greenberg exhibits a disregard for the text that is astonishing in light of her indictment of oedipal criticism's textual blindness. For in her analysis, Greenberg fails to examine, or even to mention, the purport of Echo's words. Surely it is significant that when the first-person subject is a female who repeats a male text, thereby articulating her *desire*, this repetition takes the form of a willing surrender of the *power* he has refused to grant her. Male author and female reader here collaborate to the ultimate benefit of patriarchy.[11] It is precisely this concord that Judith Fetterley tried to break in urging women to become "resisting readers." My second allegory of feminist criticism, then, would identify Echo as the feminist critic who holds "desire" and power to be mutually exclusive for women.

In my opinion, the feminist critic repeats Echo's gesture whenever she utters the Derridean notion that the quest for mastery in interpretation is a phallocentric one, which it is her business to repudiate, thereby putting "the feminine" into play. That is precisely what Greenberg does when at the end of her essay she unwittingly echoes Echo's words by cautioning us against the exercise of a critical will to power, a warning that is de rigueur in a certain kind of contemporary feminist criticism. Insisting that the reader must consider the text as "a locus of processes," Greenberg concludes: "It is not so much that roles need to be reversed; that is, for example, it is not particularly necessary that the text suddenly become seen as a male entity dominated by female critics. Instead, domination or mastery of the text must disappear as a political necessity of criticism" (p. 308).

To my mind, there is something profoundly depressing in the spectacle of female critics' avowing their eagerness to relinquish a mastery that they have never possessed. Since when have women been granted the power of interpretation or our readings accorded the status of interpretive truth by the male critical establishment? For a woman to proclaim an end to critical mastery, then, is quite different from a male critic's repudiation of the textual dominance that he in fact possesses. As Nancy Miller puts it in criticizing feminists who repeat Foucault's pronouncements on the death of the author, "only those who have it can play with not having it."[12]

I would like to be very clear. I am not advocating the kind of role reversal Greenberg imagines, whereby a text would "suddenly become seen as a male entity dominated by female critics." I do not, in fact, believe there is any cause for alarm about that, since the oedipal process outlined by Greenberg and others—according to which the female body is a text enabling the male to accede to the world of the fathers and the father's power—is not applicable to the psychic development of the female. That is not to say, however, that power is not a crucial issue for a feminist theory of interpretation, and that we should not explore our desire for power as fully as some of us have been exploring the power of desire. This will to power certainly informs Greenberg's own text and motivates her exceedingly ambitious plot to overthrow the dominant critical myth—the myth of Oedipus— and to propose an alternate myth that would explain the role of the traditionally excluded female reader. Moreover, as Greenberg makes her bid for power, she necessarily exerts a mastery over the text similar to that of the oedipal critics, whom she accuses of "attenuating" the text. She ignores the denoted meaning of Echo's statement—the rejection of power—in order to attend to the signification that pleases her better—the expression of passion.

Similarly, in my own desire to return to the issue of power, I have ignored the parts of Greenberg's text and of the Echo myth that do not seem relevant to my purposes (for example, Greenberg has much to say about another version of the myth featuring the god Pan). It seems to me self-evident that a degree of "domination or mastery of the text" is not only a "political necessity of criticism"; it is a necessity of criticism *tout court*. Rather than naively declaring power to be *passé* because of its association with phallocentricism, we should perhaps learn to use it in order to advance the feminist cause, while working to rethink its nature and effects. That is, of course, no easy task; but if we do not attempt it, we risk sabotaging feminism, just as Echo fails Juno by putting forth a "text" that is in the service of the male god and that "diverts Juno from knowledge [and, I would add, the power that is attendant on knowledge] rather than informing her" (p. 305).

Greenberg's essay nevertheless opens up onto some important issues for a feminist theory of the reader. In particular, her contention that a female "speaker" (or reader) may be articulating a different meaning when she repeats a male text is close to Luce Irigaray's notion of feminine "mimesis":

> To play with mimesis is thus, for a woman, to try to recover the place of exploitation by discourse, without allowing herself to be simply reduced to it. It means to resubmit herself . . . to ideas about herself . . . that are elaborated in/by a masculine logic, but so as to make "visible," by an effect of playful repetition, what was supposed to remain invisible: the cover-up of a possible operation of the feminine in language. It

also means "to unveil" the fact that if women are such good mimics, it is because they are not simply reabsorbed in this function. *They also remain elsewhere.* [13] (emphasis hers)

The problem with Greenberg's argument is that she crucially fails to locate an elsewhere and thus, contrary to her intention, winds up becoming "reabsorbed" in masculine meaning and masculine discourse. On the other hand, for Irigaray, who entitles the chapter dealing with feminine mimesis "The Power of Discourse," the "elsewhere" would seem to lie precisely in women's desire for power.

But lest Irigaray's thesis seem too abstract, it should be pointed out that "mimesis," or mimicry, is a time-honored tactic among oppressed groups, who often appear to acquiesce in the oppressor's ideas about it, thus producing a double meaning: the same language or act simultaneously confirms the oppressor's stereotypes of the oppressed and offers a dissenting and empowering view for those in the know. A vivid explanation of how it works can be found in Maya Angelou's *I Know Why the Caged Bird Sings.* A black con man describes to the heroine how he and his friends were able to use the white man's prejudice against him by performing a Sambo masquerade so that the "con man who could act the most stupid, won out every time over the powerful, arrogant white. . . . Anything that works for you can also work against you once you understand the Principle of Reverse," he says.[14]

Many examples of this principle can be adduced in feminist literary criticism. To take only one, in commenting on Bertha Harris's notion that the lesbian is "the prototype of the monster and 'the quintessence of all that is female and female enraged,' " Bonnie Zimmerman observes that while the image of the lesbian as monster appears to confirm popular prejudice, the fact that the image is offered by Harris in a "celebratory context" rather than a derogatory one suggests that "there is an important dialectic between how the lesbian articulates herself and how she is articulated and objectified by others."[15] The "elsewhere" in Harris's statement, for all its apparent mimicry of male stereotypes of the lesbian, surely lies in its articulation of women's rage—a rage that, in *my* interpretation of the remark, stems from women's powerlessness and oppression rather than, say, from disappointment over their lack of a penis (the patriarchal view). Thus, as Zimmerman notes, "context"—the terms of address and reception—is all-important in determining the meaning of any given utterance or text.

But while Irigaray's notion of mimesis is useful, there is, as I have said, a danger of losing sight of the "elsewhere"—a danger to which women seem especially susceptible. Maya Angelou's con man puts on an act for the gullible white men for the purpose of gaining power over them, and that power is, after all, the whole point of the stories he tells the heroine and the moral he draws from them. In my opinion, the function of feminist criticism is similarly to empower women by the force of its stories and interpretations, locating that "difference of view" so eloquently described by Mary Jacobus.[16] At least when we talk to each other—on the pages of feminist journals, special issues, or anthologies—it seems important to be clear and frank about the stakes of our work.

Both Kolodny and Greenberg, then, writing out of very different critical traditions, exhibit a typically feminine reluctance to admit to the desire for power—a reluctance that in Kolodny's case threatens to undermine the entire feminist enterprise of trying to account for the specificity of the female reader. Kolodny's concern that nothing be taken away from men leads her to assert that they can read women's texts just as women do. And though Greenberg quite rightly insists on the importance of considering gendered subjects in the activity of reading, much deconstructive criticism, for all its emphasis on "sexual difference," and for all that it frequently deplores the conventional critical habit of universalizing the male reader, nevertheless seems to be involved in a similar practice of negating the female reader.

Deconstructive theory tends to insist on the oppressiveness of gender distinctions and holds these distinctions to be products of a phallocentric order which it is the business of "the feminine" (and of writing, which is identified with the feminine) to subvert. Feminists have frequently pointed out, with some dismay, that in the work of certain theorists such as Jacques Derrida and Julia Kristeva, male authors are thought to be better practitioners of "l'écriture féminine" than female authors. Not surprisingly, along with this tendency to displace female writers, there has been a corresponding tendency to displace female readers of texts. For example, in an essay that takes feminists to task for being concerned about the gender of authors, Peggy Kamuf defines feminist criticism as "a way of reading texts that points to the masks of truth with which phallocentrism hides its fictions."[17] Such a definition obviously opens up a space for "male feminist" interpretations, and, as we shall see, it has been seized upon by at least one male critic eager to find a place for himself within the community of feminist readers.

In her article "Critical Cross-Dressing: Male Feminists and the Woman of the Year," Elaine Showalter vividly and brilliantly points out the dangers for women of adopting a "postgender" position. The essay analyzes male feminist criticism in the light of popular culture's recent preoccupation with tranvestism (as in the film *Tootsie*), and it concludes with the recounting of a nightmare featuring the *Diacritics* "covergirl" who appeared on the special feminist issue of that journal (the one with the clothes arranged in a gracefully feminine "bodiless tableau"). Showalter writes:

> I am haunted by the ambiguity of that cover. Sometimes I have a dream of the feminist literary conference of the future. The demonic woman rises to speak, but she mutates before our eyes into a mermaid, a vampire, a column of fire. The diacritical woman rises to speak but she has no head. Holding out the empty sleeves of her fashionable jacket, she beckons to the third panelist. He rises swiftly and commands the podium. He is forceful; he is articulate; he is talking about Heidegger or Derrida or Lévi-Strauss or Brecht. He is wearing a dress.[18]

Showalter, then, is rightly skeptical of the tendency of male critics to appropriate feminism. At the same time, however, she wants to allow for the possibility of male feminist readings of texts, maintaining that since (female) feminists have frequently complained about being ignored by the male critical establishment, it is hardly fair to condemn the few men who are taking us seriously at last. Showalter is heartened by the fact that the "initial recognitions"—by Robert Scholes, Wayne Booth, Terry Eagleton, and Jonathan Culler—"should have come from strong and secure writers of criticism who have little to gain by aligning themselves with a constituency or cause" (p. 134). Interestingly, she proceeds emphatically to contradict this statement by showing exactly what Terry Eagleton has at stake in appropriating feminism in his book *The Rape of Clarissa*; like Lovelace, who tries to possess Clarissa in order to allay his fear that writing is an unmanly act, Eagleton would possess feminism in order to alleviate his anxiety of authorship as a white male Marxist critic "who fears that his writing (rather than revolutionary action) is effeminate" (p. 145).

Showalter singles out Jonathan Culler as her model male-feminist critic, referring to the chapter section entitled "Reading as a Woman" in his book *On Deconstruction*. That Culler's discussion of feminist criticism is confined to these few brief pages; that he never returns to most of the issues he raises in this section; that he raises these issues primarily in order to make a single point (about the "divided" nature of the reader's experience), which he proceeds to use in his ongoing battle with the all-male critical establishment; that he thus treats feminism as a man would a wife who supports him through professional school and then is discarded once she has served her purpose—all these are points unremarked by Showalter. Showalter notes approvingly that despite his title, Culler is not himself interested in "reading as a woman"—not, that is, interested in playing Tootsie and appropriating the feminine. I, on the contrary, would argue that that is precisely part of his agenda.

In "Reading as a Woman," Culler constructs a historical account of feminist criticism, classifying it into three stages, or moments. The first moment, according to Culler, appeals to a notion of "women's experience" as a source of authority for women's responses as readers. The second moment is exemplified by Judith Fetterley's strategy of resistance to male literature and its designs on the female reader. Feminist criticism at this stage is a critique of what Mary Ellmann in *Thinking about Women* calls "phallic criticism." The third moment also entails a critique of phallic criticism, but unlike the second, which works "to prove itself more rational, serious, and reflective than male criticism," the third type of critique exposes the way "notions of the rational are tied to or in complicity with the interests of the male."[19]

For Culler, each stage of feminist criticism renders increasingly problematic the idea of "women's experience." By calling this notion into question, Culler manages to clear a space for male feminist interpretations of literary texts. Thus, at one point he quotes Peggy Kamuf's remark about feminism as a *way* of reading, and he borrows a term, ironically enough, from Elaine Showalter in order to suggest that "reading as a woman" is ultimately not a matter of any actual reader's gender: over and over again, Culler speaks of the need for the critic to adopt what Showalter has called the "hypothesis" of a woman reader in lieu of appealing to the experience of real readers. "The conclusions reached in feminist criticism of this sort are *not specific to women* in the sense that one can sympathize, comprehend and agree only if one has had certain experiences which are women's" (that is to say, I take it, only if one *is* a woman). "On the contrary, these readings demonstrate the limitations of male critical interpretations in terms that male critics would purport to accept" (p. 58). Not anyone, of course, can *be* a woman reader, but anybody can hypothesize one, and Culler goes on to offer a reading based on this hypothesis and designed to "demonstrate the limitations of male critical interpretations."

In *Moses and Monotheism*, Culler says, Freud attempts to account for the replacement of a matriarchal order by a patriarchal one. Freud writes, "This turning from the mother to the father points . . . to a victory of intellectuality over sensuality—that is, an advance of civilization, since maternity is proved by the evidence of the senses while paternity is a hypothesis, based on an inference and a premise" (p. 59). Far from exposing the limitations of Freud's account, Culler entirely accepts it and proceeds to elaborate on it, suggesting that "the promotion of the intelligible over the sensible, meaning over form, and the invisible over the visible" may be aspects of the patriarchal principle (p. 59-60). He also draws some implications of this account for literary criticism, speculating that a patriarchal literary criticism would be obsessed with ascertaining which meanings were legitimate and which illegitimate (p. 61).

Astonishingly, Culler never reflects on how this reading of Freud subverts much of his own argument. For if the privileging of the hypothetical and the invisible is indeed related to a patriarchal world view, then it follows that Culler himself is being patriarchal just at the point when he seems to be most feminist—when he arrogates to himself and to other male critics the ability to read as women by "hypothesizing" women readers. It also follows that a genuinely feminist literary criticism might wish to repudiate the *hypothesis* of a woman reader and instead promote the "sensible," visible, actual female reader.

But, of course, it would be foolish to accept out of hand an inference based on such patently patriarchal premises. According to Freud, hypothesizing is a male activity. There are, however, many more compelling reasons for feminists to be wary of a hypothesis that allows men to read as women. To illustrate, we can consider the case of a man and a woman reading Freud's text as it is glossed by Culler.

The woman, accustomed to the experience of being thought more sensual than intellectual, must certainly respond to it differently from the man, even if her response is not fully conscious, for it will be difficult not to feel at some level uncomfortable and possibly insulted by the facile use of a stereotype that once again consigns her to what Simone de Beauvoir calls "immanence." Even if the female reader ultimately chooses to assent to Freud's pronouncements, she will rarely do so with the ease of the male reader, and, more importantly, her acquiescence will mean something different from what he means. At the very least, woman's relation to texts such as Freud/Culler's is apt to be a contradictory one, since even when she accepts in theory being relegated to the realm of the sensible on the grounds that much "intelligible" discourse is patriarchal, she knows herself to be capable not only of participating in this kind of discourse but of occasionally deriving pleasure from it. Let us, then, do full justice to the contradictory situation of woman, refusing to choose either side of a sexist alternative, and suggest that to read as a woman in a patriarchal culture necessitates that the *hypothesis* of a woman reader be advanced by an *actual* woman reader: the female feminist critic.

It is crucial to employ the notion of a hypothetical woman reader (as I myself did when I speculated on her response to Freud/Culler) if as critics we wish to be able to make generalizations about the activity of reading. Yet it is equally important that we refer these generalizations to the experience of real women, in spite of Culler's attempt to assign the category of "experience" largely to a mythical "first moment" of feminist criticism, as if we should have outgrown such an immature concern. For Culler, and for a "postfeminist" such as Peggy Kamuf, the notion of a "ground" (like experience) from which to make critical judgments is anathema. At the end of the section on "Reading as a Woman," Culler quotes Kamuf in order to elucidate his own point, transposing what she ways about writing as a woman to reading as a woman:

> A woman [reading] as a woman . . . the repetition has no reason to stop there, no finite number of times it can be repeated until it closes itself off logically, with the original identity recuperated in a final term. Likewise, one can find only arbitrary beginnings for the series, and no term which is not already a repetition: . . . a woman [reading] as a woman [reading] as a. . . . (p.64)

In depicting a situation in which real women and their experience are superfluous to the process she describes (since beginnings are totally arbitrary and all notions of identity negated), Kamuf plays the role of Juno condemning Echo to a repetition that ultimately leads to her physical annihilation. With each turn of the phrase, woman seems to be further diminished. And suppose we were to repeat Kamuf's statement as repeated by Culler, only substituting the word *man* for *woman*: man reading as a man. The series has every reason to stop there, since rather than leading us into an infinite regression, it has all the tautological force that masculinity itself has in our culture (cf. "a man's gotta do what a man's gotta do"). Thus, although Kamuf and Culler want to destroy the concept of "origin," the attempt works best when "woman" is the (vanishing) subject. When we substitute *man* for *woman* in the passage, the substitution actually serves to solidify the sense of the subject as point of origin (it thus interestingly coincides with one of the definitions of *tautology* given in the *O. E. D.*: "a repetition of acts, incidents, or experiences, used for the sending of a thing back to its place of origin"). And instead of subverting the notion of masculine "identity," the substitution works to stabilize it, since this kind of tautology irresistibly suggests that man is equal to himself and his deeds.

Whereas Kamuf and Culler reject the notion of experience as a ground on which to make critical judgments, Teresa de Lauretis has used C. S. Peirce's concept of "ground" to designate precisely that place from which it is possible to theorize, construct, modify, and make conscious female experience. Far from being a simple concept, and more than the metaphor for territory that the term is for Kamuf (although, interestingly, de Lauretis begins the chapter in question with the anecdote of Virginia Woolf at Oxbridge being rudely brought back to her proper ground, the gravel path), "ground" in de Lauretis's work is a precise theoretical concept that allows for communication to occur between sender and addressee, writer and reader, and is thus a relational term rather than the simple referential entity spurned by Derridean theory. Certain political or "micropolitical" practices enable a "shifting" of the "ground" of a given sign, says de Lauretis, thus producing changes in consciousness, behavior, or "experience."[20]

Importantly for our purposes, this notion of "ground" opens onto a definition of "experience" more useful for feminism than the "individualistic, idiosyncratic sense of something belonging to" someone that Kamuf and Culler find objectionable.[21] Just as the notion of "ground" is relational, so "experience" is used to designate a *process*—"a process by which, for all social beings, subjectivity is constructed. . . . For each person, therefore, subjectivity is an ongoing contruction, not a fixed point of departure or arrival from which one then interacts with the world."[22] Needless to say—and this is the point of de Lauretis's opening the chapter with an anecdote from Woolf's *A Room of One's Own*—feminist criticism and theory play a crucial role in the process by which women's experience is made conscious, articulated, and—in the case of a Virginia Woolf—even constructed.

If, then, we wish to participate in and elucidate the ongoing process that makes up female subjectivity, feminists at this historical moment need to insist on the importance of real women as interpreters. As for men who want to show their support of feminism (which is different from wanting to *be* feminists, and certainly less presumptuous), Showalter correctly advises them to conduct a thoroughgoing and honest analysis of the way in which their gender shapes their interpretations in order truly to "demonstrate the limitations of male critical interpretations." Contrary to her claim, however, that is not what Culler does: for men to devote little sections of their big books to "reading as a woman" simply perpetuates the complacent view that man can include and, as Culler says, "comprehend" woman just as the generic term *man* in language is said to do. Man thus once again achieves universality at the expense of women.

Interpretation is, as I have insisted throughout this essay, crucially bound up with power. For feminism, power is the stake of the critical enterprise, and each and every interpretive act involves an exercise of power over a text, whether we like to admit it or not. Moreover, as female critics who are (presumably) concerned to address ourselves to other women, we are placed in a potential relation of power over female readers, including the critics whose theories and interpretations we dispute. For a variety of very good reasons, feminism has tended to downplay this aspect of power more than any other, wishing at all costs to avoid masculine kinds of rivalry and to assert sisterhood and solidarity. As laudable as this emphasis on sisterhood is, we may gain more by acknowledging the power struggles that go on among us than by perennially disavowing them.

In any case, the ultimate goal of feminist criticism and theory is female empowerment. My particular concern here has been to empower female readers of texts, in part by rescuing them from the oblivion to which some critics would consign them. Other feminists have insisted on delivering female writers from the premature burial they have suffered at the hands of those who declare the death of the author. Our very survival, as Adrienne Rich observed some time ago, hangs in the balance, so that there can be no question of *choosing* between authors and readers.[23] We must, I think, not mimic the oedipal hostility implicit in Roland Barthes's remark that the "birth of the reader must be at the cost of the death of the author."[24] By working on a variety of fronts for the survival and empowerment of women, feminist criticism performs an escape act dedicated to freeing women from *all* male captivity narratives, whether these be found in literature, criticism, or theory.

N O T E S

I would like to thank Cheryl Kader, without whose critical viewpoint this essay would not have been possible. Thanks also to Kris Straub for her thoughtful criticisms of an earlier draft.

1. Judith Fetterley, *The Resisting Reader: A Feminist Approach to American Fiction* (Bloomington: Indiana University Press, 1978), p. xxiii.

2. Nancy K. Miller, "Women's Autobiography in France: For a Dialectics of Identification," in *Women and Language in Literature and Society*, ed. Sally McConnell-Ginet, Ruth Borker, and Nelly Furman (New York: Praeger, 1980), p. 270.

3. Gayatri Chakravorty Spivak, "The Politics in Interpretation," in *The Politics of Interpretation*, ed. W. J. T. Mitchell (Chicago and London: University of Chicago Press, 1983), p. 352.

4. Annette Kolodny, "Dancing through the Minefield: Some Observations on the Theory, Practice, and Politics of a Feminist Literary Criticism," *Feminist Studies* 6, no. 1 (Spring 1980):19.

5. Catharine MacKinnon, lecture at the Conference on Cultural Studies, University of Illinois, Champagne-Urbana, July 10, 1983. See the essay by Gayatri Chakravorty Spivak, "Displacement and the Discourse of Woman," in *Displacement: Derrida and After*, ed. Mark Krupnick (Bloomington and London: Indiana University Press, 1983), for a different use of the metaphor of female orgasm to describe a possible activity of reading.

6. See also the telling critiques of Kolodny's essay by Judith Kegan Gardiner, Elly Bulkin, and Rena Grasso Patterson, "An Interchange on Feminist Criticism: On 'Dancing through the Minefield,' " *Feminist Studies* 8, no. 3 (Fall 1982):pp. 629-75.

7. Annette Kolodny, "Turning the Lens on 'The Panther Captivity': A Feminist Exercise in Practical Criticism," in *Writing and Sexual Difference*, ed. Elizabeth Abel (Chicago: University of Chicago Press, 1982), p. 159.

8. See Elaine Showalter, "Feminist Criticism in the Wilderness," in Abel, *Writing and Sexual Difference*, pp. 9-35.

9. In her reply to the articles in Abel, *Writing and Sexual Difference*, Jane Gallop makes a similar gesture toward the fathers. She counsels feminist critics to pay as much attention to "literary critics" (their "fathers") as to "feminists" (their "mothers"). It is through the metaphor of marriage and the strict division of criticism and politics along the lines of gender that Gallop formulates her notion of "sexual difference" (p. 290).

10. Caren Greenberg, "Reading Reading: Echo's Abduction of Language," in McConnell-Ginet, Borker, and Furman, *Women and Language in Literature and Society*, p. 303.

11. In a paper entitled "Feminist Theory and Lesbian Consciousness," delivered at the Women's Studies Conference, Madison, Wisconsin, September 1984, Cheryl Kader speculates that the contemporary emphasis on "desire" may be a move to displace or replace feminism's concern with power and power relations. Greenberg's essay provides an excellent case in point for her thesis.

12. Nancy K. Miller, "The Texts Heroine: A Feminist Critic and Her Fictions," *Diacritics* (Summer 1982), p. 53.

13. Luce Irigaray, *This Sex Which Is Not One*, trans. Catherine Porter (Ithaca: Cornell University Press, 1985), p. 76.

14. Maya Angelou, *I Know Why the Caged Bird Sings* (New York: Random House, 1969), pp. 214-15.

15. Bonnie Zimmerman, "What Has Never Been: An Overview of Lesbian Feminist Literary Criticism," *Feminist Studies* 7, no. 3 (Fall 1981):463-64.

16. Mary Jacobus, "The Difference of View," in *Women Writing and Writing about Women*, ed. Mary Jacobus (New York: Barnes and Noble, 1979), pp. 10-21.

17. Peggy Kamuf, "Writing like a Woman," in McConnell-Ginet, Borker, and Furman, *Women and Language in Literature and Society*, p. 286.

18. Elaine Showalter, "Critical Cross-Dressing: Male Feminists and the Woman of the Year," *Raritan* 3, no. 2 (1983):149.

19. Jonathan Culler, *On Deconstruction: Theory and Criticism after Structuralism* (Ithaca: Cornell University Press, 1982), p. 258.

20. Teresa de Lauretis, *Alice Doesn't: Feminism, Semiotics, Cinema* (Bloomington: Indiana University Press, 1984), p. 178.

21. Ibid., p. 159.

22. Ibid., p. 159.

23. Adrienne Rich, "When We Dead Awaken: Writing as Re-vision," in her *On Lies, Secrets, and Silence; Selected Prose, 1966-1978* (New York: W. W. Norton, 1979), p. 35.

24. Roland Barthes, "The Death of the Author," in *Image-Music-Text,* trans. Stephen Heath (New York: Hill and Wang, 1977), p. 147. Quoted in Greenberg, p. 304n.

Inhibiting Midwives, Usurping Creators: The Struggling Emergence of Black Women in American Fiction

Sondra O'Neale

One ostensible phenomenon in the literature by and about black Americans which has been written since the 1960s is the disclosure of those aspects of black personality that were heretofore hidden from the white world. Many of those unsurfaced aspects have been historically weapons of survival, weapons that of necessity have obfuscated the truth about black identity. The noted poet Paul Laurence Dunbar has most aptly called the veneer that blacks have worn in life and literature the "mask" we wear "that grins and lies and hides our sighs."[1]

Beyond the mask, in the ghetto of the black woman's community, in her family, and, more important, in her psyche, is and has always been another world, a world in which she functions—sometimes in sorrow but more often in genuine joy, sometimes in anger but usually in love—by doing the things that "normal" black women do. That is, they observe the feminine images of the "larger" culture, realize that these models are at best unsuitable and at worst destructive to them, and go about the business of fashioning themselves after the prevalent, historical black female role models in their own community. They then grow up, get married (or a reasonable facsimile thereof), have children, get a job (although certainly not always following these priorities), and allow their lives to touch the white world only in the sphere of economic encounter. In short, black women do not go around all the time thinking about white women, wanting to be like them or look like them or think like them. Black women just want the freedom, and the economic wherewithal, to be themselves.

One of the tasks of the black woman critic is to approach the "new" black woman's literature (an approach undertaken with some trepidation) to see if it has indeed revealed those strengths that have made possible the black woman's survival.

Perhaps the anticipated fear that certain secrets of black female survival will be cheapened and weakened by exposure to the white world should be rendered groundless. Most heroines in the post-sixties literature by black women are: 1) either too white or longing to be whiter (e.g., Jones's *Corregidora* and Morrison's *The Bluest Eye*); 2) pitiful objects of black male domestic violence (e.g., Walker's *The Third Life of Grange Copeland* and Shange's *For Colored Girls . . .*); 3) religious mystics who, because of the unique sexual racism that black women face, find ethereal reality preferable to this earthly realm (as in Morrison's *Song of Solomon* and Walker's *Meridian*); 4) redeemed from the emotional impotencies of black males through sexual union with other women (all of Anne Allen Shockley's novels, and certainly Walker's *The Color Purple*); or 5) maniacs bordering on massive self-destruction (as in Morrison's *Sula* and Bambara's *The Salt Eaters*).

While some of these literary characters triumph despite the fact that they are nearly white-skinned (in Hunter's *Lakestown Rebellion*, for example), and others perish because they are not (like Pilate's granddaughter in *Song of Solomon*), the truth is that most black women do not want to be white women. They simply want the freedom to exist as they are. Morrison says so herself:

> Black women . . . look at white women and see them as the enemy for they know that racism is not confined to white men, and that there are more white women than men in this country and that 53 percent of the population sustained an eloquent silence during times of greatest stress. . . . Black women have always considered themselves superior to white women. . . . [They] have been able to envy white women . . . fear them . . . and even love them . . . but Black women have found it impossible to respect white women. I mean they never had what Black men have had for white men: a feeling of awe at their accomplishments.[2]

Thus, much of what is in her own writing and in that of many contemporary black women novelists must be some kind of literary ploy. White women are supposed to be the demure, submissive ones. That a black woman will stay put and let any man pulverize her without lifting a foot, finger, skillet (of boiling water, lye, or ever-available hot grits), chair, knife, or some other handy instrument of self-defense, is indeed a neohistory of some other believer in passive resistance. Maybe we don't always win, but at least we do always fight back. That is certainly the note of victory in a character who leads an otherwise dismal life, Alice Walker's Mem Copeland in *The Third Life of Grange Copeland.*

There is definitely a theme of insanity woven into most of the recent fiction by and about black women. As there is simply no literary tradition of the mad black woman sequestered in the attic, one must assume that this character, too, is a wedge taken from the authorial imagination of extremes in black female experience. In Bambara's novel *The Salt Eaters*, insanity, disjointed thought, fragments of consciousness form the structure and describe the psyche of Velma Henry until they propel her into catatonic isolation. In Morrison's *Sula*, the women chop off their legs, murder their sons, set themselves ablaze, and leap from multistoried houses to self-destruct. And in Gayle Jones's *Eva's Man, Corregidora*, and *White Rat*, the madness is initiated by, perpetuated in, and resolved through sex: sexual acts, studies of sexual appendices, and the totality of sexual releases.

The ultimate identity of these fictional characters is that they are all marginal members of marginal societies. Their isolation, their wretched loneliness, or what brings Morrison to label one of her characters the "pariah" of black female existence, are hallmarks of black women who have never been wrapped in the heart of black communal love. Perhaps the depiction of such marginal characters and their "universal" insanity does make for better fiction, but these characters do not represent black life.

Certainly, there is no dispute that many black women at some time in their lives wrestle with a pervasive standard, the white female as the most desirable love object in world culture. Sexual racism is an inherent problem in integrated cultures. It is a carefully orchestrated and integral part of the white man's control over his kingdom and therefore is unfortunately adopted by some black men as a de facto part of American culture. The pervasiveness of the white female as the secular icon of femininity in our culture is so strong as to affect even the most well-meaning members of the sisterhood, not to mention those "liberated" males who think that they can write about female experience.

White men have historically manipulated the representation of femaleness, and always at the black woman's expense. Scholars of the ancient Western world clearly describe a culture in which white skin or Europeanized features were not the norm of beauty and in which African and Eastern women were set forth as exquisite models of past and contemporary reality. Both in the prevalence of interracial mar-

riages involving both white and nonwhite women and in a plethora
of religious iconography, the black woman was exhibited as a glorious
archetype in ancient Western culture. Nor was it considered odd or
exceptional that black men and black women could love one another
without social and psychological inhibitions.

In fact, a prominent early church father, Origen, points out that the
black woman in the Biblical "Song of Solomon" was a symbol of the
bride of Christ. He wrote that she was the Queen of Sheba, with
whom the great Hebrew king Solomon peopled the nation of Ethiopia.
Hundreds of years later, another queen of Ethiopia was the first mon-
arch of a non-Jewish nation to receive the gospel message of the new
age, soon after the death and resurrection of Christ. Origen further
reminded his audience of Keturah, the Ethiopian woman who married
Moses after his first wife deserted him. Again, he presented the black
woman as a type of the Christian church, a much coveted honor in
medieval times.[3]

These images of black women as equally acceptable cultural standards of beauty began to change in the fourteenth century until finally,
by the sixteenth century, through the use of thoroughly pejorative
connotations in literature and art created to accommodate the emerging slave trade, black women were presented in societal media as
icons of evil rather than examples of divine beauty. Sheba was no
longer the gracious queen whose beauty inspired Solomon to pen his
scriptural song. In the fourteenth century, church leaders painted her
hair blond so that they could continue her lionization as the bride of
Christ. Within two hundred years, the icon was changed again, first
to white skin and blond hair, and then, when the black face and woolly
hair were returned to Sheba, the fabrication was diffused throughout
medieval culture that this black queen of Ethiopia had been the cause
of Solomon's apostasy.[4] Similarly, the black woman was introduced
as Lilith, Adam's first wife, and was made responsible for his sin.

Thus, from the sixteenth century onward in Western culture, the
black woman has been the object of forbidden attention as the symbol
of devilish sensuality. From the position of queen, lover, muse, and
pedestaled wife, she became a symbol of sexual excess in the white
mind. And if black men were made studs to procreate slaves, black
women became sexual receptacles for all men.

Apparently the shift in value from woman as an international personage to woman as white—with all women arranged in a downwardly
spiraling hierarchy, in which each descending step is delineated by
skin color and hair texture—has been such a powerful torque in the
culture that nothing in the last four hundred years has been able to

dislodge it. That is especially true in kinetic America, where transitions in racial and sexual status have been the hallmark of social change. Neither the religious revivals of the eighteenth century, with their paramount theme of "restoring" scriptural accuracy; nor the "marriage" of the suffragette movement with antislavery politics in the nineteenth century; nor the militant, Afrocentric (and male-centered) civil rights movement that merged with, or was swallowed by, the white women's liberation movement in the twentieth century has disturbed the perception of black women as antitypes of femininity.

If one can comprehend Betty Friedan's detailed scenario, in *The Feminine Mystique*, of Madison Avenue's manipulative seduction of the white woman, first to make her the object of capitalist buying power and then, when it suited the needs of World War II, to transform her into Rosie the Riveter, then one should be able to see how the four-hundred-year historic "reconstruction" of the black woman's image was—and continues to be—fashioned to feed the white man's need for a poverty object, to fulfill his lust for dominance over those he thinks he has "created" to inhabit the most powerless corners of his realm.

I find it improbable to discuss the development of black women writers and characters in the language of American feminism, a political movement that is at least a hundred and fifty years old. In all that time, the black woman has never been the feminine ideal, not only in the minds of men who write literature, but, more important, she has not been the ideal of femininity through which white women obtain their self-view; nor even, lamentably, has she been an ideal of femininity for many black women.

In her *Images of Women in Fiction*, Susan Koppelman Cornillon structures the collection around the assumption that most female characters in Western literature can be divided into four categories: 1) Woman as Heroine, or the "sugar 'n' spice and everything nice" stereotype of traditional women; 2) the invisible woman, "roles women are forced to play in much fiction such as the Other, the thing, as non-cognating phenomenon for the hero"; 3) "The Woman as Hero" or "women as whole people in the process of . . . finding other metaphors for existence"; and 4) "Feminist Aesthetics" with the "determined and courageous statements [of] women's desires and determinations and their abilities to achieve, at least as much as men do."[5]

The black woman is never seen in anyone's fiction as sugar and spice; she is never in close enough proximity to the hero to even be in his sphere of vision, and, with the exception of a very few novels by black women, she is not depicted as "finding herself." Her problem usually is more to find a compatible world in which to exist. The true struggle for black women today lies precisely in Cornillon's last category. However, the black woman's "courage" statement is different from the white woman's, and the latter is often threatened by it, because the black woman's courage treads upon a world in which the white woman is "queen." Thus, too, much feminist literature serves political and social ends that white women have for themselves, ends other than the full liberation of black women, even their literary liberation in authentic characterization as mothers, role models, wives, friends, and lovers. As long as those whom I call the "midwives" of feminist literature insist that the black woman's story must be told from a perspective that the white woman can manipulate and approve, then the movement will be bogged forever in a game of facades. Black women writers must be freed from those career and economic shackles which prevent them from recreating black women as they are—as they are in history, in life, and in their own realities—rather than as white women expect them to be.

For instance, where are the Angela Davises, Ida B. Wellses, and Daisy Bateses of black feminist literature? Where are the portraits of those women who fostered their own actions to liberate themselves, other black women, and black men, as well? We see a sketch of such a character in *Meridian*, but she is never developed to a social and political success. Could it be that these black women—astounding superwomen in history but strangely muted in fiction—do not fit the political ends of white women's liberation? Would their presence in art be too threatening to the agendas of those who would use black literature to reorient the politically explosive tendencies of black life? Is that why Kristin Hunter's novel *The Lakestown Rebellion*, featuring a black woman who organizes black communal guerilla warfare against the white establishment, has been ignored by reviewers as inappropriate for this feminist age?[6] As Stephen Henderson argues in *The Militant Black Writer*,

> Black writers do not write for white people and refuse to be judged by them. They write for black people and they write about their blackness, and out of their blackness, rejecting anyone and anything that stands in the way of self-knowledge and self-celebration. They know that to assert blackness in America is to be "militant," to be dangerous, to be subversive, to be revolutionary, and they know this in a way that even the Harlem Renaissance did not. The poets and the playwrights are especially articulate and especially relevant and speak directly to the people.[7]

How long the contemporary black woman writer can continue her attempt to serve three masters is a legitimate question. Those tugging for her loyalties include the heritage of militant and political black American literature, the requirements of white feminism, and the trendyism of the literary and academic establishment, which has money, power, and control as its ultimate aims.

Thus, I am saying that even while it is presenting the views and images of selected black women, the white feminist movement is still somewhat entangled in traps of traditional, if very subtle, racism. Feminist literature, publishing, and criticism, instead of enhancing the complete emergence of black women as characters and authors in American fiction, have too often reinforced traditional literary stereotypes of black women. That is, of course, a major thesis in Bell Hooks's *Ain't I a Woman: Black Women and Feminism* and Michelle Wallace's *Black Macho and the Myth of the Superwoman*. White feminism is one of the "sexy" issues in academia in the eighties. In most of the literature, regardless of the discipline involved, the white feminist defines "female" from the assumption that the experience of white females is the "standard" female experience, from which all others must (negatively) deviate. For instance, Phyllis Chesler in *Women and Madness* writes:

> I have no theory to offer of Third World female psychology in America. No single theory will do descriptive justice to women of African, Latin-American, Mexican, Chinese and native Indian descent. Furthermore, as a white woman, I'm reluctant and unable to construct theories about experiences I haven't had; and as a psychologist and feminist, I'm really more interested in exploring the laws of *female* psychology than in exploring their various *exceptions* and *variations*.[8] (emphasis added)

In the feminist critique of literature, the quest is too often to "rediscover," and to critique the roles of white women characters in "traditional" literature by European and American white men; to "resurrect" neglected white women authors of the same culture, and to critique theories of literature by the effect that these have on the aesthetic exploration of the white woman's being. Literature by and about black women is so rarely quoted or evaluated as to be phenomenal in its appearance. Black women as feminist critics (or as commentators in other disciplines) are too often included for "token" representation because publishers require a "balanced" view, usually from selected scholars who are compatible with other agendas, as well.[9] As long as these policies continue, the uninhibited black woman as character and writer, a being who is free to be herself, will seldom be seen in the feminist canon.

The "tragic mulatto" figure is the homage that white male authors have paid to the black female character, but the foil for that stereotype has always been the loutish "mammy," whose ignorance and religiosity serve to allay his suspicions of his own banality. The third figure, the reverse of the Madonna myth, is the black woman as whore, a character seen only when American authors wish to exhibit the most frightening aspects of uninhibited, animallike sexuality, as in Carl Van Vechten's *Nigger Haven*, Richard Wright's *Native Son*, and John Wideman's *Lynchers*. In all other cases, when black men create black female characters, they usually present them as "mammies."

The mammy figure is first introduced by Washington Irving in the eighteenth century and is then taken up by James Fenimore Cooper, William Gilmore Simms, Henry Timrod, William Faulkner, Allen Tate, Robert Penn Warren, and others. Although not usually included at all in twentieth-century feminists novels, she is prominent in more traditional literature by women such as Eudora Welty, Flannery O'Connor, and Katherine Anne Porter. A shabby variation of the ultimate Mother Earth—fat, mindless, enamored with white family home life but absent and powerless in her own home—the "mammy" stereotype is perpetuated in literature by black men who, instead of attempting to redeem her into an authentic Madonna character, usually transform her into an emasculating religious savage. She is Richard Wright's smothering and hateful Seventh-Day Adventist grandmother; she is Ralph Ellison's innocuous Mary Rambo; and she is Ishmael Reed's murderous Mammy Gorbaduke in *Flight to Canada*. Earnest Gaines is the only one who attempts to show the aged black woman as an endearing character. But his Jane Pittman is an unrealistic portrayal, more idyllic than human, and really epitomizes what Michelle Wallace has identified as the myth of superior black feminine strength. The essence of this myth is that the black woman is really more like a man than the white woman.

Conversely, the black matriarch is never seen as a "mammy" in the black woman's literature. That is precisely the theme of Trudier Harris's new critical text *From Mammies to Militants*.[10] In novels by black women writers, black women of any age are treated with love and respect. Their physical features, whether thin or obese, are seldom the issue. Rather, what makes the older black female character an object of love and gratitude for both writers and readers is the immensity of her willing and sacrificial service for her people and her yearning for a better life for her daughters. Kristin Hunter laid the "mammy" figure to rest in *God Bless the Child*, when she equated Rosie's grandmother with the conduit of the capitalistic greed that eventually killed the heroine. Otherwise, in Bambara's *Salt Eaters*, Maya Angelou's *Tell Me Why the Caged Bird Sings*, and Zora Neale Hurston's *Their Eyes Were Watching God*, the grandmothers are redeemed progenitors and socially revered icons.

The mulatto figure is the most discussed black female character in American literature. She is the woeful spitfire in Mark Twain's *Puddin' Head Wilson*, the tearful, confused coquette in Warren's *Band of Angels*, and the glamorous but betrayed woman who longs for her white lover's return to her embrace in Faulkner's *Go Down Moses*. In every instance, these characters do not represent women with whom the black community is familiar. They are instead perceived as totally Europeanized, not only in facial features but in acculturation, as well.

Along with his many "mammy" figures, Faulkner decided to admit to his audience that there were indeed surreptitious liaisons between white men and black women in the South and that they persisted at the white man's behest and in spite of the black woman's willful and even organized resistance. But he simply could not admit that a white man could be amorously attracted to a "normal" looking black woman with dark skin and woolly hair. In the "Delta Autumn" chapter of *Go Down Moses*, he describes the black heroine's features as "the face indistinct and as yet only young with dark eyes, queerly colorless but not ill and not that of a country woman."[11] Like most other white male southern writers, Faulkner has a "shock of recognition" scene, wherein the mulatto character discovers that she is black and not white. That is a classic ploy in the literature which attempts to deal with interracial love relationships between black women (who do not look like black women) and white men. But in fact, if all black women raped by white men during the slavery era had looked like white women, there would have been no mulattoes, because they never would have been conceived.

Few white women have attempted to center their fiction around black heroines. An early exception is Gertrude Stein. An outspoken feminist expatriate who should have been more sensitive to the chauvinism of the mulatto trap, Stein exhibits overt racism in comparing two Black women in her novel *Three Lives*:

> Rose Johnson and Melanctha Herbert had been friends now for some years. . . . Rose Johnson was a real black, tall, well built, sullen, stupid, childlike, good looking negress. . . . Rose Johnson was careless and was lazy, but she had been brought up by white folks and she needed decent comfort. Her white training had only made for habits, not for nature. Rose had the simple, promiscuous unmorality of the black people. Melanctha Herbert was a graceful, pale yellow, intelligent, attrac-

tive negress. She had not been raised like Rose by white folks but then she had been half made with real white blood.[12]

Other than such absurd rhetoric—which reveals that "oppressed" but wealthy white women have real difficulty identifying with women of color, who instead must deal with oppression whenever they encounter the white world—most white women writers try to merge the identity of the mulatto or white woman with that of what they perceive as the "normal" black woman.

In fiction by black men, the mulatto pattern is essentially no different. In the first novel written by a black in America, William Wells Brown's *Clotel: Or The President's Daughter* (1864), the mulatto heroine thinks that she is white. When she discovers otherwise, the conflict begins. (Thus, while black writers, such as Gaines in *Of Love and Dust*, seem to be imitating Faulkner, Twain, and Warren, actually it is the white authors who are "borrowing" their theme from Brown.) Most black male writers, like their white counterparts, have tended to avoid creating black female characters who more authentically reflect the experience of most black women.

The most militant black spokesman of his time, W. E. B. DuBois, in his novel *Dark Princess* could not bear to contemplate an articulate, internationally mobile black woman who was both an ex-slave and a graceful lover, so he had his hero press his unrequited attentions upon a "princess" from India. In his popular short story "The Wife of His Youth," Charles Chestnutt, another turn-of-the-century black writer, brought a long-forgotten, dark-skinned wife into the parlor of sedate, manicured, light-skinned, northern black society to spoil their idyllic nonidentities. In another tale, "Cicely's Dream," Chestnutt describes a lithe black woman in this way: "though brown, she was not brown but that her cheek was darkly red with the blood of another race than that which gave her her name and station in life."[13] Chestnutt has Cicely dream a strange dream of being rescued by a white lover. A few days later, she finds the man anguishing in a deep stupor; he makes plans to marry Cicely, until his true love, a white school teacher, awakens him from such foolishness, and he goes off into the sunset with her.

Black men writing during the Harlem Renaissance continued to idolize the mulatto female in their works. Images of idyllic black women in Jean Toomer's *Cane*, Claude McKay's *Home to Harlem*, and Countee Cullen's poems and dramas are usually based on black women who have manipulated their features to make themselves more acceptably white for black men. McKay describes the protagonist's lover in *Home to Harlem* thus: "She was brown, but she had tinted her leaf-like face to a ravishing chestnut."[14]

Most surprising is what a perusal of currently popular works by black women writers reveals. Though of Afrocentric and liberal political orientation, and though they are black and female themselves, many of these writers still portray a psychological image of woman as white as their definitive statements on femaleness. While one suspects that they do so in order to meet the demands of what I call the publishing midwifery—that conglomerate which filters the intentions of black women writers with its own views of who "woman" should be—nonetheless, too many black women authors still present black female characters as: 1) suffering rejection from black males who are smothered by the male's longing for idealized white beauty, and thus force the women themselves into a hopeless longing to be white; 2) maladjusted tragic mulattoes, who cannot find identity or acceptance in either the black or the white worlds; or 3) "normal"-looking black women, who are triumphant heroines because they have found avenues of escape from their supposed lack of desirability, and consequently from society's rejection.

As stated earlier, the avenues of escape in the last category include religion, mysticism, insanity, suicide, and lesbianism. I am not equating these choices; I am simply stating that these are the kinds of choices that black heroines are making in the new black woman's literature. And the choices are not self-determined or uncoerced: the characters are usually forced into these choices by a society that makes no room for them to develop a sense of self which reconciles them to their sex as well as their race. Mysticism, for example, may be a choice forced upon heroines by the black, male-dominated church, which has made no room for aspiring women preachers. That is, of course, the background for Morrison's Pilate and Sula, and Walker's Meridian (the black woman as a neglected minister is presented brilliantly in Mary Helen Washington's forthcoming work on black women writers in the nineteenth century). Lesbianism, at least in the writings of Shange and Naylor, seems to be motivated by the savage cruelty that black women characters suffer at the hands of black men. Insanity is presented as a legitimate defense mechanism, as I indicated earlier; and suicide and death appear to be the only options left to female characters in *Sula*, as well as in Larsen's *Passing* and Walker's *The Third Life of Grange Copeland*.

The tragic mulatto appeared in the fiction by black women as early as the first novel, Frances E. W. Harper's *Iola Leroy, or The Shadows Uplifted* (1899). Harper left the mulatto heroine's dark-skinned sister-in-law surrounded by shadows of admiration and mystery, distancing her from women who were more nearly white, and so in effect confirming the Establishment's criterion that the black woman with dark skin was an inappropriate subject matter for American literature. And the obsidian woman character indeed remained in a state of neglect until Gwendolyn Brooks's novel *Maud Martha*.

For half a century after Harper's achievement in publishing the first black woman's novel in America—in itself a rather improbable task at the time—only the acculturated Anglo-Europeanized African woman appeared as both author and character in works by black women. That appearance reinforced the opportunities for education, breeding, and refinement (all accoutrements of the pedestaling process), which were available then mainly to those whom DuBois described as "the talented tenth" (i.e., mulatto, although he would not claim to have drawn the color line consciously). In none of the ensuing novels, until the early fifties, is the pain that society can inflict on the nonmulatto, the "unlovely" black woman, articulated. The very absence of that articulation is of enormous importance to those who wish to understand cultural manipulation and American literature's heretofore negative contribution to black female self-definition.

The stereotypical mulatto continued to be the central focus in the black woman's literature to the Harlem Renaissance period and beyond. She is the only female heroine in the novels by Nella Larsen, Jessie Fawcett, and Dorothy West. She continues on as the representative black woman throughout the fifties and the early sixties in such novels as Ann Petry's *The Street* and Margaret Walker's *Jubilee*. (In the latter book, however, Walker reconciles her heroine to the realities of black life, forcing Vyry to find her true identity in a lower-class black marriage and in fully compatible relationships with the black community.)

Zora Neale Hurston, who actually birthed black feminist literature, is another woman writer who elaborates the figure of the mulatto heroine. In her now-resurrected novel *Their Eyes Were Watching God*, Zora gave Janie Starks a "great rope of black hair swinging to her waist and unraveling in the wind like a plume" and began the task of trying to orient the mulatto woman into the pleasantries of black culture.[15] Like too many characters who would follow her in fiction written by black women, Janie was looking for artistic or spiritual substitutes outside of the self that would obviate the necessity of physical attractiveness.

Toni Morrison continues on the same path. Sula and Nel become friends when they discover that, as she writes, "they were neither white nor male," but their friendship is strained when Sula seduces Nel's husband precisely to prove that, as the epitomal changeling in the black community, she is the exception to the rule that to be a "colored woman in America is the same as being a man."[16] Pilate's granddaughter in *Song of Solomon* commits suicide when her lover, Milkman, forsakes her for a woman with light skin and straight hair. Conversely, when Pilate discovers that her skin tone, croppy hair, and navelless stomach render her unattractive to black men, she immediately whacks off her hair and begins to develop an "inner self" that finds her a niche in the community as a healer.

Alice Walker also develops the theme of black women who find or fashion themselves into "escapes" because those in their environment will not accept their femaleness. In *Meridian*, the heroine loses her femininity and effaces herself into a self-denying Madonna image, hoping to become a savior for black people. And in the celebrated *The Color Purple*, the heroine chooses lesbianism because no one who touches her life, not mother or father, children, or husband, or even most of the other women around her, will give her the attention, tenderness, and respect with which white and mulatto characters are showered. In a recent issue of *Black American Literary Forum*, Trudier Harris takes the position, with which I agree, that Walker runs the risk of presenting a black female figure who (if she is not like white females) is more like a man; that is dangerous, because it reinforces an existing stereotype and tends to serve the needs of those who use this fiction in hopes of convincing readers that such is the totality of black feminine experience.[17]

The truth is that, as Kristin Hunter portrayed it in *The Lakestown Rebellion*, the mulatto character can be redeemed in no other way than in the total recognition that she is and will always be nothing else but a black woman, and that there is nothing "tragic" about that reality. When Hunter's heroine finally sees that her only chance for independence is to take a definite stand in defiance of her husband's insistence that she should act like a white woman because she looks so much like a white woman, she tells him that she will return to him only if he accepts the terms of her new self-awareness:

> I won't play any more roles for you or with you. If that interferes with your ambitions, it's just too damned bad. I'm Bella Lakes, your black wife, not some silly white society whore. Plain old funky natural me is you'll be getting, not a mock-up of some painted white doll. How white I happen to look has nothing to do with it. I'm a black woman inside, a real *down* black woman, and you're just going to have to live with that.[18]

Until the revolutionary sixties, with one notably unnoticed exception, no American writer, whether black or white, male or female, had introduced authentic black female experience in American literature. From Harper's novel up to and including the Harlem Renaissance, the black woman writer tended to come from a very small sector of the upper-middle-class black elite, who were usually mulattoes themselves. Thus, the black woman reader could seldom approach a text that presented her as a desirable heroine unless she was depicted as having light hues and long hair. When she read a book, she felt as if someone were trying to convince her that it *is* true, blondes do have more fun. Not even the writings of black women who were not mulattoes, with the exception of one, have really tackled the issue of the black woman as the "unlovely" woman in American culture. The one writer who has recognized the demoralizing effect that literary iconography can have on those black women who cannot fulfill the mulatto mold is Gwendolyn Brooks. Her novel *Maud Martha* is that notable exception.

An unheralded landmark in American literature, *Maud Martha* marked the first departure from the superficial treatment of African women in fiction. In no novel before it is the pain that society can inflict on the "unlovely" black woman articulated. Brooks delicately implies that even in the midst of a seemingly secure and loving household, Maud was a rejected child. This rejection, based solely on appearance, is clear when Maud notices that she receives none of the admiration, concern, or special courtesies afforded to her light-skinned sister, Helen, and most specifically from the men in their lives.

Brooks selected the sister's name, of course, to symbolize adoration of the Western beauty, Helen of Troy. And Maud's sister is the objectification of that aesthetic bias toward white skin in Western iconography that is a perpetual curse to the black woman and her sometimes unaware (if not uncaring) community. Helen, who by the end of the novel marries the family doctor, thirty years her senior, thinks of Maud as untouchable; she cannot even visit her sister, who is herself married by then, because she finds Maud's poverty-stricken surroundings unbearable. Having escaped, Helen feels no emphaty for the deadly poverty and ostracism that white society imposes on her younger sister.

At first, Maud is aware only intuitively that some biological or cosmic force has subjugated her identity. Cognition, finally, is not a steppingstone to escape but rather the fulcrum of depression, a tidewater of self-hatred and self-destruction. In the chapter entitled "If You're Light and Have Long Hair," when Maud and her husband are invited to a ball, she fears that "there will only be beautiful girls, or real stylish ones. There won't be more than a handful like me."[19] Her husband, Paul, makes her fears come true by deserting her at the dance and devoting his attention to "someone red-haired and curved, and white as white" (p.211).

Following the pattern by which she has endured these inflictions in childhood, Maud does not rightly place the blame on Paul's insensitivity: she internalizes the "fault" as her own. "But it's my color that makes him mad. . . . He keeps looking at my color, which is like a wall. He has to jump over it. . . . He gets awful tired of all that jumping" (p. 213). Maud, who yearned only to be cherished, lets her spirit die in a malaise of rejection, despair, and impoverishment when she realizes that her family, her husband, and her community will not afford her love or dignity because she does not exemplify the ideal American (white) woman. As the novel closes, her only hope is that there will be a better day for her daughter, who, alas, is dark-skinned like Maud.

It is indeed a sad commentary in black American literature—one for which novelists and critics alike must share responsibility—that Maud Martha's literary daughter has yet to be "born," or if born, she has yet to mature into that character who achieves the cultural and intellectual development for which her mother yearned; who finds fulfillment in a marriage based on equality of intellectual potential (not on facial qualifications) and who, by the novel's ending, has attained a full freedom of self within the possibilities of her own horizons and in spite of the limitations that white or black or male-oriented criteria would impose upon her.

Such a heroine is almost "born" in Sula and Pilate, but these are distorted images of her self. She certainly exists in Marshall's *Brown Girls, Brown Stones*, where she is seen as a young woman searching for fulfillment in an artistic career. But this heroine never returns to the fiction as a fully liberated artist. Nor does one see Maud's daughter settled in a compatible marriage. We don't even see her settled in a compatible divorce. We never see her in the joyful role of mother, teacher, lover, or appreciated community leader—behind either the church pulpit or the political rostrum. Lamentably, we are still seeing the black woman in roles that the prevailing cultural manipulators ascribe to her—always on the fringes of society, always alone.

As for the liberation of her creators—those black women writers who must, and undoubtedly soon will, bring forth the complete black female character in American literature—they must speak in a feminist voice which creates freedom for all black women and which therefore reinforces the African American literary heritage. Indeed, the task is formidable: it may be impossible to distribute "free" artistic creation in a society that is both racist and sexist. But if there is any avenue where that can be accomplished, a feminist movement with a redefined feminine ideal would offer the best hope. In the process, these writers must resist the mentoring of publishing midwives and return to the totality of feminine experience in the black community. Herein lie the foundations of black life, and consequently of black literature, and herein should lie the foundations of black feminist expression, as well. W. E. B. DuBois spoke of the duality of black identity as "two souls warring in one body." In her "Double Jeopardy: To Be Black and Female," Frances Beale raised the possibility that for the black woman there are perhaps three souls in that one body.[20] The black woman's full emergence as author, character, and critic will go a long way toward reconciling those identities by giving more representative and enhancing self-images to black women readers.

N O T E S

1. "We Wear the Mask" is among the most popular poems in black American literature. It is certainly Dunbar's most anthologized poem, and has been a fundamental reference since it was first published in the late nineteenth century. See, for instance, *Black Writers of America: A Comprehensive Anthology*, ed. Richard Barksdale and Kenneth Kinnamon (New York: Macmillan, 1972); and, of course, Paul Laurence Dunbar, *Complete Poems* (New York: Dodd Mead, 1913).

2. Toni Morrison, "What the Black Woman Thinks about Women's Lib," *New York Times Magazine*, August 22, 1971.

3. See Frank Snowden, *Before Color Prejudice: The Ancient View of Blacks* (Cambridge, Mass.: Harvard University Press, 1983) and *Blacks in Antiquity: Ethiopians in the Greco-Roman Experience* (Cambridge, Mass.: Harvard University Press, 1970).

4. In addition to Snowden's texts, see Jean Devisse and Michel Moliat, *The Image of the Black in Western Art: From the Early Christian Era to the "Age of Discovery," Africans in the Christian Ordinance of the World*, trans. William Granger Ryan (New York: William Morrow and Co., 1979).

5. Susan Koppelman Cornillon, ed., *Images of Women in Fiction: Feminist Perspectives* (Bowling Green, Ohio: Bowling Green University Popular Press, 1973), pp. ix-xiii. See also Barbara Warren, *The Feminine Image in Literature* (Rochelle Park, N.J.: Hayden Book Co., 1973). Warren also divides her examples of "typical" Western women into four types: "Marble/Plastic Doll," "The Virgin," "Masked Wearers," and those women of "The Androgynous Mind." Again her selections are exclusively of Anglo-Western women. The same mindset controls Nancy Reeves, *Womankind: Beyond the Stereotypes* (New York: Aldine-Atherton, 1971) and the introduction to *Women in Sexist Society: Studies in Power and Powerlessness*, ed. Vivian Gornick and Barbara K. Moran (New York: Basic Books, 1971).

6. Kristin Hunter, *The Lakestown Rebellion* (New York: Charles Scribner's Sons, 1978). Al Young, Ishmael Reed's sometimes coeditor, was hired by the *New York Times* to review *Lakestown Rebellion*. Although the paper paid him for the review, the *Times* then refused to print the finished article, which commented favorably on the text as one having viable ideas for community action. Hunter and Young believe that the censure was due to the "incendiary" nature of the book. Subsequently, the novel went quickly out of print. Hunter is among the most ignored contemporary black writers. Despite the fact that she was the only woman writing during the sixties whose book (*The Landlord*) was made into a movie (an accomplishment achieved by few black male writers, such as Chester Himes and Bisheri), Hunter is barely mentioned in *Some of Us Are Brave*, ed. Gloria T. Hull, Patricia Bell Scott, and Barbara Smith (Old Westbury, N.Y.: Feminist Press, 1982), and in Barbara Christian, *Black Women Novelists: The Development of a Tradition, 1892-1976* (Westport, Conn.: Greenwood Press, 1980). She is, however, included in Claudia Tate, ed., *Black Women Writers at Work* (New York: Continuum, 1983), as is Sherley Anne Williams, another writer who has been similarly ignored, and, I believe, for similar reasons. Because Hunter is not included in texts such as these, with which most white feminists are familiar, she is virtually unknown to them.

7. Mercer Cook and Stephen E. Henderson, *The Militant Black Writer in Africa and the United States* (Madison: University of Wisconsin Press, 1969), p. 65.

8. Phyllis Chesler, *Women and Madness* (Garden City, N.Y.: Doubleday, 1972), p. 210.

9. Let me say here that I consider Teresa de Lauretis's conference, from which this volume evolves, to be a salient exception to that "rule." Not only was the conference very well integrated and without a sense of quota treatment, but Third World women participants seemed to have been selected precisely because they did have new contributions to make to existing feminist perspectives, including prevalent black feminist views. The essays in this collection augment and continue that laudable precedent.

10. Trudier Harris, *From Mammies to Militants: Domestics in Black American Literature* (Philadelphia: Temple University Press, 1982).

11. William Faulkner, "Delta Autumn," in *Go Down Moses* (New York: Random House, 1942), pp. 335-65.

12. Gertrude Stein, *Three Lives* (New York: Random House, 1936), pp.85-86.

13. Charles Chestnutt, *The Wife of His Youth and Other Stories of the Color Line* (Ridgewood, N.J.: Gregg Press, 1967, reprint).

14. Claude McKay, *Home to Harlem* (Chatham, N.J.: Chatham Booksellers, 1973, reprint).

15. Zora Neale Hurston, *Their Eyes Were Watching God* (Urbana: University of Illinois Press, 1978).

16. Toni Morrison, *Sula* (New York: Bantam Books, 1973), pp. 44 and 123.

17. Trudier Harris, "On *The Color Purple*, Stereotypes and Silence," *Black American Literary Forum* 18 (Winter 1984):155-61.

18. Hunter, *Lakestown Rebellion*, pp.260-61.

19. Gwendolyn Brooks, *Maud Martha* (1953). I quote from *The World of Gwendolyn Brooks* (New York: Harper and Row, 1971), pp. 205-214. In her recent article " 'Taming All That Anger Down': Rage and Silence in Gwendolyn Brooks's *Maud Martha*," *Massachusetts Review* 24 (1983):453-66, Mary Helen Washington observes the heroine's collapse as her family and society deny her the right to develop her full intellectual potential. Washington also charts

the curious and very sexist reception that this novel received as compared to Ralph Ellison's *Invisible Man*, also published in the same era.

20. Frances Beale, "Double Jeopardy: To Be Black and Female," in *The Black Woman: An Anthology*, ed. Toni Cade (New York: New American Library, 1970), pp. 90-100.

Considering Feminism as a Model for Social Change

Sheila Radford-Hill

Breaking the Silence/Keeping the Faith

> The following analysis is offered as one small cut
> against that stone of silence and secrecy. It is not
> intended to be original or all-inclusive. I dedicate
> this work to all the women hidden from history whose suffering
> and triumph have made it possible for me to call my name
> out loud.
>
> —CHERYL CLARKE,
> "Lesbianism: An Act of Resistance" (1981)
> *This Bridge Called My Back*

There she was, standing in my room
not loudly condemning that day and
not remembering that I grew hearing her
curse the factory where she "cut uh slave" . . .
not remember that I heard the tears when
they told her a high school diploma was not enough
and her now, not able to understand, what she had
been forced to deny, still—
she pushed into my kitchen so
she could open my refrigerator to see
what I had to eat, and pressed fifty
bills in my hand saying "pay the talk bill and buy
some food; you got folks who care about you."

My mother, religious-negro, proud of
having waded through a storm, is very obviously,
a sturdy Black bridge that I
crossed over, on.

—CAROLYN RODGERS,
"It is Deep" (1975),
How I Got Ovah

but now you've passed on your chores to me and I give
you up to God to rest. I wanted you to know, I'll
try to do my best for mine and all the rest.
                                          —RUTH RADFORD,
                  "To My Mother" (1984), unpublished, written by
                  my mother on the occasion of the death of hers.

The stuggle continues, begins anew. This effort is dedicated to all
black women whom feminism in its present presence has never
touched or has failed to help. This new walk through the valley of
the shadows, through pain and fear, through sullen dreams and burnt
emotions to timid strides is for those of us whose hands are too weary,
too rough to have ever been girls.
For those of us who
have no home.
        What y'all do don't concern, ain't about—is/me.
        Angry. Pushing the raging sounds pass the lumps and hard empty
places to talk to them "feminists" who say they speak for us/me.
Who look/feel like me but don't talk/say/act/be/do like it.
        Tell me Ms. Anne, what do I do about my sistuhs—I
mean 3rd world wimmen who ain't gettin enough to eat.

        White folks is defendin' they country with bread from my
                sistuhs' mouths.
        Patriarchy the foe whose lover I'm unprepared to despise.
        If struggle was easy they'd call it something else.

        Tell me Ms. Annie Mae what about them black womens who
stops me on the way home from work asking for spare change?
Say what?? nobody gon' save us but us, organize around our own
oppression, victimized, brutalized, anti-socialized, terrorized. Well,
Ms. Annie Mae you speaks intelligent, your words—seem fine but
they ain't none too fillin.

        Some of us are fucked over at levels deeper than our present
visions. Revolution? A new designer lip gloss. Color
        Purple/the rain. Social change?
baby change your clothes so we can go party. Power for girl/people.
Drop dead, you silly bitches. Drop dead, like your

*history. Onward, upward to the cult of prosperity wear callous
masks of indifference by Valenti/Blass/Jordache complete
with Coach bag known for wearing its age better than I do mine.*

*This act of resistance keeps faith with those whose tears are still
silent. For those still concerned with the survival of our race, our
culture, our families and our communities. With those who simply
want a man to love the emptiness away from their thighs. With/for
the unaware/I don't care/get blow'd ones. With those whose lovers
have honey dipped breasts. With those who straightened their hair
but strengthened their commitment.*

The Primacy of Questions: Feminist Ideology as a Model of Social Change

Mine is a lifetime commitment to empowerment. Empowerment
occurs when individuals recognizing their common oppression mobilize against the exploitation, victimization, marginality, expendabil-
ity, powerlessness, suppressed rage, and degradation that characterize
both the reality of oppression and the experience of being oppressed.
The central task of any movement for social change is empowerment.
That is to say that the genesis of any social movement is a struggle to
control one's own destiny. Empowerment is existentially felt as individuals develop a shared conception of how they are systematically
exploited to benefit another group. It is strengthened through forms
of action consistent with alternative values generated with/through/
because of/in the developmental process of social change.

Empowerment endures, i.e., people continue to feel empowered
when their collective struggles result in fundamental alterations in
social hierarchies that are experienced on a day-to-day basis as an
improvement in the quality of life.

Implicit in the articulation of a feminist ideology, therefore, is the
promise of a mediation structure, a set of actions and practices that
are directed toward the empowerment of women.

Given the continued lack of participation by black women in the
feminist movement, it is appropriate—in fact, critical—to struggle with
a fundamental question; namely, is feminism an effective model for
social change for black women? In other words, can feminist ideology—an ideology that professes the empowerment of women as its
expressed goal—compel black women to organize for their own liberation?

Feminists—black, brown, and white—have struggled with issues regarding the relevance of feminism to minority women. In most of these discussions, however, the question of what feminism should, could, or would do for black women is merely used as a rhetorical platform from which to launch arguments for or against a variety of feminist positions. The relevance of feminism to the lives of black women is, however, the question that reconciles the interests of black women to the demands of social, political, and economic empowerment. Accordingly, posing the question, Does feminist ideology serve the needs, goals, and aspirations of black women? is not an exercise in political rhetoric; it is the basis of a legitimate critique of feminist praxis in terms of its usefulness as a vehicle for improving the day-to-day experiences of minority women.

The question of whether or not any feminist ideology should count black women among its adherents can never be raised legitimately in abstract terms. The essential issue that black women must confront when assessing a feminist position is as follows: If I, as a black woman, "become a feminist," what basic tools will I gain to resist my individual and group oppression? Questions such as these challenge feminist theorists to examine the political implications inherent in specific women-centered or gender-based ideological initiatives, social interventions, or brave new social orders.

This paper is by no means a complete discussion of current feminist theory and practice; it suggests, however, a framework for minority women to assess whether or not they should espouse a particular feminist practice. I propose that minority women assess feminist praxis in terms of its implication for improving the quality of their daily lives. This assessment defines the outcome of feminist praxis in terms of empowerment; that is, in terms of fundamental and lasting changes which assure the equitable distribution of power and privileges in a new social order.

A self-interested critique of current feminist theory challenges its credibility, forcing it to come to terms with itself, i.e., with its implications for minority women who seek the power to control their own destinies.

Power relationships, including cultural values about what those relationships are and whom they ultimately serve, constitute a standard by which a gender-based ethic can ultimately be judged. Put another way, the relevance of feminism as a vehicle for social change can be effectively assessed in terms of its ability to factor black women and other women of color into alternative conceptions of power and the consequences of its use. Thus, the degree to which black women can and should "become" feminist is related to the power ethics of feminist praxis. Related, that is, to whether in the transformations and mutual interactions of ethics, ideology, and praxis, feminism can dispense power options equitably across lines of race, ethnicity, class, and sexual preference.

Consideration of feminism as a model for social change also raises questions about which cultural values achieve hegemony in the feminist world view. Gender-based or women-centered analyses of social, cultural, sexual, and heterosexual exploitation must engender shared values consistent with the social needs and cultural imperatives of all women—black, white, lesbian, heterosexual, young, and old.

Whether or not feminism is a viable model for social change is an open question that cannot be closed by debate. Closure can be reached only by the tensions between action and analysis that accompany women-centered social interventions. Thus, the efficacy of feminism as a change agency depends on:

1) the correctness of its analysis of the social, historical, and experiential forces that produce and constitute oppression.
2) the degree to which ideology can satisfy demands for empowerment among its constituent base.
3) the degree to which values consistent with the imperatives of the newly empowered are reflected in the resulting cultural hegemony (that separates the newly empowered from the truly empowered).

Minority women must employ these criteria when debating whether or not to participate in any movement calling itself feminist. In other words, no corpus of feminist ideology should be supported by minority women without a thorough understanding of its practical implications. Moreover, it is this process of questioning and debate that engenders a perspective of feminist struggle in the process of social change itself.

The Struggle against Racism within the Feminist Movement

> I have always felt that Black women's ability to function with dignity, independence, and imagination in the face of total adversity—that is, in the face of white America—points to an innate feminist potential. To me the phrase, "Act like you have some sense," probably spoken by at least one Black woman to every Black child who ever lived, is a cryptic warning that says volumes about keeping your feet on the ground and your ass covered. . . .
> Although our involvement has increased considerably in recent years, there are countless rea-

sons why Black and other Third World women
have not identified with contemporary feminism
in large numbers. The racism of white women in
the women's movement has certainly been a
major factor.
—BARBARA SMITH (1982),
Home Girls

Black feminists have been struggling for decades with increasingly
mixed success to help white feminists transcend their socialization.
This protracted struggle has placed black feminists in the awkward
position of urging their sisters to join a movement that they openly
attacked as racist. This "no-win" situation accounts for the fact that
more print has been devoted to reshaping "their" movement to fit
"our" needs than to creating the ideological basis for a politically
active core constituency within the black community. This core constituency must be built essentially by black women, with black women,
for themselves. Once politicized, black women can join with other
enemies of gender oppression, effectively supporting a feminist agenda
designed to meet the needs of women and their families.

The struggle against racism within the movement increased the visibility of minority women's concerns and rightly asserted the essential
point that white women have benefited and continue to benefit from
black female oppression. This point, however well taken, was widely
known by black women, as told to them by their own parents, and
as such the analysis did little to attract black women to the movement.
More important, black women have become increasingly alienated by
the self-righteous anger of black feminists who label white women as
racists because these women best understand their own oppression
as a struggle against male dominance rather than as a movement for
social justice.

Black feminists, enraged by what they viewed as the cultural ar-
rogance and political excess of the "women's movement," constructed a crucible against white feminists who organized politically
around their class interests. Although the bitterness black feminists
feel over racism and classism within the movement has a legitimacy
that lingers still, black women now realize that part of the problem
within the movement was our insistence that white women
do for/with us what we must do for/with ourselves: namely, frame
our own social action around our own agenda for change. In the long
run, it does little good to attack white women for their failure to
organize on behalf of black interests.

Critical to this discussion is the right to organize on one's own behalf.
This "right" is also a necessity, given the developmental process of

social change. Criticism by black feminists must reaffirm this principle. Thus, it must acknowledge the right of white women to organize on behalf of their own self-interest. To the extent that these interests directly threaten our own, we must engage in organized resistance; i.e., we must mobilize black women as a group both to protect their interests and to design political, social, or economic alternatives consistent with the demands of social justice.

Given these considerations, black feminists' initial emphasis on racism within an essentially white women's movement was, in many ways, misplaced. Furthermore, the angry focus on racism essentially undercut the goal of black involvement in the movement by framing our options for participation in ways that were short-sighted and reactionary.

Ultimately, the struggle against racism within feminism cannot deny the right of minority women to organize themselves. By the same token, this struggle cannot deny either the legitimacy of alternative views of feminist praxis or the contributions made by white feminists, whether theoretical, social, historical, political, cultural, or economic.

Naturally, in cases where white feminists have appointed themselves or allowed themselves to be appointed as official spokespersons representing the entire feminist movement, defining it only out of their experience and solely in terms of their needs, white feminists have been rightly criticized. However, an ideological perspective that denies any group of women the right to see feminism in a different way—i.e., as a specialized critique, or as a movement for equal rights, or as a mobilized constituency against rape, or as a mass movement against female violence, or as a struggle for or against reproductive rights—places minority feminists in the peculiar position of trying to organize black women on behalf of their own interests while attacking other women for doing the same thing.

Organizing around such an apparent contradiction can charitably be described as futile. Clearly, the issue is what feminism is or is not, and who has the power to define; however, issues such as these are best resolved through consensus building, not through mudslinging. Caterwauling and namecalling misplace our emotional and political energies into attacking each other rather than organizing to dislodge a social order that provides women with few ethically responsible ways to escape the consequences of their inferior status in the patriarchal social order.

Black women who want to be feminist have every right to be angry at white women who seek to deny their own social and economic privilege, bestowed by a social order that values white skin. Black women do not want to be tokenized, consulted as an afterthought, written about as a monolithic presence, or excluded from the reward system of professional feminist practice.

A viable constituency of black women, however, cannot be successful if built primarily as a reaction against white women. Neither will minority women effectively raise their political consciousness by restating the obvious: educating white women, and sharing with them so that they can read at their leisure what every black woman already knows, namely, that black women are oppressed by white men, white women, and black men.

Rather, black feminists must build an agenda that meets the needs of black women by helping black women to mobilize around issues that they perceive to have a direct impact on the overall quality of their lives. Such is the challenge that defines our struggle and constitutes our legacy. Within that challenge lies the secret of how black women endure, survive, overcome, and transcend societies that force us to live out our lives in the web of contradiction that surrounds racial and sexual oppression.

Thus, black women need to develop their own leadership and their own agenda based on the needs of their primary constituent base; that is, based around black women, their families, and their communities. This task cannot be furthered by dialoguing with white women about their inherent racism.

The history of the feminist movement proves the fact that the oppressions of white and black women are equally compelling but mutually exclusive. The reality of this statement rightly suggests that bonding across lines of race, and to a lesser extent across class lines, is not possible at the present time and will become possible in the future only to the extent that each group generates a collective sense of its own struggle.

Black feminists lullabied by the liberal cult of sisterhood, on the one hand, and vilified by black antifeminists, on the other, have been sensitive to charges of racism, separatism, and political correctness within their own ranks. They have stressed coalitioning at every turn, even when such coalitioning directly threatens the fragile solidarity between white and black militant feminists and will, in the long run, be detrimental to the emerging political consciousness of black women and other women of color. Building premature coalitions merely increases the echo of a failed constituency. Responsible feminist leadership, whether black, white, militant, liberal, academic, activist, lesbian, celibate, or otherwise, should seek to avoid probable failure by any means necessary.

Organizing separately on behalf of your own interests allows groups to build even stronger coalitions when issues cut across the interests of several groups. Such a strategy is preferable to sticking with global issues for which the grassroots constituency is too weak to mount the necessary offensive to secure victory.

Black Feminists and Black Feminism

> Although contemporary feminist movement should have provided a training ground for women to learn about political solidarity, Sisterhood was not viewed as a revolutionary accomplishment women would work and struggle to obtain. The vision of Sisterhood evoked by women's liberationists was based on the idea of common oppression. . . . The idea of "common oppression" was a false and corrupt platform disguising and mystifying the true nature of women's varied and complex social reality. Women are divided by sexist attitudes, racism, class privilege, and a host of other prejudices. Sustained woman bonding can occur only when these divisions are confronted and the necessary steps are taken to eliminate them.
>
> —BELL HOOKS (1984),
> *Feminist Theory: From Margin to Center*

Not all black feminists practice or believe in black feminism. Many see black feminism as a vulgar detraction from the goal of female solidarity. Others of us, myself included, see black feminism as a necessary step toward ending racisexism, given the nature of gender oppression and the magnitude of society's resistance to racial justice. I would like to point out, however, that both black feminists and feminists who are black agree that feminism must become a mass political movement if its goals are to be achieved. Both groups recognize, therefore, that the failure of large numbers of black women to organize specifically on behalf of their needs undermines the legitimacy of feminist values and the efficacy of the feminist enterprise.

Currently, black feminism is building from a tradition of leftist activism, adapting models of socialist feminism and advocating active involvement in a variety of progressive struggles.

Its ideology rightly affirms that meaningful change in a social order repressive to both men and women can be accomplished by building coalitions between women of color and progressive movements. It also has the added advantage of stimulating class consciousness among black women by its rigorous critique of monopoly capitalism.

These advantages notwithstanding, black feminism has yet to mediate a necessary "fit" between its ideology and black women in the real world. Thus black feminism often alienates black women as much as white feminism does. Put another way, black women are just as "turned off" by the leftist militancy and radical posturing of black feminism as they are by the antimen, antifamily thrust that they associate with white feminism.

Both black feminists and feminists who are black must realize that the business of social change is risky. They must understand that attempts to effect some meaningful change in the conditions under which people live can be accomplished for the people (that is, on behalf of the people) by the people or with the people. Meaningful change is never accomplished despite the people or without the people. That means that unless the target group participates in specific actions around collective goals, no viable change occurs. Furthermore, social change demands the organization of oppressed groups in ways that link the goals of social action to where the people are, where they see themselves going, and how they see themselves getting there.

Mass political constituencies are not solely the result of a correct definition of a given social problem. They require organizing people so that they are committed to the struggle, knowledgeable about the systems that oppress them, persistent in their tactics, focused on specific institutional policies, organized for action over the long term, and willing to develop and to follow responsive leaders; leaders who have alternative visions of the present power structures; leaders who can build strategy and implement tactics around the strengths of those who are intervening on their own behalf.

Thus, the significance of black feminism to day-to-day improvement in the lives of the masses of black women must be stated clearly and often. Rather than attack or ignore black women who see their men as partners in oppression or who are male-identified, we must fashion an analysis that speaks to their needs and translates less poorly downward to their political and economic interests. Black feminism must translate its analysis of the social, economic, and sexist oppressions in ways consistent with the group experience of its constituent base. Street organizing around the interests that black women have today is essential if we are to have the opportunity to take our sisters to the next phase of the struggle.

Movements that are too far ahead of the people are always elitist and often reactionary. All social change is based in struggle; this struggle is both from within the movement itself, based on empowerment demands, and outside the movement, based on the resistance to change. Mobilization tactics must be fashioned to the strength of the people whose struggle it is. In the case of black women, that has not been done, and although black feminist writers have cited the multiple oppressions of black women—i.e., their abject victimization—as reason for our failure to organize, I submit that we simply have yet to find and to use the correct organizing tactics.

I further submit that the reality of oppression in the black community has been underestimated by feminist writers who do not wish to be seen as criticizing our community and thus prefer to romanticize it. Black women in the black community are neither too oppressed nor too apathetic to organize. They are, however, profoundly immobilized. This immobilization is the result of a deep-seated rupture in the structure of self-identity that black women have experienced and been forced to live through within the last twenty years. I call this rupture the crisis of black womanhood. It is to this crisis that I now turn my attention.

The Crisis of Black Womanhood

May 30, 1984. Award-winning Tribune columnist Leanita McClain, 32, was the first black member of the Tribune's editorial board and was selected as one of the 10 most outstanding young working women in America in the March 1984 edition of Glamour Magazine. Ms. McClain was found dead Tuesday in her southside home by a neighbor. Police said it appeared Miss McClain had taken her life.

—Obituary, Leanita McClain,
Chicago Tribune
May 31, 1985

Our mother was glad . . . to have occasion to address a large group of educated and successful black women. . . . She spoke praisingly of black herstory; she spoke, as she often did, deliberately, of her mother (formerly missing from both literature and history); she spoke of the alarming rise in the suicide rate of young black women all over America. She asked that these black women address themselves to this crisis. Address themselves, in effect, to themselves. Our mother was halted in mid-speech. She was told that "those to address were black men," that, though it appeared more black women than men were com-

mitting suicide, still everyone knew black women
to be the stronger of these two. Those women
who committed suicide were merely sick, apparently with an imaginary or in any case a
causeless disease.

—ALICE WALKER (1979),
In Search of Our Mothers' Gardens

The crisis of black womanhood began in the mid-sixties. Prior to that
time, in fact, since our earliest recorded history, black women have
collectively structured roles within self-identities that assured the survival of our race.

This fit of role, image, and self-identity was cognitively mapped
across institutions within and to some extent outside of the black
community. Through the struggle to survive, black women created a
standard for womanhood that stressed independence, resistance, self-
affirmation, and race pride.

The role of black women as culture makers and culture bearers was
nothing less than a major struggle for culture against extinction. Our
culture of resistance has ensured the survival of our race and our
community.

The power of black women was the power to make culture, to
transmit folkways, norms, and customs, as well as to build shared ways
of seeing the world that insured our survival. This power, needless to
say, was neither economic nor political; nor did it translate into female
dominance, as social scientists and social commentators would have
an ignorant public believe.

The confluence of new left militarism and black macho, the emergence of the welfare state, and the rise of a women's liberation perceived as "for white middle-class women only" were blows rendered
with lightning speed. The aftermath of the 1960s brought the economic dislocation of the 1970s and the rise of conservatism in the
1980s. The resulting cuts in social programs occasioned by conservative social policy have plunged thousands of women into poverty,
creating a widening gap between black women who are middle-class
and those who are poor.

Black macho constituted a betrayal by black men; a psychosexual
rejection of black women experienced as the capstone to our fall from
cultural power, from the power of integrated self-identities consistent
with our legacy of race survival. Without the power to influence the
purpose and the direction of our collective experience, without the
power to influence our culture from within, we are increasingly immobilized, unable to integrate self and role identities, unable to resist

the cultural imperialism of the dominant culture which assures our continued oppression by destroying us from within.

Thus, the crisis manifests itself as social dysfunction in the black community—as genocide, fratricide, homicide, and suicide. It is also manifested by the abdication of personal responsibility by black women for themselves and for each other. The abdicators are middle-class black women who deny the crisis, preferring to connect their destinies to alien standards of womanhood promoted in the general culture rather than to identify with working-class or poor women.

Poor and working-class black women are also abdicating personal responsibility for their families and their communities, preferring to remain male-identified in an attempt to undo the profound damage to their sexual identities that the crisis has caused. The pursuit of ultra-femininity—or fachoism—is rampant, as many black women are profoundly alienated from their sexuality.

The crisis of black womanhood is a form of cultural aggression; a form of exploitation so vicious, so insidious, that it is currently destroying an entire generation of black women and their families.

Black women must move against this destruction now, whether they are feminists or not, and it may be that black feminists or black feminism can facilitate our understanding of this crisis and move us toward standards of black womanhood that will help resolve it. In other words, the extent to which black feminists can articulate and solve the crisis of black womanhood is the extent to which black women will undergo a feminist transformation.

The political viability of feminism as an agency of change depends in the final analysis both on its ability to foster women's solidarity and on its ability to build a movement that is inclusive rather than exclusive, one that can mobilize against sexist oppression from a broad base of support. Building such a base implies politicizing a strong primary constituency; a nucleus that allows feminist praxis to expand outward from its core.

Constitutency building demands a correct assessment of the nature and scope of problems of race, class, and gender. It also requires an ability to link the impact of these oppressions to the interests of the group's major secondary constituencies. What holds the constituent base at its center includes responsive leadership, coherent ideology, theoretical propositions that are accessible to the masses, and multifaceted interventions designed to win local victories and to increase support among progressive people.

Black feminists must build local community-based organizations that
address the needs of women in the community in ways consistent
with the movement's long-range goals. Street organizing must employ
tactics designed to halt the malaise currently affecting black women.
Bonding between women must be fostered between class lines, and
organizing must place a renewed emphasis on historical standards of
black womanhood, black female sexuality, basic literacy and education, health care, economic exploitation, and employment. Issues regarding sexual exploitation must be reaffirmed or recut within the
context of family and community. In short, the crisis of black womanhood must be acknowledged, analyzed, and attacked.

Mobilizing Black Women: Feminist Practice and Social Change

> If you tryin' to take somebody someplace, that is
> if you lookin' to move a person from one place
> to another,—first—you got to meet up with
> them. You got to git up, leave your house, and
> go get the person. You can't wait for the person
> to come to you—You can't organize spit
> from across the street.
>
> You got to be right there—right with the peoples you
> tryin' to move.
> Seeing what they see.
> Eatin' what they eat.
> Doin' what they do.
>
> All the time tryin' to git 'em to figure out what
> they want and how they gon' get it.
> —SHEILA RADFORD-HILL,
> internal monologue
> (circa 1983)

The successful mobilization of black women as feminists will not
succeed simply by organizing us around a variety of national and
international issues. The basic agenda for black women must be one
that helps us understand the relationship between economic exploitation and sexist exploitation; one that helps us to accept responsibility
for ourselves and our sisters; one that gets us out of the stores and
into the streets, committed to a better quality of life for ourselves and
our children; committed to our own empowerment.

Thus, the basic agenda for black women should
—attack the cultural aggression that perpetuates the crisis of black
womanhood.

—build local organizations of black women able to work on behalf of their own interests as women and ready, when necessary, to join coalitions to achieve mutually desired goals.

—educate middle-class black women regarding class exploitation so that they can view their long-term interests in terms of working-class and poor women.

—support progressive movements to end imperialism and militarism.

—build a domestic agenda supported by black women and women of color.

—develop black feminist leadership dedicated to expanding the core constituency.

There is much to do and little time to waste. Women who call themselves feminists (no matter what their color) cannot sit back and debate politically correct solutions or fret over the ever-increasing numbers of us who conscientiously fail to toe the party line. Those of us interested in social justice for people in general and for women in particular need to develop useful theoretical models of feminist practice. These models should be informed by those of us who use various intervention strategies to organize women. The goal of feminist organizing is to mobilize around issues that constitute a gender-based agenda for social change. This agenda must be supported by well-disciplined organizations of black women who vigorously pursue this agenda working with viable coalitions on issues as situations dictate.

As the current state of feminist theory and practice would indicate, we must dig in for the long haul and accept the challenges of our history. The struggle continues, begins anew.

R E F E R E N C E S

Bell, Roseann P. et al. *Sturdy Black Bridges: Visions of Black Women in Literature.* New York: Anchor Books, 1979.

Cabral, Amilcar. *Return to the Source.* New York: African Information Service and the Party for the Independence of Guinea (Bissau) and the Cape Verde Islands.

Cade, Toni [Bambara]. *The Black Woman: An Anthology.* New York; New American Library, 1970.

Cox, Fred M. et al. *Strategies of Community Organization: A Book of Readings.* Itasca, Ill.: F. E. Peacock Publishers, 1974.

Davis, Angela. *If They Come in the Morning.* New York: Third Press, 1971.

———. "Reflections on the Black Woman's Role in the Community of Slaves," in Robert Chrisman et al., *Contemporary Black Thought.* Indianapolis: Bobbs-Merrill, 1973.

———. *Women, Race, and Class.* New York: Random House, 1981.

Exum, Pat Crutchfield. *Keeping the Faith: Writings by Contemporary Black American Women.* Greenwich, Conn.: Fawcett Publications, 1974.

Gerhart, Gail M. *Black Power in South Africa: The Evolution of an Ideology.* Berkeley: University of California Press, 1978.

Hooks, Bell. *Ain't I a Woman: Black Women and Feminism.* Boston: South End Press, 1981.

———. *Feminist Theory: From Margin to Center.* Boston: South End Press, 1984.

Hull, Gloria T. et al. *All The Women Are White, All the Blacks Are Men, But Some of Us Are Brave.* Old Westbury, N.Y.: Feminist Press, 1982.

Lorde, Audre. *Sister Outsider: Essays and Speeches.* Trumansburg, N.Y.: Crossing Press, 1984.

Moraga, Cherríe, and Anzaldúa, Gloria, eds. *This Bridge Called My Back: Writings by Radical Women of Color.* Watertown Mass.: Persephone Press, 1981.

Perkins, Eugene. *Home Is a Dirty Street: The Social Oppression of Black Children.* Chicago: Third World Press, 1975.

Rich, Adrienne. *On Lies, Secrets, and Silence: Selected Prose, 1966-1978.* New York: W. W. Norton and Co., 1979.

Rodgers, Carolyn. *How I Got Ovah: New and Selected Poems.* New York: Doubleday/Anchor, 1975.

Smith, Barbara, ed. *Home Girls: A Black Feminist Anthology.* New York: Kitchen Table: Women of Color Press, 1983.

Tate, Claudia. *Black Women Writers at Work.* New York: Continuum Publishing, 1983.

Walker, Alice. *In Search of Our Mothers' Gardens.* San Diego: Harcourt, Brace, Jovanovich, 1983.

Wallace, Michele. *Black Macho and the Myth of the Superwoman.* New York: Dial Press, 1978.

From a Long Line of Vendidas: Chicanas and Feminism

Cherríe Moraga

If somebody would have asked me when I was a teenager what it means to be Chicana, I would probably have listed the grievances done me. When my sister and I were fifteen and fourteen, respectively, and my brother a few years older, we were still waiting on him. I write "were" as if now, nearly two decades later, it were over. But that would be a lie. To this day in my mother's home, my brother and father are waited on, including by me. I do this out of respect for my mother and her wishes. In those early years, however, it was mainly in relation to my brother that I resented providing such service. For unlike my father, who sometimes worked as much as seventy hours a week to feed my face every day, the only thing that earned my brother my servitude was his maleness.

***

What looks like betrayal between women on the basis of race originates, I believe, in sexism/heterosexism. Chicanas begin to turn our backs on each other either to gain male approval or to avoid being sexually stigmatized by them under the name of puta, vendida, jota. This phenomenon is as old as the day is long, and first learned in the school yard, long before it is played out with a vengeance within political communities.

In the seventh grade, I fell in love with Manuel Poblano. A small-boned boy. Hair always perfectly combed and oiled. Uniform shirt pressed neatly over shoulder blades jutting out. At twelve, Manuel was growing in his identity—sexually, racially—and Patsy Juárez, my

Editor's Note: This contribution is excerpted from Moraga's essay "A Long Line of Vendidas," originally published in her book *Loving in the War Years: Lo que nunca pasó por sus labios* (Boston: South End Press, 1983), pp. 90-144. The essay, combining critical analysis with poems, journal entries, and other autobiographical material, was dedicated to Gloria Anzaldúa. The excerpts are reprinted here with the author's permission. Gracias, Cherríe.

one-time fifth-grade friend, wanted him too. Manuel was pals with Leticia and Connie. I remember how they flaunted a school picture of his in front of my face, proving how *they* could get one from him, although I had asked first. The two girls were conspiring to get him to "go" with Patsy, which in the end, he finally did. I, knowing all along I didn't have a chance. Not brown enough. And the wrong last name.

At puberty, it seemed identity alliances were beginning to be made along rigid and immovable lines of race, as it combined with sex. And everyone—boy, girl, anglo, and Chicano—fell into place. Where did *I* stand?

I did not move away from other Chicanos because I did not love my people. I gradually became anglocized because I thought it was the only option available to me toward gaining autonomy as a person without being sexually stigmatized. I can't say that I was conscious of all this at the time, only that at each juncture in my development, I instinctively made choices which I thought would allow me greater freedom of movement in the future. This primarily meant resisting sex roles as much as I could safely manage and this was far easier in an anglo context than in a Chicano one. That is not to say that anglo culture does not stigmatize its women for "gender-transgressions"— only that its stigmatizing did not hold the personal power over me which Chicano culture did.

Chicanas' negative perceptions of ourselves as sexual persons and our consequential betrayal of each other find their roots in a four-hundred-year-long Mexican history and mythology. They are further entrenched by a system of anglo imperialism which long ago put Mexicanos and Chicanos in a defensive posture against the dominant culture.

The sexual legacy passed down to the Mexicana/Chicana is the legacy of betrayal, pivoting around the historical/mythical female figure of Malintzin Tenepal. As translator and strategic advisor and mistress to the Spanish conqueror of México, Hernan Cortez, Malintzin is considered the mother of the mestizo people. But unlike La Virgen de Guadalupe, she is not revered as the Virgin Mother, but rather slandered as La Chingada, meaning the "fucked one," or La Vendida, sell-out to the white race.[1]

Upon her shoulders rests the full blame for the "bastardization" of the indigenous people of México. To put it in its most base terms: Malintzin, also called Malinche, fucked the white man who conquered the Indian peoples of México and destroyed their culture. Ever since, brown men have been accusing her of betraying her race, and over the centuries continue to blame her entire sex for this "transgression."

As a Chicana and a feminist, I must, like other Chicanas before me, examine the effects this myth has on my/our racial/sexual identity and my relationship with other Chicanas. There is hardly a Chicana growing up today who does not suffer under her name even if she never hears directly of the one-time Aztec princess.

The Aztecs had recorded that Quetzalcoatl, the feathered serpent god, would return from the east to redeem his people in the year One Reed according to the Aztec calendar. Destiny would have it that on this very day, April 21, 1519 (as translated to the Western calendar), Cortez and his men, fitting the description of Quetzalcoatl, light-haired and bearded, landed in Vera Cruz.[2]

At the time of Cortez's arrival in México, the Aztecs had subjugated much of the rest of the Indian population, including the Mayans and Tabascans, who were much less powerful militarily. War was a necessity for the Aztecs in order to take prisoners to be used for sacrificial offerings to the warrior-god, Huitzilopochtli. As slaves and potential sacrificial victims to the Aztecs, then, these other Indian nations, after their own negotiations and sometimes bloody exchanges with the Spanish, were eager to join forces with the Spanish to overthrow the Aztec empire. The Aztecs, through their systematic subjugation of much of the Mexican Indian population, decreed their own self-destruction.[3]

Aleida Del Castillo, Chicana feminist theorist, contends that as a woman of deep spiritual commitment, Malinche aided Cortez because she understood him to be Quetzalcoatl returned in a different form to save the peoples of México from total extinction. She writes, "The destruction of the Aztec empire, the conquest of México, and as such, the termination of her indigenous world," were, in Malinche's eyes, "inevitable" in order to make way for the new spiritual age that was imminent.[4]

Del Castillo and other Chicana feminists who are researching and re-interpreting Malinche's role in the conquest of México are not trying to justify the imperialism of the Spanish. Rather, they are attempting to create a more realistic context for, and therefore a more sympathetic view of, Malinche's actions.

The root of the fear of betrayal by a woman is not at all specific to the Mexican or Chicano. The resemblance between Malinche and the Eve image is all too obvious. In chronicling the conquest of México and founding the Catholic Church there, the Spanish passed on to the mestizo people as legacy their own European-Catholic interpretation of Mexican events. Much of this early interpretation originated from Bernal del Castillo's eye-witness account of the conquest. As the primary source of much contemporary analysis as well, the picture we have of Mexican Indian civilization during that period often contains a strong Catholic and Spanish bias.

In his writings, Bernal Diaz del Castillo notes that upon the death of Malinche's father, the young Aztec princess was in line to inherit his estate. Malinche's mother wanted her son from her second marriage to inherit the wealth instead. She therefore sold her own daughter into slavery.

According to Gloria Anzaldúa, there are writings in México to refute this account.[5] But it was nevertheless recorded—or commonly believed—that Malinche was betrayed by her own mother. It is this myth of the inherent unreliability of women, our natural propensity for treachery, which has been carved into the very bone of Mexican/ Chicano collective psychology.

Traitor begets traitor.

Little is made of this early betrayal, whether or not it actually occurred, probably because no man was immediately affected. In a way, Malinche's mother would only have been doing her Mexican wifely duty: *putting the male first.*

There is none so beautiful as the Latino male. I have never met any kind of Latino who, although he may have claimed his family was very woman-dominated ("mi mamá made all the real decisions"), did not subscribe to the basic belief that men are better. It is so ordinary a statement as to sound simplistic and I am nearly embarrassed to write it, but that's the truth in its kernel.

Ask, for example, any Chicana mother about her children and she is quick to tell you she loves them all the same, but she doesn't. *The boys are different.* Sometimes I sense that she feels this way because she wants to believe that through her mothering, she can develop the kind of man she would have liked to have married, or even have been. That through her son she can get a small taste of male privilege, since without race or class privilege that's all there is to be had. The daughter can never offer the mother such hope, straddled by the same forces that confine the mother. As a result, the daughter must constantly earn the mother's love, prove her fidelity to her. The son—he gets her love for free.

After ten years of feminist consciousness and activism, why does this seem so significant to me—to write of the Mexican mother favoring the son? I think because I had never quite gone back to the source.

Never said in my own tongue, *the boys, they are men, they can do
what they want . . . after all, he's a man.*

Journal Entry: April 1980
*Three days ago, my mother called me long distance full of tears,
loving me, wanting me back in her life after such a long period of
separation. My mother's tears succeed in getting me to break down
the edge in my voice, the protective distance. My mother's pleading
"mi'jita, I love you, I hate to feel so far away from you," succeeds in
opening my heart again to her.*

*I don't remember exactly why my heart had been shut, only that it
had been very necessary to keep my distance, that in a way we had
agreed to that. But, it only took her crying to pry my heart open again.*

*I feel myself unriveting. The feelings begin to flood my chest. Yes,
this is why I love women. This woman is my mother. There is no love
as strong as this, refusing my separation, never settling for a secret
that would split us off, always at the last minute, like now, pushing
me to the brink of revelation, speaking the truth.*

*I am as big as a mountain! I want to say, "Watch out, Mamá! I love
you and I am as big as a mountain!" And it is on the brink of this
precipice where I feel my body descending into the places where we
have not spoken, the times I did not fight back. I am descending,
ready to speak the truth, finally.*

*And then suddenly, over the phone, I hear another ring. My mother
tells me to wait. There is a call on my father's work phone. Moments
later, "It is your brother," she says. My knees lock under me, bracing
myself for the fall . . . Her voice lightens up. "Okay, mi'jita. I love you.
I'll talk to you later," cutting off the line in the middle of the connection.*

*I am relieved when I hang up that I did not have the chance to say
more. The graceful reminder. This man doesn't have to earn her love.
My brother has always come first.*

*Seduction and betrayal. Since I've grown up, no woman cares for
me for free. There is always a price. My love.*

What I wanted from my mother was impossible. It would have
meant her going against Mexican/Chicano tradition in a very fundamental way. You are a traitor to your race if you do not put the man
first. The potential accusation of "traitor" or "vendida" is what hangs
above the heads and beats in the hearts of most Chicanas seeking to
develop our own autonomous sense of ourselves, particularly through
sexuality.

***

Because heterosexism—the Chicana's sexual commitment to the Chicano male—is proof of her fidelity to her people, the Chicana feminist attempting to critique the sexism in the Chicano community is certainly between a personal rock and a political hard place.

Although not called "the sexism debate," as it has been in the literary sectors of the Black movement, the Chicano discussion of sexism within our community has like that movement been largely limited by heterosexual assumption: "How can we get our men right." The feminist-oriented material which appeared in the late 70s and early 80s for the most part strains in its attempt to stay safely within the boundaries of Chicano—male-defined and often anti-feminist—values.

Over and over again, Chicanas trivialize the women's movement as being merely a white middle-class thing, having little to offer women of color. They cite only the most superficial aspects of the movement. For example, in "From Woman to Woman," Silvia S. Lizarraga writes:

> class distinction is a major determinant of attitudes toward other subordinated groups. In the U.S. we see this phenomenon operating in the goals expressed in the Women's Liberation Movement. . . . The needs represent a large span of interests—from those of *capitalist women*, women in business and professional careers, to *witches* and *lesbians*. However, the needs of the unemployed and working class women of different ethnic minorities are generally overlooked by this movement.[6] (my emphasis)

This statement typifies the kind of one-sided perspective many Chicanas have given of the women's movement in the name of Chicana liberation. My question is *who* are they trying to serve? Certainly not the Chicana who is deprived of some very critical information about a ten-year grassroots feminist movement where women of color, including lesbians of color (certainly in the minority and most assuredly encountering "feminist' racism) have been actively involved in reproductive rights, especially sterilization abuse, battered women's shelters, rape crisis centers, welfare advocacy, Third World women's conferences, cultural events, health and self-help clinics and more.

Interestingly, it is perfectly acceptable among Chicano males to use white theoreticians, e.g. Marx and Engels, to develop a theory of Chicano oppression. It is unacceptable, however, for the Chicana to use white sources by women to develop a theory of Chicana oppression. Even if one subscribes to a solely economic theory of oppression, how can she ignore that over half of the world's workers are females who suffer discrimination not only in the workplace, but also at home and in all the areas of sex-related abuse I just cited? How can she afford not to recognize that the wars against imperialism occurring both domestically and internationally are always accompanied by the rape of women of color by both white and Third World men? Without a feminist analysis what name do we put to these facts? Are these not deterrents to the Chicana developing a sense of "species being?" Are these "women's issues" not also "people's issues?" It is far easier for the Chicana to criticize white women who on the face of things could never be familia, than to take issue with or complain, as it were, to a brother, uncle, father.

The most valuable aspect of Chicana theory thus far has been its re-evaluation of our history from a woman's perspective through unearthing the stories of Mexican/Chicana female figures that early on exhibited a feminist sensibility. The weakness of these works is that much of it is undermined by what I call the "alongside-our-man-knee-jerk-phenomenon." In speaking of María Hernández, Alfredo Mirande and Evangelina Enríquez offer a typical disclaimer in *La Chicana*:

> Although a feminist and leader in her own right, she is always quick to point to the importance of family unity in the movement and to acknowledge the help of her husband . . .[7]

And yet we would think nothing of the Chicano activist never mentioning the many "behind-the-scenes" Chicanas who helped him!

In the same text, the authors fall into the too-common trap of coddling the Chicano male ego (which should be, in and of itself, an insult to Chicano men) in the name of cultural loyalty. Like the Black Superwoman, the Chicana is forced to take on extra-human proportions. She must keep the cultural home-fires burning while going out and making a living. She must fight racism alongside her man, but challenge sexism single-handedly, all the while retaining her "femininity" so as not to offend or threaten *her man*. This is what being a Chicana feminist means.

In recent years, however, truly feminist Chicanas are beginning to make the pages of Chicano, feminist, and literary publications. This, of course, is only a reflection of a fast-growing Chicana/Third World feminist movement. I am in debt to the research and writings of Norma Alarcón, Martha Cotera, Gloria Anzaldúa, and Aleida Del Castillo, to name a few. Their work reflects a relentless commitment to putting the female first, even when it means criticizing el hombre.[8]

To be critical of one's culture is not to betray that culture. We tend to be very righteous in our criticism and indictment of the dominant culture and we so often suffer from the delusion that, since Chicanos are so maligned from the outside, there is little room to criticize those aspects from within our oppressed culture which oppress us.

I am not particularly interested in whether or not Third World people learned sexism from the white man. There have been great cases made to prove how happy men and women were together before the white man made tracks in indigenous soil. This reflects the same mentality of white feminists who claim that all races were in harmony when the "Great Mother" ruled us all. In both cases, history tends to prove different. In either case, the strategy for the elimination of racism and sexism cannot occur through the exclusion of one problem or the other. As the Combahee River Collective, a Black feminist organization, states, women of color experience these oppressions "simultaneously."[9] The only people who can afford not to recognize this are those who do not suffer this multiple oppression.

I remain amazed at how often so-called "Tercermundistas" in the U.S. work to annihilate the concept and existence of white supremacy, but turn their faces away from male supremacy. Perhaps this is because when you start to talk about sexism, the world becomes increasingly complex. The power no longer breaks down into neat little hierarchical categories, but becomes a series of starts and detours. Since the categories are not easy to arrive at, the enemy is not easy to name. It is all so difficult to unravel. It *is* true that some men hate women even in their desire for them. And some men oppress the very women they love. But unlike the racist, they allow the object of their contempt to share the table with them. The hatred they feel for women does not translate into separatism. It is more insidiously intra-cultural, like class antagonism. But different, because it lives and breathes in the flesh and blood of our families, even in the name of love.

In Toni Cade Bambara's novel, *The Salt Eaters*, the curandera asks the question, *Can you afford to be whole?*[10] This line represents the question that has burned within me for years and years through my growing politicization. *What would a movement bent on the freedom of women of color look like?* In other words, what are the implications of not only looking outside of our culture, but into our culture and ourselves and from that place beginning to develop a strategy for a movement that could challenge the bedrock of oppressive systems of belief globally?

The one aspect of our identity which has been uniformly ignored by every existing political movement in this country is sexuality, both as a source of oppression and a means of liberation. Although other movements have dealt with this issue, sexual oppression and desire have never been considered specifically in relation to the lives of women of color. Sexuality, race, and sex have usually been presented in contradiction to each other, rather than as part and parcel of a complex web of personal and political identity and oppression.

***

Unlike most white people, with the exception of the Jews, Third World people have suffered the threat of genocide to our races since the coming of the first European expansionists. The family, then, becomes all the more ardently protected by oppressed peoples, and the sanctity of this institution is infused like blood into the veins of the Chicano. At all costs, la familia must be preserved: for when they kill our boys in their own imperialist wars to gain greater profits for American corporations; when they keep us in ghettos, reservations, and barrios which ensure that our own people will be the recipients of our frustrated acts of violence; when they sterilize our women without our consent because we are unable to read the document we sign; when they prevent our families from getting decent housing, adequate child care, sufficient fuel, regular medical care; then we have reason to believe—although they may no longer technically be lynching us in Texas or our sisters and brothers in Georgia, Alabama, Mississippi—they intend to see us dead.

So we fight back, we think, with our families—with our women pregnant, and our men, the indisputable heads. We believe the more severely we protect the sex roles within the family, the stronger we will be as a unit in opposition to the anglo threat. And yet, our refusal to examine *all* the roots of the lovelessness in our families is our weakest link and softest spot.

Our resistance as a people to looking at the relationships within our families—between husband and wife, lovers, sister and brother, father, son, and daughter, etc.—leads me to believe that the Chicano male does not hold fast to the family unit merely to safeguard it from the death-dealings of the anglo. Living under Capitalist Patriarchy, what is true for "the man" in terms of misogyny is, to a great extent, true for the Chicano. He, too, like any other man, wants to be able to determine how, when, and with whom his women—mother, wife, and daughter—are sexual. For without male imposed social and legal control of our reproductive function, reinforced by the Catholic Church, and the social institutionalization of our roles as sexual and domestic servants to men, Chicanas might very freely "choose" to do otherwise, including being sexually independent *from* and/or *with* men. In fact, the forced "choice" of the gender of our sexual/love partner seems to precede the forced "choice" of the form (marriage and family) that partnership might take. The control of women begins through the institution of heterosexuality.

Homosexuality does not, in and of itself, pose a great threat to society. Male homosexuality has always been a "tolerated" aspect of Mexican/Chicano society, as long as it remains "fringe." A case can even be made that male homosexuality stems from our indigenous Aztec roots.[11] But lesbianism, in any form, and male homosexuality which openly avows both the sexual and emotional elements of the bond, challenges the very foundation of la familia. The "faggot" is the object of the Chicano/Mexicano's contempt because he is consciously choosing a role his culture tells him to despise. That of a woman.

The question remains. Is the foundation as it stands now sturdy enough to meet the face of the oppressor? I think not. There is a deeper love between and amongst our people that lies buried between the lines of the roles we play with each other. It is the earth beneath the floor boards of our homes. We must split wood, dig barefisted into the packed ground to find out what we really have to hold in our hands as muscle.

Family is *not* by definition the man in a dominant position over women and children. Familia is cross-generational bonding, deep emotional ties between opposite sexes, and within our sex. It is sexuality, which involves, but is not limited to, intercourse or orgasm. It springs forth from touch, constant and daily. The ritual of kissing and the sign of the cross with every coming and going from the home. It is finding familia among friends where blood ties are formed through suffering and celebration shared.

The strength of our families never came from domination. It has only endured in spite of it—like our women.

* * *

Chicanos' refusal to look at our weaknesses as a people and a movement is, in the most profound sense, an act of self-betrayal. The Chicana lesbian bears the brunt of this betrayal, for it is she, the most visible manifestation of a woman taking control of her own sexual identity and destiny, who so severly challenges the anti-feminist Chicano/a. What other reason is there than that for the virtual dead silence among Chicanos about lesbianism? When the subject *is* raised, the word is used pejoratively.

For example, Sonia A. López writes about the anti-feminism in El Movimiento of the late 60s.

> The Chicanas who voiced their discontent with the organizations and
> with male leadership were often labeled "women's libbers," and "les-
> bians." This served to isolate and discredit them, a method practiced
> both covertly and overtly.[12]

This statement appears without qualification. López makes no value
judgment on the inherent homophobia in such a divisive tactic. Without comment, her statement reinforces the idea that lesbianism is not
only a white thing, but an insult to be avoided at all costs.

Such attempts by Chicana feminists to bend over backwards to
prove criticism of their people is love (which, in fact, it is) severely
undermines the potential radicalism of the ideology they are trying to
create. Not quite believing in their love, suspecting their own anger,
and fearing ostracism from Chicano males (being symbolically "kicked
out of bed" with the bait of "lesbian" hanging over their work), the
Chicana's imagination often stops before it has a chance to consider
some of the most difficult, and therefore, some of the most important,
questions.

It is no wonder that the Chicanas I know who *are* asking "taboo"
questions are often forced into outsiderhood long before they begin
to question el carnal in print. Maybe like me they now feel they have
little to lose.

It is important to say that fearing recriminations from my father never
functioned for me as an obstacle in my political work. Had I been
born of a Chicano father, I sometimes think I never would have been
able to write a line or participate in a demonstration, having to repress
all questioning in order that the ultimate question of my sexuality
would never emerge. Possibly, even some of my compañeras whose
fathers died or left in their early years would never have had the
courage to speak out as Third World lesbians the way they do now,
had their fathers been a living part of their daily lives. The Chicana
lesbians I know whose fathers are very much a part of their lives are
seldom "out" to their families.

During the late 60s and the early 70s, I was not an active part of la
causa. I never managed to get myself to walk in the marches in East
Los Angeles (I merely watched from the sidelines); I never went to
one meeting of MECHA on campus. No soy tonta. I would have been
murdered in El Movimiento-—light-skinned, unable to speak Spanish
well enough to hang; miserably attracted to women and fighting it;
and constantly questioning all authority, including men's. I felt I did
not belong there. Maybe I had really come to believe that "Chicanos"
were "different," not "like us," as my mother would say. But I fully

knew that there was a part of me that was a part of that movement, but it seemed that part would have to go unexpressed until the time I could be a Chicano and the woman I had to be, too.

The woman who defies her role as subservient to her husband, father, brother, or son by taking control of her own sexual destiny is purported to be a "traitor to her race" by contributing to the "genocide" of her people—whether or not she has children. In short, even if the defiant woman is *not* a lesbian, she is purported to be one; for, like the lesbian in the Chicano imagination, she is una *Malinchista*. Like the Malinche of Mexican history, she is corrupted by foreign influences which threaten to destroy her people. Norma Alarcón elaborates on this theme of sex as a determinant of loyalty when she states:

> The myth of Malinche contains the following sexual possibilities: woman is sexually passive, and hence at all times open to potential use by men whether it be seduction or rape. The possible use is double-edged: that is, the use of her as pawn may be intracultural—"amongst us guys"— or intercultural, which means if we are not using her then "they" must be using her. Since woman is highly pawnable, nothing she does is perceived, as choice.[13]

Lesbianism can be construed by the race then as the Chicana being used by the white man, even if the man never lays a hand on her. *The choice is never seen as her own.* Homosexuality is *his* disease with which he sinisterly infects Third World people, men and women alike. (Because Malinche is female, Chicano gay men rebelling against their prescribed sex roles, although still considered diseased, do not suffer the same stigma of traitor.) Further, the Chicana lesbian who has relationships with white women may feel especially susceptible to such accusations, since the white lesbian is seen as the white man's agent. The fact that the white woman may be challenging the authority of her white father, and thereby could be looked upon as a potential ally, has no bearing on a case closed before it was ever opened.

* * *

The line of reasoning goes:

Malinche sold out her indio people by acting as courtesan and translator for Cortez, whose offspring symbolically represent the birth of the bastardized mestizo/Mexicano people. My mother then is the modern-day Chicana, Malinche marrying a white man, my father, to produce the bastards my sister, my brother, and I are. Finally, I—a half-breed Chicana—further betray my race by *choosing* my sexuality which excludes all men, and therefore most dangerously, Chicano men.

I come from a long line of Vendidas.

I am a Chicana lesbian. My own particular relationship to being a sexual person; and a radical stand in direct contradiction to, and in violation of, the woman I was raised to be.

* * *

Coming from such a complex and contradictory history of sexual exploitation by white men and from within our own race, it is nearly earth-shaking to begin to try and separate the myths told about us from the truths; and to examine to what extent we have internalized what, in fact, is not true.

Although intellectually I knew different, early on I learned that women were the willing cooperators in rape. So over and over again in pictures, books, movies, I experienced rape and pseudo-rape as titillating, sexy, as what sex was all about. Women want it. Real rape was dark, greasy-looking bad men jumping out of alleys and attacking innocent blonde women. Everything short of that was just sex; the way it is: dirty and duty. We spread our legs and bear the brunt of penetration, but we do spread our legs. In my mind, inocencia meant dying rather then being fucked.

I learned these notions about sexuality not only from the society at large, but more specifically and potently from Chicano/Mexicano culture, originating from the myth of La Chingada, Malinche. In the very act of intercourse with Cortez, Malinche is seen as having been violated. She is not, however, an innocent victim, but the guilty party—ultimately responsible for her own sexual victimization. Slavery and slander is the price she must pay for the pleasure our culture imagined she enjoyed. In *The Labyrinth of Solitude*, Octavio Paz gives an explanation of the term "chingar," which provides valuable insights into how Malinche, as symbolized by La Chingada, is perceived. He writes:

> The idea of breaking, of ripping open. When alluding to a sexual act, violation or deception gives it a particular shading. The man who commits it never does so with the consent of the chingada.
>
> Chingar then is to do violence to another, i.e., rape. The verb is masculine, active, cruel: it stings, wounds, gashes, stains. And it provokes a bitter, resentful satisfaction. The person who suffers this action is passive, inert, and open, in contrast to the active, aggressive, and closed person who inflicts it. The chingón is the macho, the male; he rips open the chingada, the female, who is pure passivity, defenseless against the exterior world.[14]

If the simple act of sex then—the penetration itself—implies the female's filthiness, non humanness, it is no wonder Chicanas often divorce ourselves from the conscious recognition of our own sexuality.

Even if we enjoy having sex, draw pleasure from feeling fingers, tongue, penis inside us, there is a part of us that must disappear in the act, separate ourselves from realizing what it is we are actually doing. Sit, as it were, on the corner bedpost, watching the degradation and violence some "other" woman is willing to subject herself to, not us. And if we have lesbian feelings—want not only to be penetrated, but to penetrate—what perverse kind of monstrosities we must indeed be! It is through our spirits that we escape the painful recognition of our "base" sexual selves.

* * *

What the white women's movement tried to convince me of is that lesbian sexuality was *naturally* different than heterosexual sexuality. That the desire to penetrate and be penetrated, to fill and be filled, would vanish. That retaining such desires was "reactionary," not "politically correct," "male-identified." And somehow reaching sexual ecstasy with a woman lover would never involve any kind of power struggle. Women were different. We could simply magically "transcend" these "old notions," just by seeking spiritual transcendence in bed.

The fact of the matter was that all these power struggles of "having" and "being had" were being played out in my own bedroom. And in my psyche, they held a particular Mexican twist. White women's feminism did little to answer my questions. As a Chicana feminist my concerns were different. As I wrote in 1982:

> What I need to explore will not be found in the feminist lesbian bedroom, but more likely in the mostly heterosexual bedrooms of South Texas, L.A., or even Sonora, México. Further, I have come to realize that the boundaries white feminists confine themselves to in describing sexuality are based in white-rooted interpretations of dominance, submission, power-exchange, etc. Although they are certainly *part* of the psychosexual lives of women of color, these boundaries would have to be expanded and translated to fit my people, in particular, the women in my family. And I am tired, always, of these acts of translation.[15]

Mirtha Quintanales corroborates this position and exposes the necessity for a Third World feminist dialogue on sexuality when she states:

> The critical issue for me regarding the politics of sexuality is that as a Latina Lesbian living in the U.S., I do not really have much of an opportunity to examine what constitutes sexual conformity and sexual defiance in my own culture, in my own ethnic community, and how that may affect my own values, attitudes, sexual life *and* politics. There is virtually no dialogue on the subject anywhere and I, like other Latinas

and Third World women, especially Lesbians, am quite in the dark about what we're up against besides negative feminist sexual politics.[16]

During the late 70s, the concept of "women's culture" among white lesbians and "cultural feminists" was in full swing; it is still very popular today. "Womon's history," "wommin's music," "womyn's spiritual-ity," "wymyn's language," abounded—all with the "white" modifier implied and unstated. In truth, there was/is a huge amount of denial going on in the name of female separatism. Women do not usually grow up in women-only environments. Culture is sexually-mixed. As Bernice Reagon puts it:

> . . . we have been organized to have our primary cultural signals come from factors other than that we are women. We are not from our base, acculturated to be women people, capable of crossing our first people boundaries: Black, White, Indian, etc.[17]

Unlike Reagon, I believe that there are certain ways we *have* been acculturated to be "women people," and there is therefore such a thing as "women's culture." This occurs, however, as Reagon points out, within a context formed by race, class, geography, religion, eth-nicity, and language.

I don't mean to imply that women need to have men around to feel at home in our culture, but that the way one understands culture is influenced by men. The fact that some aspects of that culture are indeed oppressive does not imply, as a solution, throwing out the entire business of racial/ethnic culture. To do so would mean risking the loss of some very essential aspects of identity, especially for Third World women.

In failing to approach feminism from any kind of materialist base, failing to take race, ethnicity, class into account in determining where women are at sexually, many feminists have created an analysis of sexual oppression (often confused with sexuality itself) which is a political dead-end. "Radical Feminism," the ideology which sees men's oppression of women as the root of and paradigm for all other oppres-sions allows women to view ourselves as a class and to claim our sexual identity as the *source* of our oppression and men's sexual iden-tity as the *source* of the world's evil. But this ideology can never then fully integrate the concept of the "simultaneity of oppression" as Third World feminism is attempting to do. For, if race and class suffer the woman of color as much as her sexual identity, then the Radical Fem-inist must extend her own "identity" politics to include her "identity" as oppressor as well. (To say nothing of having to acknowledge the fact that there are men who may suffer more than she.) This is something that, for the most part, Radical Feminism as a movement has refused to do.

Radical Feminist theorists have failed to acknowledge how their position in the dominant culture—white, middle-class, often Christian—has influenced every approach they have taken to implement feminist political change—to "give women back their bodies." It follows then that the anti-pornography movement is the largest organized branch of Radical Feminism. For unlike battered women's, anti-rape, and reproductive rights workers, the anti-porn "activist" never has to deal with any live woman outside of her own race and class. The tactics of the anti-pornography movement are largely symbolic and theoretical in nature. And, on paper, the needs of the woman of color are a lot easier to represent than in the flesh. Therefore, her single-issued approach to feminism remains intact.

It is not that pornography is not a concern to many women of color. But the anti-materialist approach of this movement makes little sense in the lives of poor and Third World women. Plainly put, it is our sisters working in the sex industry.

Many women involved in the anti-porn movement are lesbian separatists. Because the Radical Feminist critique is there to justify it, lesbianism can be viewed as the logical personal response to a misogynist political system. Through this perspective, lesbianism has become an "idea"—a political response to male sexual aggression, rather than a sexual response to a woman's desire for another woman. In this way, many ostensibly heterosexual women who are not active sexually can call themselves lesbians. Lesbians "from the neck up." This faction of the movement has grown into a kind of cult. They have taken whiteness, class privilege, and an anglo-american brand of "return-to-the-mother" which leaps back over a millenium of patriarchal domination, attempted to throw out the man, and call what is left female. While still retaining their own racial and class-biased cultural superiority.

The lesbian separatist retreats from the specific cultural contexts that have shaped her and attempts to build a cultural-political movement based on an imagined oppression-free past. It is understandable that many feminists opt for this kind of asexual separatist/spiritualist solution rather than boldly grappling with the challenge of wresting sexual autonomy from such a sexually exploitative system. Every oppressed group needs to imagine through the help of history and mythology a world where our oppression did not seem the pre-ordained order. Aztlán for Chicanos is another example. The mistake lies in believing in this ideal past or imagined future so thoroughly and single-mindedly that finding solutions to present-day inequities loses priority, or we attempt to create too-easy solutions for the pain we feel today.

As culture—our race, class, ethnicity, etc.—influences our sexuality, so too does heterosexism, marriage, and men as the primary agents of those institutions. We can work to tumble those institutions so that when the rubble is finally cleared away we can see what we have left to build on sexually. But we can't ask a woman to forget everything she understands about sex in a heterosexual and culturally-specific context or tell her what she is allowed to think about it. Should she forget and not use what she knows sexually to untie the knot of her own desire, she may lose any chance of ever discovering her own sexual potential.

**

Among Chicanas, it is our tradition to conceive of the bond between mother and daughter as paramount and essential in our lives. It is the daughters that can be relied upon. Las hijas who remain faithful a la madre, a la madre de la madre.

When we name this bond between the women of our race, from this Chicana feminism emerges. For too many years, we have acted as if we held a secret pact with one another never to acknowledge directly our commitment to one another. Never to admit the fact that we count on one another *first*. We were never to recognize this in the face of el hombre. But this is what being a Chicana feminist means—making bold and political the love of the women of our race.

**

A political commitment to women does not equate with lesbianism. As a Chicana lesbian, I write of the connection my own feminism has had with my sexual desire for women. This is my story. I can tell no other one than the one I understand. I eagerly await the writings by heterosexual Chicana feminists that can speak of their sexual desire for men and the ways in which their feminism informs that desire. What is true, however, is that a political commitment to women must involve, by definition, a political commitment to lesbians as well. To refuse to allow the Chicana lesbian the right to the free expression of her own sexuality, and her politicization of it, is in the deepest sense to deny one's self the right to the same. I guarantee you, there will be no change among heterosexual men, there will be no change in heterosexual relations, as long as the Chicano community keeps us lesbians and gay men political prisoners among our own people. Any movement built on the fear and loathing of anyone is a failed movement. The Chicano movement is no different.

N O T E S

1. Norma Alarcón examines this theme in her article "Chicana's Feminist Literature: A Re-Vision Through Malintzin/or Malintzin: Putting Flesh Back on the Object," in *This Bridge Called My Back: Writings by Radical Women of Color*, ed. Cherríe Moraga and Gloria Anzaldúa (Watertown, Mass.: Persephone Press, 1981).

2. Aleida R. Del Castillo, "Malintzin Tenepal: A Preliminary Look into a New Perspective," in *Essays on La Mujer*, ed. Rosaura Sánchez and Rosa Martínez Cruz (University of California at Los Angeles: Chicano Studies Center Publications, 1977), p. 133.

3. Ibid., p. 131.

4. Ibid., p. 141.

5. Gloria Anzaldúa, unpublished work in progress. Write: The Third World Women's Archives, Box 159, Bush Terminal Station, Brooklyn, NY 11232.

6. Silvia S. Lizarraga, "From a Woman to a Woman," in *Essays on La Mujer*, p. 91.

7. Alfredo Mirandé and Evangelina Enríquez, *La Chicana; The Mexican-American Woman* (Chicago: University of Chicago Press, 1979), p. 225.

8. Some future writings by Latina feminists include: Gloria Anzaldúa's *La Serpiente Que Se Come Su Cola: The Autobiography of a Chicana Lesbian* (Write: The Third World Women's Archives, see address above); *Cuentos: Stories by Latinas*, ed. Alma Gómez, Cherríe Moraga, and Mariana Romo-Carmona (Kitchen Table: Women of Color Press, Box 2753 Rockefeller Center Station, New York, NY 10185, 1983); and *Compañeras: Antología Lesbiana Latina*, ed. Juanita Ramos and Mirtha Quintanales (Write: The Third World Women's Archives, see address above).

9. The Combahee River Collective, "A Black Feminist Statement," in *But Some of Us Are Brave: Black Women's Studies*, ed. Gloria T. Hull, Patricia Bell Scott, and Barbara Smith (Old Westbury, N.Y.: The Feminist Press, 1982), p. 16.

10. Toni Cade Bambara, *The Salt Eaters* (New York: Random House, 1980), pp. 3 and 10.

11. Bernal Díaz del Castillo, *The Bernal Diaz Chronicles*, trans. and ed. Albert Idell (New York: Doubleday, 1956), pp. 86-87.

12. Sonia A. López, in *Essays on La Mujer*, p. 26.

13. Norma Alarcón, in *This Bridge Called My Back*, p. 184.

14. Octavio Paz, *The Labyrinth of Solitude: Life and Thought in Mexico* (N.Y.: Grove Press, 1961), p. 77.

15. Cherríe Moraga, "Played between White Hands," in *Off Our Backs*, July 1982, Washington, D.C.

16. Mirtha Quintanales with Barbara Kerr, "The Complexity of Desire: Conversations on Sexuality and Difference," in *Conditions: Eight*, Box 56 Van Brunt Station, Brooklyn, N.Y., p. 60.

17. Bernice Reagon, "Turning the Century Around" in *Home Girls: A Black Feminist Anthology*, ed. Barbara Smith (Brooklyn, N.Y.: Kitchen Table: Women of Color Press, 1983).

Feminist Politics: What's Home Got to Do with It?

Biddy Martin and
Chandra Talpade Mohanty

We began working on this project after visiting our respective "homes" in Lynchburg, Virginia and Bombay, India in the fall of 1984—visits fraught with conflict, loss, memories, and desires we both considered to be of central importance in thinking about our relationship to feminist politics. In spite of significant differences in our personal histories and academic backgrounds, and the displacements we both experience, the political and intellectual positions we share made it possible for us to work on, indeed to write, this essay together. Our separate readings of Minnie Bruce Pratt's autobiographical narrative entitled "Identity: Skin Blood Heart" became the occasion for thinking through and developing more precisely some of the ideas about feminist theory and politics that have occupied us. We are interested in the configuration of home, identity, and community; more specifically, in the power and appeal of "home" as a concept and a desire, its occurrence as metaphor in feminist writings, and its challenging presence in the rhetoric of the New Right.

Both leftists and feminists have realized the importance of not handing over notions of home and community to the Right. Far too often, however, both male leftists and feminists have responded to the appeal of a rhetoric of home and family by merely reproducing the most conventional articulations of those terms in their own writings. In her recent work, Zillah Eisenstein identifies instances of what she labels revisionism within liberal, radical, and socialist feminist writings: texts by women such as Betty Friedan, Andrea Dworkin, and Jean Bethke Elshtain, in which the pursuit of safe places and ever-narrower conceptions of community relies on unexamined notions of home, family, and nation, and severely limits the scope of the feminist inquiry and struggle.[1] The challenge, then, is to find ways of conceptualizing community differently without dismissing its appeal and importance.

It is significant that the notion of "home" has been taken up in a range of writings by women of color, who cannot easily assume "home" within feminist communities as they have been constituted.[2] Bernice Johnson Reagon's critique of white feminists' incorporation of "others" into their "homes" is a warning to all feminists that "we are going to have to break out of little barred rooms" and cease holding tenaciously to the invisible and only apparently self-evident boundaries around that which we define as our own, "if we are going to have anything to do with what makes it into the next century." Reagon does not deny the appeal and the importance of "home" but challenges us to stop confusing it with political coalition and suggests that it takes what she calls an old-age perspective to know when to engage and when to withdraw, when to break out and when to consolidate.[3]

For our discussion of the problematics of "home," we chose a text that demonstrates the importance of both narrative and historical specificity in the attempt to reconceptualize the relations between "home," "identity," and political change. The volume in which Pratt's essay appears, *Yours in Struggle: Three Feminist Perspectives on Anti-Semitism and Racism* (Brooklyn, N.Y.: Long Haul Press, 1984), is written by Elly Bulkin, Minnie Bruce Pratt, and Barbara Smith, each of whom ostensibly represents a different experience and identity and consequently a different (even if feminist) perspective on racism and anti-Semitism. What makes this text unusual, in spite of what its title may suggest, is its questioning of the all-too-common conflation of experience, identity, and political perspective.

What we have tried to draw out of this text is the way in which it unsettles not only any notion of feminism as an all-encompassing home but also the assumption that there are discrete, coherent, and absolutely separate identities—homes within feminism, so to speak—based on absolute divisions between various sexual, racial, or ethnic identities. What accounts for the unsettling of boundaries and identities, and the questioning of conventional notions of experience, is the task that the contributors have set for themselves: to address certain specific questions and so to situate themselves in relation to the tensions between feminism, racism, and anti-Semitism. The "unity" of the individual subject, as well as the unity of feminism, is situated and specified as the product of the interpretation of personal histories; personal histories that are themselves situated in relation to the development within feminism of particular questions and critiques.

Pratt's autobiographical narrative is the narrative of a woman who identifies herself as white, middle-class, Christian-raised, southern, and lesbian. She makes it very clear that unity through incorporation has too often been the white middle-class feminist's mode of adding on difference without leaving the comfort of home. What Pratt sets out to explore are the exclusions and repressions which support the seeming homogeneity, stability, and self-evidence of "white identity," which is derived from and dependent on the marginalization of differences within as well as "without."

Our decision to concentrate on Pratt's narrative has to do with our shared concern that critiques of what is increasingly identified as "white" or "Western" feminism unwittingly leave the terms of West/East, white/nonwhite polarities intact; they do so, paradoxically, by starting from the premise that Western feminist discourse is inadequate or irrelevant to women of color or Third World women. The implicit assumption here, which we wish to challenge, is that the terms of a totalizing feminist discourse *are adequate* to the task of articulating the situation of white women in the West. We would contest that assumption and argue that the reproduction of such polarities only serves to concede "feminism" to the "West" all over again. The potential consequence is the repeated failure to contest the feigned homogeneity of the West and what seems to be a discursive and political stability of the hierarchical West/East divide.

Pratt's essay enacts as much as it treats the contradictory relations between skin, blood, heart, and identity and between experience, identity, and community in ways that we would like to analyze and discuss in more detail. Like the essays that follow it, it is a form of writing that not only anticipates and integrates diverse audiences or readers but also positions the narrator as reader. The perspective is multiple and shifting, and the shifts in perspective are enabled by the attempts to define self, home, and community that are at the heart of Pratt's enterprise. The historical grounding of shifts and changes allows for an emphasis on the pleasures and terrors of interminable boundary confusions, but insists, at the same time, on our responsibility for remapping boundaries and renegotiating connections. These are partial in at least two senses of the word: politically partial, and without claim to wholeness or finality.

It is this insistence that distinguishes the work of a Reagon or a Pratt from the more abstract critiques of "feminism" and the charges of totalization that come from the ranks of antihumanist intellectuals. For without denying the importance of their vigilante attacks on humanist beliefs in "man" and Absolute Knowledge wherever they appear, it is equally important to point out the political limitations of an insistence on "indeterminacy" which implicitly, when not explicitly, denies the critic's own situatedness in the social, and in effect refuses to acknowledge the critic's own institutional home.

Pratt, on the contrary, succeeds in carefully taking apart the bases of her own privilege by resituating herself again and again in the social, by constantly referring to the materiality of the situation in which she finds herself. The form of the personal historical narrative forces her to reanchor herself repeatedly in each of the positions from which she speaks, even as she works to expose the illusory coherence of those positions. For the subject of such a narrative, it is not possible to speak from, or on behalf of, an abstract indeterminacy. Certainly, Pratt's essay would be considered a "conventional" (and therefore suspect) narrative from the point of view of contemporary deconstructive methodologies, because of its collapsing of author and text, its unreflected authorial intentionality, and its claims to personal and political authenticity.

Basic to the (at least implicit) disavowal of conventionally realist and autobiographical narrative by deconstructionist critics is the assumption that difference can emerge only through self-referential language, i.e., through certain relatively specific formal operations present in the text or performed upon it. Our reading of Pratt's narrative contends that a so-called conventional narrative such as Pratt's is not only useful but essential in addressing the politically and theoretically urgent questions surrounding identity politics. Just as Pratt refuses the methodological imperative to distinguish between herself as actual biographical referent and her narrator, we have at points allowed ourselves to let our reading of the text speak for us.

It is noteworthy that some of the American feminist texts and arguments that have been set up as targets to be taken apart by deconstructive moves are texts and arguments that have been critiqued from within "American" feminist communities for their homogenizing, even colonialist gestures; they have been critiqued, in fact, by those most directly affected by the exclusions that have made possible certain radical and cultural feminist generalizations. Antihumanist attacks on "feminism" usually set up "American feminism" as a "straw man" and so contribute to the production—or, at the very least, the reproduction—of an image of "Western feminism" as conceptually and politically unified in its monolithically imperialist moves.

We do not wish to deny that too much of the conceptual and political work of "Western" feminists is encumbered by analytic strategies that do indeed homogenize the experiences and conditions of women across time and culture; nor do we wish to deny that "Western" feminists have often taken their own positions as referent, thereby participating in the colonialist moves characteristic of traditional humanist scholarship. However, such critiques run the risk of falling into culturalist arguments, and these tend to have the undesired effect of solidifying the identification of feminism with the West rather than challenging the hegemony of specific analytic and political positions. The refusal to engage in the kind of feminist analysis that is more differentiated, more finely articulated, and more attentive to the problems raised in poststructuralist theory makes "bad feminism" a foil supporting the privilege of the critics' "indeterminacy." Wary of the limitations of an antihumanism which refuses to rejoin the political, we purposely chose a text that speaks from within "Western feminist discourse" and attempts to expose the bases and supports of privilege even as it renegotiates political and personal alliances.[4]

One of the most striking aspects of "Identity: Skin Blood Heart" is the text's movement away from the purely personal, visceral experience of identity suggested by the title to a complicated working out of the relationship between home, identity, and community that calls into question the notion of a coherent, historically continuous, stable identity and works to expose the political stakes concealed in such equations. An effective way of analyzing Pratt's conceptualization of these relationships is to focus on the manner in which the narrative works by grounding itself in the geography, demography, and architecture of the communities that are her "homes"; these factors function as an organizing mode in the text, providing a specific concreteness and movement for the narrative.

Correspondingly, the narrative politicizes the geography, demography, and architecture of these communities—Pratt's homes at various times of her history—by discovering local histories of exploitation and struggle. These are histories quite unlike the ones she is familiar with, the ones with which she grew up. Pratt problematizes her ideas about herself by juxtaposing the assumed histories of her family and childhood, predicated on the invisibility of the histories of people unlike her, to the layers of exploitation and struggles of different groups of people for whom these geographical sites were also home.

Each of the three primary geographical locations—Alabama (the home of her childhood and college days), North Carolina (the place of her marriage and coming out as a lesbian), and Washington, D.C. (characterized by her acute awareness of racism, anti-Semitism, class, and global politics)—is constructed on the tension between two specific modalities: being home and not being home. "Being home" refers to the place where one lives within familiar, safe, protected boundaries; "not being home" is a matter of realizing that home was an illusion of coherence and safety based on the exclusion of specific histories of oppression and resistance, the repression of differences even within oneself. Because these locations acquire meaning and function as sites of personal and historical struggles, they work against the notion of an unproblematic geographic location of home in Pratt's narrative. Similarly, demographic information functions to ground and concretize race, class, and gender conflicts. Illusions of home are always undercut by the discovery of the hidden demographics of particular places, as demography also carries the weight of histories of struggle.

Pratt speaks of being "shaped" in relation to the buildings and streets in the town in which she lived. Architecture and the layouts of particular towns provide concrete, physical anchoring points in relation to which she both sees and does not see certain people and things in the buildings and on the streets. However, the very stability, familiarity, and security of these physical structures are undermined by the discovery that these buildings and streets witnessed and obscured particular race, class, and gender struggles. The realization that these "growing up places" are home towns where Pratt's eye "has only let in what I have been taught to see" politicizes and undercuts any physical anchors she might use to construct a coherent notion of home or her identity in relation to it.

> Each of us carries around those growing up places, the institutions, a sort of backdrop, a stage set. So often we act out the present against the backdrop of the past, within a frame of perception that is so familiar, so safe that it is terrifying to risk changing it even when we know our perceptions are distorted, limited, constricted by that old view.

The traces of her past remain with her but must be challenged and reinterpreted. Pratt's own histories are in constant flux. There is no linear progression based on "that old view," no developmental notion of her own identity or self. There is instead a constant expansion of her "constricted eye," a necessary reevaluation and return to the past in order to move forward to the present. Geography, demography, and architecture, as well as the configuration of her relationships to particular people (her father, her lover, her workmate), serve to indicate the fundamentally relational nature of identity and the negations on which the assumption of a singular, fixed, and essential self is based. For the narrator, such negativity is represented by a rigid identity such as that of her father, which sustains its appearance of stability by defining itself in terms of what it is not: not black, not female, not Jewish, not Catholic, not poor, etc. The "self" in this narrative is not an essence or truth concealed by patriarchal layers of deceit and lying in wait of discovery, revelation, or birth.[5]

It is this very conception of self that Pratt likens to entrapment, constriction, a bounded fortress that must be transgressed, shattered, opened onto that world which has been made invisible and threatening by the security of home. While Pratt is aware that stable notions of self and identity are based on exclusion and secured by terror, she is also aware of the risk and terror inherent in breaking through the walls of home. The consciousness of these contradictions characterizes the narrative.

In order to indicate the fundamentally constructive, interpretive nature of Pratt's narrative, we have chosen to analyze the text following its own narrative organization in three different scenarios: scenarios that are characterized not by chronological development but by discontinuous moments of consciousness. The scenarios are constructed around moments in Pratt's own history which propel her in new directions through their fundamental instability and built-in contradictions.

Scenario 1

I live in a part of Washington, D.C. that white suburbanites called "the jungle" during the uprising of the '60s—perhaps still do, for all I know. When I walk the two-and-a-half blocks to H St. NE, to stop in at the bank, to leave my boots off at the shoe-repair-and-lock shop, I am most usually the only white person in sight. I've seen two other whites, women, in the year I've lived here. [This does not count white folks in cars, passing through. In official language, H St. NE, is known as "The H Street Corridor," as in something to be passed through quickly, going from your place, on the way to elsewhere.]

This paragraph of the text locates Minnie Bruce Pratt in a place that does not exist as a legitimate possibility for home on a white people's map of Washington, D.C. That place is H Street N.E., where Pratt lives, a section of town referred to as "the jungle" by white suburbanites in the sixties, also known as "the H. Street Corridor as in something to be passed through quickly, going from your place to elsewhere" (p. 11). That, then, is *potentially* Pratt's home, the community in which she lives. But this "jungle," this corridor, is located at the edge of homes of white folk. It is a place outside the experience of white people, where Pratt must be the outsider because she is white. This "being on the edge" is what characterizes her "being in the world as it is," as opposed to remaining within safe bounded places with their illusion of acceptance. "I will try to be at the edge between my fear and outside, on the edge at my skin, listening, asking what new thing will I hear, will I see, will I let myself feel, beyond the fear," she writes. It is her situation on the edge that expresses the desire and the possibility of breaking through the narrow circle called home without pretense that she can or should "jump out of her skin" or deny her past.

The salience of demography, a white woman in a black neighborhood, afraid to be too familiar and neighborly with black people, is acutely felt. Pratt is comforted by the sounds of the voices of black people, for they make her "feel at home" and remind her of her father's southern voice, until she runs into Mr. Boone, the janitor with the downcast head and the "yes ma'ams," and Pratt responds in "the horrid cheerful accents of a white lady." The pain is not just the pain of rejection by this black man; it is the pain of acknowledging the history of the oppression and separation of different groups of people which shatters the protective boundaries of her self and renders her desire to speak with others problematic. The context of this personal interaction is set immediately in terms of geographical and political history.

Mr. Boone's place of origin (hometown) is evoked through the narration of the history of local resistance struggles in the region from which he comes.

> He's a dark, red-brown man from the Yemessee in South Carolina—that swampy land of Indian resistance and armed communities of fugitive slaves, that marshy land at the headwaters of the Combahee, once site of enormous rice plantations and location of Harriet Tubman's successful military action that freed many slaves.

This history of resistance has the effect of disrupting forever all memories of a safe, familiar southern home. As a result of this interaction, Pratt now remembers that home was repressive space built on the surrendering of all responsibility. Pratt's self-reflection, brought on by a consciousness of difference, is nourished and expanded by thinking contextually of other histories and of her own responsibility and implication in them. What we find extraordinary about Pratt as narrator (and person) is her refusal to allow guilt to trap her within the boundaries of a coherent "white" identity. It is this very refusal that makes it possible for her to make the effort to educate herself about the histories of her own and other peoples—an education that indicates to her her own implication in those histories.

Pratt's approach achieves significance in the context of other white feminists' responses to the charge of racism in the women's movement. An all-too-common response has been self-paralyzing guilt and/or defensiveness; another has been the desire to be educated by women of color. The problem is exacerbated by the tendency on the part of some women of color to assume the position of ultimate critic or judge on the basis of the authenticity of their personal experience of oppression. An interesting example of the assignment of fixed positions—the educator/critic (woman of color) and the guilty and silent listener (white woman)—is a recent essay written collaboratively by Elizabeth Spelman and Maria Lugones. The dynamics set up would seem to exempt both parties from the responsibilities of working through the complex historical relations between and among structures of domination and oppression.

In this scenario, the street scene is particularly effective, both spatially and metaphorically. The street evokes a sense of constant movement, change, and temporality. For instance, Pratt can ask herself why the young black woman did not speak to her, why she herself could not speak to the professional white woman in the morning but does at night, why the woman does not respond—all in the space of one evening's walk down three blocks. The meetings on the street also allow for a focus on the racial and ethnic demography of the community as a way of localizing racial, sexual, and class tensions. Since her present location is nowhere (the space does not exist for white people), she constantly has to problematize and define herself anew in relation to people she meets in the street. There is an acute consciousness of being white, woman, lesbian, and Christian-raised, and of which of these aspects is salient in different "speakings."

> Instead, when I walk out in my neighborhood, each speaking to another person has become fraught for me, with the history of race and sex and class; as I walk I have a constant interior discussion with myself, questioning how I acknowledge the presence of another, what I know or don't know about them, and what it means how they acknowledge me.

Thus, walking down the street and speaking to various people—a young white man, young black woman, young professional white woman, young black man, older white woman are all rendered acutely complex and contradictory in terms of actual speakings, imagined speakings, and actual and imagined motivations, responses, and implications—there is no possibility of a coherent self with a continuity of responses across these different "speaking-to's." History intervenes.

For instance, a respectful answer from a young black man might well be "the response violently extorted by history." The voices, sounds, hearing, and sight in particular interactions or within "speaking to's" carry with them their own particular histories; this narrative mode breaks the boundaries of Pratt's experience of being protected, of being a majority.

Scenario 2
Yet I was shaped by my relation to those buildings and to the people in the buildings, by ideas of who should be in the Board of Education, of who should be in the bank handling money, of who should have the guns and the keys to the jail, of who should be *in* the jail; and I was shaped by what I didn't see, or didn't notice, on those streets.

The second scenario is constructed in relation to her childhood home in Alabama and deals very centrally with her relation to her father. Again, she explores that relationship to her father in terms of the geography, demography, and architecture of the hometown; again she reconstructs it by uncovering knowledges, not only the knowledge of those Others who were made invisible to her as a child but also the suppressed knowledge of her own family background. The importance of her elaborating the relation to her father through spatial relations and historical knowledges lies in the contextualization of that relation, and the consequent avoidance of any purely psychological explanation. What is effected, then, is the unsettling of any self-evident relation between blood, skin, heart. And yet, here as elsewhere, the essential relation between blood, skin, heart, home, and identity is challenged without dismissing the power and appeal of those connections.

Pratt introduces her childhood home and her father in order to explain the source of her need to change "what she was born into," to explain what she, or any person who benefits from privileges of class and race, has to gain from change. This kind of self-reflexivity characterizes the entire narrative and takes the form of an attempt to avoid the roles and points of enunciation that she identifies as the legacy of her culture: the roles of judge, martyr, preacher, and peace-maker, and the typically white, Christian, middle-class, and liberal pretense of a concern for Others, an abstract moral or ethical concern for what is right. Her effort to explain her own need to change is elaborated through the memory of childhood scenes, full of strong and suggestive architectural/spatial metaphors which are juxtaposed with images suggesting alternative possibilities.

The effort to explain her motivation for change reminds her of her father. "When I try to think of this, I think of my father. . . ." Pratt recounts a scene from her childhood in which her father took her up the marble steps of the courthouse in the center of the town, the courthouse in which her grandfather had judged for forty years, to the clock tower in order to show her the town from the top and the center. But the father's desire to have her see as he saw, to position her in relation to her town and the world as he was positioned, failed. She was unable, as a small child, to make it to the top of the clock tower and could not see what she would have seen had she been her father or taken his place.

From her vantage point as an adult, she is now able to reconstruct and analyze what she would have seen and would not have seen from the center and the top of the town. She would have seen the Methodist church, the Health Department, for example, and she would not have seen the sawmill of Four Points where the white mill folks lived, or the houses of blacks in Veneer Mill quarters. She had not been able to take that height because she was not her father and could not become like him: she was a white girl, not a boy. This assertion of her difference from the father is undercut, however, in a reversal characteristic of the moves enacted throughout the essay, when she begins a new paragraph by acknowledging: "Yet I was shaped by my relation to those buildings and to the people in the buildings."

What she has gained by rejecting the father's position and vision, by acknowledging her difference from him, is represented as a way of looking, a capacity for seeing the world in overlapping circles, "like movement on the millpond after a fish has jumped, instead of the courthouse square with me at the middle, even if I am on the ground." The contrast between the vision that her father would have her learn and her own vision, her difference and "need," emerges as the contrast between images of constriction, of entrapment, or ever-narrowing circles with a bounded self at the center—the narrow steps to the roof of the courthouse, the clock tower with a walled ledge—and, on the other hand, the image of the millpond with its ever shifting centers. The apparently stable, centered position of the father is revealed to be profoundly unstable, based on exclusions, and characterized by terror.

Change, however, is not a simple escape from constraint to liberation. There is no shedding the literal fear and figurative law of the father, and no reaching a final realm of freedom. There is no new place, no new home. Since neither her view of history nor her construction of herself through it is linear, the past, home, and the father leave traces that are constantly reabsorbed into a shifting vision. She lives, after all, on the edge. Indeed, that early experience of separation and difference from the father is remembered not only in terms of the possibility of change but also in relation to the pain of loss, the loneliness of change, the undiminished desire for home, for familiarity, for some coexistence of familiarity and difference. The day she couldn't make it to the top of the tower "marks the last time I can remember us doing something together, just the two of us; thereafter, I knew on some level that my place was with women, not with him, not with men."

This statement would seem to make the divisions simple, would seem to provide an overriding explanation of her desire for change, for dealing with racism and anti-Semitism, would seem to make her one of a monolithic group of Others in relation to the white father. However, this division, too, is not allowed to remain stable and so to be seen as a simple determinant of identity.

Near the end of her narrative, Pratt recounts a dream in which her father entered her room carrying something like a heavy box, which he put down on her desk. After he left, she noticed that the floor of her room had become a field of dirt with rows of tiny green seed just sprouting. We quote from her narration of the dream, her ambivalence about her father's presence, and her interpretation of it:

> He was so tired; I flung my hands out angrily, told him to go, back to my mother; but crying, because my heart ached; he was my father and so tired. . . . The box was still there, with what I feared: my responsibility for what the men of my culture have done. . . . I was angry: why should I be left with this: I didn't want it: I'd done my best for years to reject it: I wanted no part of what was in it: the benefits of my privilege, the restrictions, the injustice, the pain, the broken urgings of the heart, the unknown horrors. And yet it is mine: I am my father's daughter in the present, living in a world he and my folks helped create. A month after I dreamed this he died; I honor the grief of his life by striving to change much of what he believed in: and my own grief by acknowledging that I saw him caught in the grip of racial, sexual, cultural fears that I still am trying to understand in myself.

Only one aspect of experience is given a unifying and originating function in the text: that is, her lesbianism and love for other women, which has motivated and continues to motivate her efforts to reconceptualize and recreate both her self and home. A careful reading of the narrative demonstrates the complexity of lesbianism, which is constructed as an effect, as well as a source, of her political and familial positions. Its significance, that is, is demonstrated in relation to other experiences rather than assumed as essential determinant.

What lesbianism becomes as the narrative unfolds is that which makes "home" impossible, which makes her self nonidentical, which makes her vulnerable, removing her from the protection afforded those women within privileged races and classes who do not transgress a limited sphere of movement. Quite literally, it is her involvement with another woman that separates the narrator not only from her husband but from her children, as well. It is that which threatens to separate her from her mother, and that which remains a silence between herself and her father. That silence is significant, since, as she points out— and this is a crucial point—her lesbianism is precisely what she can deny, and indeed must deny, in order to benefit fully from the privilege of being white and middle-class and Christian. She can deny it, but only at great expense to herself. Her lesbianism is what she experiences most immediately as the limitation imposed on her by the family, culture, race, and class that afforded her both privilege and comfort, at a price. Learning at what price privilege, comfort, home, and secure notions of self are purchased, the price to herself and ultimately to others is what makes lesbianism a political motivation as well as a personal experience.

It is significant that lesbianism is neither marginalized nor essentialized, but constructed at various levels of experience and abstraction. There are at least two ways in which lesbianism has been isolated in feminist discourse: the homophobic oversight and relegation of it to the margins, and the lesbian-feminist centering of it, which has had at times the paradoxical effect of removing lesbianism and sexuality from their embeddedness in social relations. In Pratt's narrative, lesbianism is that which exposes the extreme limits of what passes itself off as simply human, as universal, as unconstrained by identity, namely, the position of the white middle class. It is also a positive source of solidarity, community, and change. Change has to do with the transgression of boundaries, those boundaries so carefully, so tenaciously, so invisibly drawn around white identity.[6] Change has to do with the transgression of those boundaries.

The insight that white, Christian, middle-class identity, as well as comfort and home, is purchased at a high price is articulated very compellingly in relation to her father. It is significant that there is so much attention to her relation to her father, from whom she describes herself as having been estranged—significant and exemplary of what we think is so important about this narrative.[7] What gets articulated are the contradictions in that relation, her difference from the father, her rejection of his positions, and at the same time her connections to him, her love for him, the ways in which she is his daughter. The complexity of the father-daughter relationship and Pratt's acknowledgment of the differences within it—rather than simply between herself and her father—make it impossible to be satisfied with a notion of difference from the father, literal or figurative, which would (and in much feminist literature does) exempt the daughter from her implication in the structures of privilege/oppression, structures that operate in ways much more complex than the male/female split itself. The narrator expresses the pain, the confusion attendant upon this complexity.

The narrative recounts the use of threat and of protections to consolidate home, identity, community, and privilege, and in the process exposes the underside of the father's protection. Pratt recalls a memory of a night, during the height of the civil rights demonstrations in Alabama, when her father called her in to read her an article in which Martin Luther King, Jr. was accused of sexually abusing young teen-aged girls. "I can only guess that he wanted me to feel that my danger, my physical, sexual danger, would be the result of the release of others from containment. I felt frightened and profoundly endangered, by King, by my father: I could not answer him. It was the first, the only time, I could not answer him. It was the first, the only time, he spoke of sex, in any way, to me."

What emerges is the consolidation of the white home in response to a threatening outside. The rhetorics of sexual victimization or vulnerability of white women is used to establish and enforce unity among whites and to create the myth of the black rapist.[8] Once again, her experience within the family is reinterpreted in relation to the history of race relations in an "outside" in which the family is implicated. What Pratt integrates in the text at such points is a wealth of historical information and analysis of the ideological and social/political operations beyond her "home." In addition to the historical information she unearths both about the atrocities committed in the name of protection, by the Ku Klux Klan and white society in general, and about the resistance to those forms of oppression, she points to the underside of the rhetoric of home, protection, and threatening Others that is currently promoted by Reagan and the New Right. "It is this threatening 'protection' that white Christian men in the U.S. are now offering."

When one conceives of power differently, in terms of its local, institutional, discursive formations, of its positivity, and in terms of the production rather than suppression of forces, then unity is exposed to be a potentially repressive fiction.[9] It is at the moment at which groups and individuals are conceived as agents, as social actors, as desiring subjects that unity, in the sense of coherent group identity, commonality, and shared experience, becomes difficult. Individuals do not fit neatly into unidimensional, self-identical categories. Hence the need for a new sense of political community which gives up the desire for the kind of home where the suppression of positive differences underwrites familial identity. Pratt's narrative makes it clear that connections have to be made at levels other than abstract political interests. And the ways in which intimacy and emotional solidarity figure in notions of political community avoid an all-too-common trivialization of the emotional, on the one hand, and romanticization of the political, on the other.

Scenario 3

Every day I drove around the market house, carrying my two boys between home and grammar school and day care. To me it was an impediment to the flow of traffic, awkward, anachronistic. Sometimes in early spring light it seemed quaint. I had no knowledge and no feeling of the sweat and blood of people's lives that had been mortared into its bricks: nor of their independent joy apart from that place.

The third scenario involves her life in an eastern rural North Carolina town, to which she came in 1974 with her husband and two children. Once again Pratt characterizes her relation to the town, as well as to her husband and children, by means of demographic and architectural markers and metaphors that situate her at the periphery of this "place which is so much like home": a place in which everything would seem to revolve around a stable center, in this case the market house.

I drove around the market house four times a day, traveling on the surface of my own life: circular, repetitive, like one of the games at the county fair. . . .

Once again she is invited to view her home town from the top and center, specifically from the point of view of the white "well-to-do folks," for whom the history of the market house consisted of the fruits, the vegetables, and the tobacco exchanged there. "But not slaves, they said." However, the black waiter serving the well-to-do in the private club overlooking the center of town contests this account, providing facts and dates of the slave trade in that town. This contradiction leaves a trace but does not become significant to her view of her life in that town, a town so much like the landscape of her childhood. It does not become significant, that is, until her own resistance to the limitations of home and family converges with her increasing knowledge of the resistance of other people; converges but is not conflated with those other struggles.

What Pratt uncovers of the town histories is multilayered and complex. She speaks of the relation of different groups of people to the

town and their particular histories of resistance—the breaking up of
Klan rallies by Lumbee Indians, the long tradition of black culture and
resistance, Jewish traditions of resistance, anti-Vietnam protest, and
lesbians' defiance of military codes—with no attempt to unify or equate
the various struggles under a grand polemics of oppression. The coexistence of these histories gives the narrative its complex, rich texture. Both the town and her relation to it change as these histories of
struggle are narrated. Indeed, there is an explicit structural connection
between moments of fear and loss of former homes with the recognition of the importance of interpretation and struggle.

From our perspectives, the integrity of the narrative and the sense
of self have to do with the refusal to make easy divisions and with
the unrelenting exploration of the ways in which the desire for home,
for security, for protection—and not only the desire for them, but the
expectation of a right to these things—operates in Pratt's own conception of political work. She describes her involvement in political
work as having begun when feminism swept through the North Carolina town in which she was living with husband and her two sons in
the 1970s, a period in her life when she felt threatened as a woman
and was forced to see herself as part of a class of people; that she
describes as anathema to the self-concept of middle-class white people, who would just like to "be," unconstrained by labels, by identities,
by consignment to a group, and would prefer to ignore the fact that
their existence and social place are anything other than self-evident,
natural, human.

What differentiates her narration of her development from other
feminist narratives of political awakening is its tentativeness, its con-
sisting of fits and starts, and the absence of linear progress toward a
visible end.[10] This narrator pursues the extent and the ways in which
she carried her white, middle-class conceptions of home around with
her, and the ways in which they informed her relation to politics. There
is an irreconcilable tension between the search for a secure place from
which to speak, within which to act, and the awareness of the price
at which secure places are bought, the awareness of the exclusions,
the denials, the blindnesses on which they are predicated.

The search for a secure place is articulated in its ambivalence and
complexity through the ambiguous use of the words *place* and *space*
in precisely the ways they have become commonplace within feminist
discourse. The moments of terror when she is brought face to face
with the fact that she is "homesick with nowhere to go," that she has
no place, the "kind of vertigo" she feels upon learning of her own
family's history of racism and slaveholding, the sensation of her body

having no fixed place to be, are remembered concurrently with moments of hope, when "she thought she had the beginning of a place for myself."

What she tried to recreate as a feminist, a woman aware of her position vis-à-vis men as a group, is critiqued as a childish place:

> Raised to believe that I could be where I wanted and have what I wanted, as a grown woman I thought I could simply claim what I wanted, even the making of a new place to live with other women. I had no understanding of the limits that I lived within, nor of how much my memory and my experience of a safe space to be was based on places secured by omission, exclusions or violence, and on my submitting to the limits of that place."

The self-reflexiveness that characterizes the narrative becomes especially clear in her discussion of white feminists' efforts at outreach in her North Carolina community. She and ner NOW fellow workers had gone forward "to a new place": "Now we were throwing back safety lines to other women, to pull them in as if they were drowning, to save them. . . . What I felt, deep down, was hope that they would join me in my place, which would be the way I wanted it. I didn't want to have to limit myself."

However, it is not only her increasing knowledge of her exclusion of Others from that place that initiates her rethinking. What is most compelling is her account of her realization that her work in NOW was also based on the exclusion of parts of herself, specifically her lesbianism.[11] Those moments when she would make it the basis of a sameness with other women, a sameness that would make a new place possible, are less convincing than the moments when that possibility too is undercut by her seeing the denials, the exclusions, and the violence that are the conditions of privilege and indeed of love in its Christian formulation. The relationship between love and the occlusion or appropriation of the Other finds expression in her description of her attempts to express her love for her Jewish lover in a poem filled with images from the Jewish tradition, a way of assuming, indeed insisting upon, their similarity by appropriating the other's culture.

The ways in which appropriation or stealth, in the colonial gesture, reproduces itself in the political positions of white feminists is formulated convincingly in a passage about what Pratt calls "cultural impersonation," a term that refers to the tendency among white women to respond with guilt and self-denial to the knowledge of racism and anti-Semitism, and to borrow or take on the identity of the Other in order to avoid not only guilt but pain and self-hatred.[12] It is Pratt's discussion of the negative effects, political and personal, of cultural impersonation that raises the crucial issue of what destructive forms a monolithic (and overly theoretical) critique of identity can take. The claim to a lack of identity or positionality is itself based on privilege, on a refusal to accept responsibility for one's implication in actual historical or social relations, on a denial that positionalities exist or that they matter, the denial of one's own personal history and the claim to a total separation from it. What Minnie Bruce Pratt refuses over and over is the facile equation of her own situation with that of other people.

> When, after Greensboro, I groped toward an understanding of injustice done to others, injustice done outside my narrow circle of being, and to folks not like me, I began to grasp, through my own experience, something of what that injustice might be. . . .
> But I did not feel that my new understanding simply moved me into a place where I joined others to struggle *with* them against common injustices. Because *I* was implicated in the doing of some of these injustices, and I held myself, and my people, responsible.

The tension between the desire for home, for synchrony, for sameness, and the realization of the repressions and violence that make home, harmony, sameness imaginable, and that enforce it, is made clear in the movement of the narrative by very careful and effective reversals which do not erase the positive desire for unity, for Oneness, but destablilize and undercut it. The relation between what Teresa de Lauretis has called the negativity of theory and the positivity of politics is a tension enacted over and over again by this text.[13] The possibility of recreating herself and of creating new forms of community not based on "home" depends for Minnie Bruce Pratt upon work and upon knowledge, not only of the traditions and culture of Others but also of the positive forms of struggle within her own. It depends on acknowledging not only her ignorance and her predjudices but also her fears, above all the fear of loss that accompanies change.

The risk of rejection by one's own kind, by one's family, when one exceeds the limits laid out or the self-definition of the group, is not made easy; again, the emphasis on her profoundly ambivalent relationship to her father is crucial. When the alternatives would seem to be either the enclosing, encircling, constraining circle of home, or nowhere to go, the risk is enormous. The assumption of, or desire for, another safe place like "home" is challenged by the realization that "unity"—interpersonal as well as political—is itself necessarily fragmentary, itself that which is struggled for, chosen, and hence unstable

by definition; it is not based on "sameness," and there is no perfect
fit. But there is agency as opposed to passivity.

The fear of rejection by one's own kind refers not only to the family
of origin but also to the potential loss of a second family, the women's
community, with its implicit and often unconscious replication of the
conditions of home.[14] When we justify the homogeneity of the wom-
en's community in which we move on the basis of the need for community, the need for home, what, Pratt asks, distinguishes our community from the justifications advanced by women who have joined
the Klan for "family, community, and protection"? The relationship
between the loss of community and the loss of self is crucial. To the
extent that identity is collapsed with home and community and based
on homogeneity and comfort, on skin, blood, and heart, the giving
up of home will necessarily mean the giving up of self and vice versa.

> Then comes the fear of nowhere to go: no old home with family: no
> new one with women like ourselves: and no place to be expected with
> folks who have been systematically excluded by ours. And with our
> fear comes the doubt: Can I maintain my principles against my need
> for the love and presence of others like me? It is lonely to be separated
> from others because of injustice, but it is also lonely to break with our
> own in opposition to that injustice.

The essay ends with a tension between despair and optimism over
political conditions and the possibilities for change. Pratt walks down
Maryland Avenue in Washington, D.C.—the town that is now her
"hometown"—protesting against U.S. invasions, Grenada, the marines
in Lebanon, the war in Central America, the acquittals of the North
Carolina Klan and Nazi perpetrators. The narrative has come full circle,
and her consciousness of her "place" in this town—the Capital—en-
compasses both local and global politics, and her own implication in
them. The essay ends with the following statement: "I continue the
struggle with myself and the world I was born in."

Pratt's essay on feminism, racism, and anti-Semitism is not a litany
of oppression but an elaboration, indeed an enactment, of careful and
constant differentiations which refuses the all-too-easy polemic that
opposes victims to perpetrators. The exposure of the arbitrariness and
the instability of positions within systems of oppression evidences a
conception of power that refuses totalizations, and can therefore account for the possibility of resistance. "The system" is revealed to be
not one but multiple, overlapping, intersecting systems or relations
that are historically constructed and recreated through everyday practices and interactions, and that implicate the individual in contradic-

tory ways. All of that without denying the operations of actual power differences, overdetermined though they may be. Reconceptualizing power without giving up the possibility of conceiving power.

Community, then, is the product of work, of struggle; it is inherently unstable, contextual; it has to be constantly reevaluated in relation to critical political priorities; and it is the product of interpretation, interpretation based on an attention to history, to the concrete, to what Foucault has called subjugated knowledges.[15] There is also, however, a strong suggestion that community is related to experience, to history. For if identity and community are not the product of essential connections, neither are they merely the product of political urgency or necessity. For Pratt, they are a constant recontextualizing of the relationship between personal/group history and political priorities.

It is crucial, then, to avoid two traps, the purely experiential and the theoretical oversight of personal and collective histories. In Pratt's narrative, personal history acquires a materiality in the constant rewriting of herself in relation to shifting interpersonal and political contexts. This rewriting is an interpretive act which is itself embedded in social and political practice.

> In this city where I am no longer of the majority by color or culture, I tell myself every day: In this *world* you aren't the superior race or culture, and never were, whatever you were raised to think: and are you getting ready to be *in* this world?
> And I answer myself back: I'm trying to learn how to live, to have the speaking-to extend beyond the moment's word, to act so as to change the unjust circumstances that keep us from being able to speak to each other; I'm trying to get a little closer to the longed-for but unrealized world, where we each are able to live, but not by trying to make someone less than us, not by someone else's blood or pain: yes, that's what I'm trying to do with my living now.

We have used our reading of this text to open up the question of how political community might be reconceptualized within feminist practice. We do not intend to suggest that Pratt's essay, or any single autobiographical narrative, offers "an answer." Indeed, what this text has offered is a pretext for posing questions. The conflation of Pratt the person with the narrator and subject of this text has led us and our students to want to ask, for example, how such individual self-reflection and critical practice might translate into the building of political collectivity. And to consider more specifically, the possible political implications and effects of a white middle-class woman's "choice" to move to H St. NE. Certainly, we might usefully keep in mind that the approach to identity, to unity, and to political alliances in Pratt's text is itself grounded in and specific to her complex positionalities in a society divided very centrally by race, gender, class, ethnicity, and sexualities.

N O T E S

1. Zillah Eisenstein, *Feminism and Sexual Equality* (New York: Monthly Review, 1984).

2. See, for example, Bernice Johnson Reagon, "Coalition Politics: Turning the Century" and Barbara Smith's introduction in *Home Girls: A Black Feminist Anthology* (New York: Kitchen Table Press, 1984), and Cherríe Moraga, *Loving in the War Years* (Boston: South End Press, 1984).

3. Of course, feminist intellectuals have read various antihumanist strategies as having made similar arguments about the turn of the last century and the future of this one. In her contribution to a *Yale French Studies* special issue on French feminism, Alice Jardine argues against an "American" feminist tendency to establish and maintain an illusory unity based on incorporation, a unity and centrism that relegate differences to the margins or out of sight. "Feminism," she writes, "must not open the door to modernity then close it behind itself." In her Foucauldian critique of American feminist/humanist empiricism, Peggy Kamuf warns against the assumption that she sees guiding much feminist thought, "an unshaken faith in the ultimate arrival at essential truth through the empirical method of accumulation of knowledge, knowledge about women" ("Replacing Feminist Criticism," *Diacritics*, Summer 1982, p. 45). She goes on to spell out the problem of humanism in a new guise:

> There is an implicit assumption in such programs that this knowledge about women can be produced in and of itself without seeking any support within those very structures of power which—or so it is implied—have prevented knowledge of the feminine in the past. Yet what is it about those structures which could have succeeded until now in excluding such knowledge if it is not a similar appeal to a "we" that has had a similar faith in its own eventual constitution as a delimited and totalizable object?

4. For incisive and insistent analyses of the uses and limitations of deconstructive and poststructuralist analytic strategies for feminist intellectual and political projects, see in particular the work of Teresa de Lauretis, *Alice Doesn't: Feminism, Semiotics, Cinema* (Bloomington: Indiana University Press, 1984), and Alice Jardine, *Gynesis: Configurations of Woman and Modernity* (Ithaca: Cornell University Press, 1985).

5. This notion of a female "true self" underlying a male-imposed "false consciousness" is evident in the work of cultural feminists such as Mary Daly, *Gyn/ecology: The Metaethics of Radical Feminism* (Boston: Beacon Press, 1978); Susan Brownmiller, *Against Our Will: Men, Women, and Rape* (New York: Simon and Schuster, 1975); and Susan Griffin, *Woman and Nature: The Roaring inside Her* (New York: Harper and Row, 1978) and *Pornography and Silence* (New York: Harper and Row, 1981).

6. For analyses and critiques of tendencies to romanticize lesbianism, see essays by Carole Vance, Alice Echols, and Gayle Rubin in *Pleasure and Danger*, ed. Carole S. Vance (Boston; Routledge and Kegan Paul, 1984), on the "cultural feminism" of such writers as Griffin, Rich, Daly, and Gearheart.

7. Feminist theorists such as Nancy Chodorow (*The Reproduction of Mothering: Psychoanalysis and the Sociology of Gender* [Berkeley: University of California Press, 1978]), Carol Gilligan (*In a Different Voice* [Boston: Harvard University Press, 1983]), and Adrienne Rich (*Of Woman Born* [New York: W. W. Norton, 1976]) have focused exclusively on the psychosocial configuration of mother/daughter relationships. Jessica Benjamin, in her paper in this volume, "A Desire of One's Own," points to the problem of not theorizing "the father" in feminist psychoanalytic work, emphasizing the significance of the father in the construction of sexuality within the family.

8. See critiques of Brownmiller (1975) by Angela Davis (*Women, Race, and Class* [Boston: Doubleday, 1983]), Bell Hooks (*Ain't I a Woman: Black Women and Feminism* [Boston; South End Press, 1981]), and Jacqueline Dowd Hall ("The Mind That Burns in Each Body: Women, Rape, and Racial Violence," in *Powers of Desire*, ed. Ann Snitow, Christine Stansell, and Sharon Thompson [New York: Monthly Review Press, 1983], pp. 328-49).

9. For a discussion of the relevance of Foucault's reconceptualization of power to feminist theorizing, see Biddy Martin, "Feminism, Criticism, and Foucault," *New German Critique*, no. 27 (1982), pp. 3-30.

10. One good example of the numerous narratives of political awakening in feminist work is the transformation of the stripper in the film *Not A Love Story* (directed by Bonnie Klein, 1982) from exploited sex worker to enlightened feminist. Where this individual's linear and unproblematic development is taken to be emblematic of problems in and feminist solutions to pornography, the complexities of the issues involved are circumvented and class differences are erased.

11. For a historical account of the situation of lesbians and attitudes toward lesbianism in NOW, see Sidney Abbot and Barbara Love, *Sappho Was A Right On Woman: A Liberated View of Lesbianism* (New York: Stein and Day, 1972).

12. For writings that address the construction of colonial discourse, see Homi Bhabha, "The Other Question—the Stereotype and Colonial Discourse," *Screen* 24 (November-December 1983):18-36; Franz Fanon, *Black Skin White Masks* (London: Paladin, 1970); Albert Memmi, *The Colonizer and the Colonized* (Boston: Beacon Press, 1965); Chandra Talpade Mohanty, "Under Western Eyes: Feminist Scholarship and Colonial Discourses," forthcoming in *boundary 2* (1985); Edward Said, *Orientalism* (New York: Vintage, 1979); and Gayatri Chakravorty Spivak, "French Feminism in an International Frame," *Yale French Studies*, no. 62 (1981), pp. 154-84.

13. See especially the introduction in de Lauretis, *Alice Doesn't*, and Teresa de Lauretis, "Comparative Literature among the Disciplines: Politics" (unpublished manuscript).

14. For an excellent discussion of the effects of conscious and unconscious pursuits of safety, see Carole Vance's introduction to *Pleasure and Danger*, in which she elaborates upon the obstacles to theorizing embedded in such pursuits.

15. Michel Foucault, *The History of Sexuality: Vol. 1* (New York: Vintage, 1980).

THIRTEEN

Female Grotesques: Carnival and Theory

Mary Russo

Pretext

There is a phrase that still resonates from childhood. Who says it? The mother's voice—not my own mother's, perhaps, but the voice of an aunt, an older sister, or the mother of a friend. It is a harsh, matronizing phrase, and it is directed toward the behavior of other women:

"She" [the other woman] is making a spectacle out of herself.

Making a spectacle out of oneself seemed a specifically feminine danger. The danger was of an exposure. Men, I learned somewhat later in life, "exposed themselves," but that operation was quite deliberate and circumscribed. For a woman, making a spectacle out of herself had more to do with a kind of inadvertency and loss of boundaries: the possessors of large, aging, and dimpled thighs displayed at the public beach, of overly rouged cheeks, of a voice shrill in laughter, or of a sliding bra strap—a loose, dingy bra strap especially—were at once caught out by fate and blameworthy. It was my impression that these women had done something wrong, had stepped, as it were, into the limelight out of turn—too young or too old, too early or too late—and yet anyone, any *woman*, could make a spectacle out of herself if she was not careful. It is a feature of my own history and education that in contemplating these dangers, I grew to admire both the extreme strategies of the cool, silent, and cloistered St. Clare (enclosed, with a room of her own) and the lewd, exuberantly parodistic Mae West.

Although the models, of course, change, there is a way in which radical negation, silence, withdrawal, and invisibility, and the bold affirmations of feminine performance, imposture, and masquerade (purity and danger) have suggested cultural politics for women.

Theory of Carnival and the Carnival of Theory

These extremes are not mutually exclusive, and in various and interesting ways they have figured round each other. Feminist theory and cultural production more generally have most recently brought together these strategies in approaching the questions of difference and the reconstruction or counterproduction of knowledge. In particular, the impressive amount of work across the discourse of carnival, or, more properly, the carnivalesque—much of it in relation to the work of the Russian scholar Mikhail Bakhtin[1]—has translocated the issues of bodily exposure and containment, disguise and gender masquerade, abjection and marginality, parody and excess, to the field of the social constituted as a symbolic system. Seen as a productive category, affirmative and celebratory (a Nietzschean gay science), the discourse of carnival moves away from modes of critique that would begin from some Archimedean point of authority without, to models of transformation and counterproduction situated within the social system and symbolically at its margins.[2]

The reintroduction of the body and categories of the body (in the case of carnival, the "grotesque body") into the realm of what is called the political has been a central concern of feminism. What would seem to be of great interest at this critical conjuncture in relation to this material would be an assessment of how the materials on carnival as historical performance may be configured with the materials on carnival as semiotic performance; in other words, how the relation between the symbolic and cultural constructs of femininity and Womanness and the experience of *women* (as variously identified and subject to multiple determinations) might be brought together toward a dynamic model of a new social subjectivity. The early work of Julia Kristeva on semiotics, subjectivity, and textual revolution and the more recent contributions of Teresa de Lauretis in mapping the terrain of a genuinely sociological and feminist semiotics are crucial to this undertaking.[3] This project is the grand one. More modestly, an examination of the materials on carnival can also recall limitations, defeats, and indifferences generated by carnival's complicitous place in dominant culture. There are especial dangers for women and other excluded or marginalized groups within carnival, though even the double jeopardy that I will describe may suggest an ambivalent redeployment of taboos around the female body as grotesque (the pregnant body, the aging body, the irregular body) and as unruly when set loose in the public sphere.

I would begin by citing briefly some of the important work on carnival in various fields (I could not pretend to be exhaustive, since the volume of recent work on Bakhtin alone is staggering). Here, I can only indicate some major lines of interest and weakness in the theory of carnival and cite some similar instances in what might be called the carnival of theory, that is, in the rhetorical masking, gesturing, and mise-en-scène of contemporary writing.

Not at all surprisingly, much of the early work on carnival in anthropology and social history dates from the late sixties, when enactments of popular protest, counterculture, experimental theater, and multimedia art were all together suggestive of the energies and possibilities of unlimited cultural and social transformation. In many ways this essay is generated from the cultural surplus of that era. The work of Mary Douglas and Victor Turner, which was as influential in social history as, more recently, the work of Clifford Geertz, saw in the human body the prototype of society, the nation-state, and the city, and in the social dramas of transition and "rituals of status reversal" evidence of the reinforcement of social structure, hierarchy, and order through inversion. In liminal states, thus, temporary loss of boundaries tends to redefine social frames, and such topsy-turvy or time-out is inevitably set right and on course.[4] This structural view of carnival as essentially conservative is both strengthened and enlarged by historical analysis, which tends, of course, to be the political history of domination. The extreme difficulty of producing lasting social change does not diminish the usefulness of these symbolic models of transgression, and the histories of subaltern and counterproductive cultural activity are never as neatly closed as structural models might suggest.

Natalie Davis, in what remains the most interesting piece on carnival and gender, "Women on Top," argues dialectically that in early modern Europe, carnival and the image of the carnivalesque woman "undermined as well as reinforced" the renewal of existing social structure:

> The image of the disorderly woman did not always function to keep women in their place. On the contrary, it was a multivalent image that could operate, first, to widen behavioral options for women within and even outside marriage, and second, to sanction riot and political disobedience for both men and women in a society that allowed the lower orders few formal means of protest. Play with an unruly woman is partly a chance for temporary release from the traditional and stable hierarchy; but it is also part of the conflict over efforts to change the basic distribution of power within society.[5]

Among Davis's very interesting examples of the second possibility—that is, that the image of the unruly or carnivalesque woman actually worked to incite and embody popular uprisings—is the Wiltshire enclosure riots of 1641, where rioting men were led by male cross-dressers who called themselves "Lady Skimmington" (a skimmington was a ride through the streets mocking a henpecked husband, the name probably referring to the big skimming ladle that could be used for husband beatings).[6] The projection of the image of the fierce virago onto popular movements, especially a movement such as this one, involving the transgression of boundaries, is suggestive from the point of view of social transformation. What may it tell us about the construction of the female subject in history within this political symbology? Merely to sketch out the obvious problems in working toward an answer to this question, one might begin with the assumption that the history of the enclosure riots and the image of the unruly woman are not direct reflections of one another; both contain ambiguities and gender asymmetries that require historical and textual readings.

These readings are difficult in both areas. First, the history of popular movements has been largely the history of men; a stronger history of women in mixed and autonomous uprisings is needed to assess the place of women as historical subjects in relation to such uprisings. Second, as a form of representation, masquerade of the feminine (what psychoanalytic theory will insist is femininity par excellence) has its distinct problems. The carnivalized woman such as Lady Skimmington, whose comic female masquerade of those "feminine" qualities of strident wifely aggression, behind whose skirts men are protected and provoked to actions, is an image that, however counterproduced, perpetuates the dominant (and in this case misogynistic) representation of women by men. In the popular tradition of this particular example, Lady Skimmington is mocked alongside her henpecked husband, for she embodies the most despised aspects of "strong" femininity, and her subordinate position in society is in part underlined in this enactment of power reversal.

Furthermore, although the origins of this image in male-dominated culture may be displaced, there remain questions of enactment and gender-layering. Are women who have taken on this role (as opposed to men cross-dressing) as effective as male cross-dressers? Or is it, like the contemporary "straight" drag of college boys in the amateur theatricals of elite universities, a clear case of sanctioned play for men, while it is something always risking self-contempt for women to put on "the feminine"? In addition, one must ask of any representation other questions—questions of style, genre, and contextuality which may cut across the issue of gender. Is the parodistic and hyperbolic style of Lady Skimmington as a leader of men a sign of insurgency and lower-class solidarity for women and men? Does this comic female style work to free women from a more confining aesthetic? Or are women again so identified with style itself that they are as estranged from its liberatory and transgressive effects as they are from their own bodies as signs in culture generally? In what sense can women really produce or make spectacles out of themselves?

Historical inquiry may yield instances of performance (symbolic and political) that may bypass the pessimism of psychoanalytically oriented answers to this last question, but only if that history begins to understand the complexity of treating signifying systems and "events" together. In this regard, even the work on female political iconography and social movements by very distinguished historians, such as Maurice Agulhon and Eric Hobsbawm, remains problematic.[7] This methodological difficulty does not prevent historians from becoming increasingly aware of gender differences in relation to the carnivalesque. Other social historians have documented the insight of the anthropologist Victor Turner that the marginal position of women and others in the "indicative" world makes their presence in the "subjunctive" or possible world of the topsy-turvy carnival "quintessentially" dangerous; in fact, as Emmanuel Le Roy Ladurie shows in *Carnival at Romans*, Jews were stoned, and there is evidence that women were raped, during carnival festivities.[8] In other words, in the everyday indicative world, women and their bodies, certain bodies, in certain public framings, in certain public spaces, are always already transgressive—dangerous, and in danger.

With these complexities no doubt in mind, Davis concluded her brilliant article with the hope that "the woman on top might even facilitate innovation in historical theory and political behavior" (p. 131). Since the writing of her article, the conjuncture of a powerful women's movement and feminist scholarship has facilitated further interrogation of the relationship between symbology and social change. The figure of the female transgressor as public spectacle is still powerfully resonant, and the possibilities of redeploying this representation as a demystifying or utopian model have not been exhausted.

The Carnivalesque Body

Investigation of linguistic and cultural contexts in relation to categories of carnival and the body have been recently inspired by a new reception in English-speaking countries of the work of the Russian scholar and linguist Mikhail Bakhtin. Like the work of Davis and Le Roy Ladurie, Bakhtin's work on carnival is at one level a historical description of carnival in early modern Europe. It offers, as well, a proscriptive model of a socialist collectivity.

In his introduction to his study of Rabelais, Bakhtin enumerates three forms of carnival folk culture: ritual spectacles (which include feasts, pageants, and marketplace festivals of all kinds); comic verbal compositions, parodies both oral and written; and various genres of billingsgate (curses, oaths, profanations, marketplace speech). The laughter of carnival associated with these spectacles and unconstrained speech in the Middle Ages was for Bakhtin entirely positive. The Romantic period, in contrast, saw laughter "cut down to cold humour, irony, sarcasm" (RW, pp. 37-38). The privatism and individualism of this later humor make it unregenerative and lacking in communal hilarity. Without pretense to historical neutrality, Bakhtin's focus on carnival in early modern Europe contains a critique of modernity and its stylistic effects as a radical diminishment of the possibilities of human freedom and cultural production. He considers the culture of modernity to be as austere and bitterly isolating as the official religious culture of the Middle Ages, which he contrasts with the joy and heterogeneity of carnival and the carnivalesque style and spirit. Bakhtin's view of Rabelais and carnival is in some ways nostalgic for a socially diffuse oppositional context which has been lost, but which is perhaps more importantly suggestive of a future social horizon that may release new possibilities of speech and social performance.

The categories of carnivalesque speech and spectacle are heterogeneous, in that they contain the protocols and styles of high culture in and from a position of debasement. The masks and voices of carnival resist, exaggerate, and destabilize the distinctions and boundaries that mark and maintain high culture and organized society. It is as if the carnivalesque body politic had ingested the entire corpus of high culture and, in its bloated and irrepressible state, released it in fits and starts in all manner of recombination, inversion, mockery, and degradation. The political implications of this heterogeneity are obvious: it sets carnival apart from the merely oppositional and reactive; carnival and the carnivalesque suggest a redeployment or counterproduction of culture, knowledge, and pleasure. In its multivalent oppositional play, carnival refuses to surrender the critical and cultural tools of the dominant class, and in this sense, carnival can be seen above all as a site of insurgency, and not merely withdrawal.

The central category under which Bakhtin organizes his reading of Rabelais as a carnivalesque text is "grotesque realism," with particular emphasis on the grotesque body. The grotesque body is the open, protruding, extended, secreting body, the body of becoming, process, and change. The grotesque body is opposed to the classical body, which is monumental, static, closed, and sleek, corresponding to the aspirations of bourgeois individualism; the grotesque body is connected to the rest of the world. Significantly, Bakhtin finds his concept of the grotesque embodied in the Kerch terracotta figurines of senile, pregnant hags. Here is Bakhtin describing the figurines:

> This is typical and very strongly expressed grotesque. It is ambivalent. It is pregnant death, a death that gives birth. There is nothing completed, nothing calm and stable in the bodies of these old hags. They combine senile, decaying, and deformed flesh with the flesh of new life, conceived but as yet unformed. (*RW*, pp. 25-26) "Moreover," he writes, "the old hags are laughing" (*RW*, p. 25).

Homologously, the grotesque body is the figure of the socialist state to come, a state unfinished, which, as it "outgrows itself, transgresses its own limits" (*RW*, p. 26). For Bakhtin, this body is, as well, a model for carnival language; a culturally productive linguistic body in constant semiosis. But for the feminist reader, this image of the pregnant hag is more than ambivalent. It is loaded with all of the connotations of fear and loathing associated with the biological processes of reproduction and of aging. Bakhtin, like many other social theorists of the nineteenth and twentieth centuries, fails to acknowledge or incorporate the social relations of gender in his semiotic model of the body politic, and thus his notion of the Female Grotesque remains, in all directions, repressed and undeveloped.

Yet, Bakhtin's description of these ancient crones is at least exuberant. Almost to prove his point about the impossibility of collective mirth over such images in the period of late capitalism, here is a version of the same female grotesque in the voice of Paul Céline:

> Women you know, they wane by candlelight, they spoil, melt, twist, ooze! [. . . The end of tapers is a horrible sight, the end of ladies too. . . .][9]

Quoted and glossed by Julia Kristeva as a portrait of "a muse in the true tradition of the lowly genres—apocalyptic, Menippean, and carnevalesque," this passage suggests the dark festival of transgression that she charts in *Powers of Horror*. This book, which contrasts in tone with Kristeva's indispensable application of Bakhtin in, for instance,

"Word, Dialogue, and the Novel" and *Polylogue*, draws on Mary Douglas's categories of purity and defilement to arrive, through the analytical processes of transference, at the brink of abjection.

Through the convolutions of Céline's relentlessly misogynist and anti-Semitic writing, Kristeva as author and problematized subject has projected herself toward the grotesque, which she sees as the "undoer of narcissism and of all imaginary identity as well" (p. 208). Her study is richly intertextual. As Kristeva focusses on Céline, her own text increasingly takes on his rhetoric of abjection, which interestingly comes to rest in the category of the maternal. Kristeva writes: "Abject . . . the jettisoned object, is radically excluded and draws me toward the place where meaning collapses . . . on the edge of non-existence and hallucination" (p. 2). And elsewhere: "Something maternal . . . bears upon the uncertainty of what I call abjection" (p. 208). The fascination with the maternal body in childbirth, the fear of and repulsion from it throughout the chosen texts of Céline, constitutes it here again as a privileged sight of liminality and defilement. Kristeva writes:

> When Céline locates the ultimate of abjection—and thus the supreme and sole interest of literature—in the birth-giving scene, he makes amply clear which fantasy is involved: something horrible to see at the impossible doors of the invisible—the mother's body. The scene of scenes is here not the so-called primal scene but the one of giving birth, incest turned inside out, flayed identity. Giving birth: the height of bloodshed and life, scorching moment of hesitation (between inside and outside, ego and other, life and death), horror and beauty, sexuality and the blunt negation of the sexual. . . . At the doors of the feminine, at the doors of abjection, as I defined the term earlier, we are also, with Céline, given the most daring X-ray of the "drive foundations" of fascism.[10]

While there are many general reasons for questioning the use of the maternal in recent French criticism, here, I think, the point may be that the accumulated horror and contempt that these descriptions of the maternal body suggest generate a subliminal defense of the maternal, which then reemerges in Kristeva as an idealized category far from the realities of motherhood, either as a construction or as a lived experience.[11] Jews, unlike mothers, would seem to merely drop out of the field of abjection, as the anti-Semitism of Céline becomes for Kristeva a problem of maintaining the categorical imperatives of identity and the political.[12]

The book ends on a note of mystical subjectivity: near "the quiet shore of contemplation" (p. 210), far from the polis. On the verge, at the limit of this avant-garde frontier, there remains, for Kristeva, only writing.[13] Peter Stallybrass and Allon White, in their book on the politics and poetics of transgression, have called the exclusion of the already marginalized in moves such as these "displaced abjection."[14] As I have argued, both in the history of carnival and in its theory, the category of the female body as grotesque (in, for instance, pregnancy or aging) brings to light just such displacements. How this category might be used affirmatively to destabilize the idealizations of female beauty or to realign the mechanisms of desire, would be the subject of another study.

Carnival of Theory

There has been, as well, a carnival of theory at the discursive level, in the poetics of postmodernist criticism and feminist writing. It has included all manner of textual travesty, "mimetic rivalry," semiotic delinquency, parody, teasing, posing, flirting, masquerade, seduction, counterseduction, tight-rope walking, and verbal aerialisms of all kinds. Performances of displacement, double displacements, and more have permeated much feminist writing in our attempts to survive or muscle in on the discourses of Lacanian psychoanalysis, deconstruction, avant-garde writing, and postmodernist visual art. It could even be said, with reservation, that in relation to academic institutions, what has come to be called "theory" has constituted a kind of carnival space. The practice of criticism informed by this theory has taken great license stylistically, and in its posing posed a threat of sorts.

It is interesting to consider the discourse of carnival and poststructuralism together. In 1980, Michèle Richman, in her essay entitled "Sex and Signs: Language of French Feminist Criticism," saw in the proliferation of literature on festival in France a reaction primarily to structuralism and to the structuralist economy of exchange within which, as Lévi-Strauss described it, women circulate as signs but are not theorized as sign producers.[15] The festival or carnival discourse drew upon the work of Marcel Mauss (and, as importantly, on the writing of Georges Bataille) on the gift or *dépense* as that which exceeds this linguistically modeled economy. As Richman indicates, the discussion of *dépense* was relocated within a more general libidinal economy of desire. The generosity of femininity and feminine writing (*écriture féminine*) is privileged over male *dépense*, which is understood as being simultaneously a demand. The female body is the site of this desirous excess.

In terms strikingly similar to Bakhtin's formulation of the grotesque body as continuous process, Hélène Cixous calls this body "the body without beginning and without end."[16] Female sexuality and especially the mother's body, as it figures simultaneously demarcation and dissolution of identity, serve this cultural project of disrupting the political economy of the sign as it is produced in dominant discourse. This *écriture féminine*, which has been admirably discussed elsewhere by many American feminists, can be and has been done by men (in fact, modernist writers such as Joyce are often mentioned as models); how the male-authored or travestied "feminine" is different, and how the inscription of the female body in the texts produced by women may be usefully contextualized elsewhere are still important and unanswered questions, although the critiques of this feminization of writing as essentialist must be taken into account in reconsiderations of these topics.[17]

Beyond essentialism, there are, as I have indicated earlier, other historical and anthropological warnings to heed. Even within France there have been critiques of the feminine textual festival. Annie Leclerc has chided the "delirious adultors of the festival," and Catherine Clément in *La jeune née* parallels the carnivalesque with hysterical crisis. In terms similar to earlier critiques of carnival, she sees the cultural category of hysteria as

> the only form of contestation possible in certain types of social organization, within the context of the village community; it is also a safety valve. This language not yet at the point of verbal expression, restrained within the bond of the body ... remains convulsive. Men look but they do not hear.[18]

Historically, Clément is right: hysterics and madwomen generally have ended up in the attic or in the asylum, their gestures of pain and defiance having served only to put them out of circulation. As a figure of representation, however, hysteria may be less recuperable. The famous photographs commissioned by Charcot, which chart the various stages of hysteria in the patients of Salpêtrière, fix in attitude and gesture, in grimaces and leaps, a model of performance not unlike the fashionable histrionics of the great Romantic actresses and circus artists of the late nineteenth century. These paid performers were, like women hysterics, "seen but not heard," in one sense, since the scene of their livelihood, their context, it can be argued, was arranged by and for the male viewer. Nonetheless, they used their bodies in public, in extravagant ways that could have only provoked wonder and ambivalence in the female viewer, as such latitude of movement and attitude was not permitted most women without negative consequences.

This hyperbolic style, this "overacting," like the staged photographs of Salpêtrière (whatever Charcot's claims were to scientific documentation), can be read as double representations: as mimicries of the somatizations of the women patients whose historical performances were lost to themselves and recuperated into the medical science and medical discourse which maintain their oppressive hold on women. The photographs of Salpêtrière especially strike us as uncanny because of the repetitiveness of the hysterical performance. It is not only the content of hysterical behavior that strikes us as grotesque but its representation: if hysteria is a dis-play, these photographs display the display. If hysteria is understood as feminine in its image, accoutrements, and stage business (rather than in its physiology), then it may be used to rig us up (for lack of the phallic term) into discourse. The possibility, indeed the necessity, of using the female body in this sense allows for the distance necessary for articulation. Luce Irigaray describes this provisional strategy as follows:

> To play with mimesis is thus, for a woman, to try to recover the place of her exploitation by discourse, without allowing herself simply to be reduced to it. It means to resubmit herself—inasmuch as she is on the side of "perceptible," of "matter"—to "ideas," in particular to ideas about herself, that are elaborated in/by masculine logic, but so as to make "visible," by an effect of playful repetition, what was supposed to remain invisible: the cover-up of a possible operation of the feminine in language. It also means to "unveil" the fact that, if women are such good mimics, it is because they are not simply reabsorbed into this function.[19]

What is called mimesis here is elsewhere, with various modifications, called masquerade. (Irigaray herself reserves the latter term to refer negatively to the false position of women experiencing desire only as male desire for them.) Female sexuality as masquerade is a well-noted psychoanalytic category. Jacques Lacan, a great *poseur* himself, has written of female sexuality as masking a lack, pretending to hide what is in fact not there:

> Paradoxical as this formulation might seem, I would say that it is in order to be the phallus, that is to say, the signifier of the desire of the Other, that the woman will reject an essential part of her femininity, notably all its attributes through masquerade. It is for what she is not that she expects to be desired as well as loved.[20]

The mask here is seen as feminine (for men and women) rather than something that hides a stable feminine identity. Femininity is a mask

which masks nonidentity. According to Lacan, that produces an unexpected side effect for the man anxious to appear manly:

> The fact that femininity takes refuge in this mask, because of the *Ver-
> drangung* inherent to the phallic mark of desire, has the strange con-
> sequence that, in the human being, virile display itself appears as fem-
> inine.[21]

In film theory, Mary Ann Doane has problematized the female spectator, using the essay of Joan Riviere on "Womanliness and Masquerade."[22] Her argument is that masquerade can "manufacture a
distance from the image, to generate a problematic within which the
image is manipulable, producible, and readable by the women."[23] It
is, in other words, a way around the theorization of the spectator only
in terms of the male gaze and male categories of voyeurism and fe-
tishistic pleasure. More generally, her discussion of Riviere is extremely useful in explaining the asymmetries of transvestism, which
for a woman has always been necessary in some sense in order for
her to take part in a man's world. For a woman to dress, act, or position
herself in discourse as a man is easily understandable and culturally
compelling. To "act like a woman" beyond narcissism and masochism
is, for psychoanalytic theory, trickier. That is the critical and hopeful
power of the masquerade. Deliberately assumed and foregrounded,
femininity as mask, for a man, is a take-it-or-leave-it proposition; for
a woman, a similar flaunting of the feminine is a take-it-*and*-leave-it
possibility. To put on femininity with a vengeance suggests the power
of taking it off.

These considerations account for some of the interest in masquerade for those contemporary artists and critics whose work on imposture and dissimulation tends to stress the constructed, the invented,
and (to use Gayatri Spivak's wonderful phrase) the "scrupulously
fake."[24] Spivak reads Nietzsche's characterization of female sexual
pleasure as masquerade ("they 'give themselves,' even when they—
give themselves. The female is so artistic") as an originary displacement, occluding "an unacknowledged envy: a man cannot fake an
orgasm."[25] Reading Derrida, she sees the figure of woman displaced
twice over. "Double displacement," she suggests, might be undone
in carefully fabricated "useful and scrupulous fake readings in place
of the passively active fake orgasm." Such readings may suggest new
ways of making new spectacles of oneself.

Other work on masquerade has a more explicitly sociopolitical dimension, which greatly enriches psychoanalytic and deconstructive
approaches to the material (I am thinking, for instance, of Dick Heb-

dige's work on subculture and Homi Bhabha's recent work on mimicry and the colonial subject).[26] For feminist theory, particularly, a more specifically historical and social use of masquerade may be needed, perhaps in the context of larger discussions of social groups and categories of the feminine mask in colonized and subcultural contexts, or in relation to other guises of the carnivalesque body. Nonetheless, the hyperboles of masquerade and carnival suggest, at least, some preliminary "acting out" of the dilemmas of femininity.

General Laughter and the Laughter of Carnival

Feminist theory itself has been travestied, hidden, and unacknowledged in many discussions of subjectivity and gender. It is part of what Elaine Showalter has called "critical cross-dressing."[27] The fathers of French theory alluded to here are in fact all masters of *mise-en-scène*. Even Derrida, whose persona has been more diffidently drawn in his writings, has been recently showcased as a carnival master.

The interview with Derrida published in *Critical Exchange*, in which he speaks of women and feminism, is quite as interesting for what he says about feminists as for the *mise-en-scène*.[28] Derrida restates his reservations about feminism as a form of phallogocentrism (fair enough). Later, he says that feminism is tantamount to phallogocentrism (not so fair).[29] James Creech, who edited and translated the interview, states that he attempted "to reproduce its conversational tone, with interruptions, ellipses, suspensions and laughter that marked a very cordial and freeform discussion. Essentially nothing has been edited out, and the reader can follow the sub-text of associations which lead from one moment of discussion to another" (p. 30). The transcription is punctuated by parenthetical laughter and occasionally, in bold face, "General Laughter." For instance:

> Certain feminists, certain women struggling in the name of feminism—may see in deconstruction only what will not allow itself to be feminist. That's why they try to constitute a sort of target, a silhouette, a shooting gallery almost, where they spot phallocentrism and beat up on it [*tappent dessus*]. Just as Said and others constitute an enemy in the image [LAUGHTER] of that against which they have ready arms, in the same way, I think certain feminists as they begin to read certain texts, focus on particular themes out of haste and say, "Well, there you have it. ..." (I don't know exactly who one could think of in this regard, but I know it goes on.) In France I recall a very violent reaction from a feminist who upon reading *Spurs* and seeing the multiplication of phallic images—spurs, umbrellas, etc.—said, "So, it's a phallocentric text," and

started kicking up a violent fuss, charging about like a bull perhaps.
. . . [GENERAL LAUGHTER] (p. 30)

This is a startling scene—the feminist as raging bull ("I don't know
exactly who one can think of in this regard, but I know it goes on").
The bull in the shooting gallery, spotting and targeting, "kicking up a
violent fuss, charging about." Is this textual spotting and targeting a
reverse image? Is phallogocentrism really tantamount to feminism here?
Is this a male dressed as a female dressing as a male? What kind of
drag is this? Who is waving the red flag? And, who must join this
"general laughter"? The laughter of carnival is communal and spontaneous, but general laughter in this context is coercive, participated
in, like much comedy, by the marginalized only in an effort to pass.
But it can be heard from another position.

A counter scene is offered in the films of Yvonne Rainer, whose
past as a performance artist puts her in a particularly good position
to stage theory and intellectual comedy. In her film *The Man Who
Envied Women* (1985) ("I don't know exactly who one can think of
in this regard, but I know it goes on"), the man stands behind a female
student, his hands gripping her shoulders as she asks the difference
between the subject-in-process and the everyday individual with
choices and identifications to make. He replies (paraphrasing Foucault): in the very enactment of the power relations that are being
almost simultaneously affirmed and denied.

In another film, *Journeys from Berlin/1971* (1980), the joke is Jean-
Paul Sartre's in another interview. Reference is made to Sartre's trip
to West Germany to visit the imprisoned terrorists awaiting trial. When
asked why he visited only the cell of Andreas Baader and not that of
his accomplice Ulrike Meinhof, he replies, "The gang is called Baader-
Meinhof not Meinhof-Baader, isn't it?" In the voice-over, two people
laugh, the man because he is pleased with the old intellectual's intellectual prowess, the woman because she hears the joke as on Sartre
himself in decadence.

What Rainer stages is a dialogical laughter, the laughter of intertext
and multiple identifications. It is the conflictual laughter of social subjects in a classist, racist, ageist, sexist society. It is the laughter we
have now: other laughter for other times. Carnival and carnival laughter remain on the horizon with a new social subjectivity.

For now, right now, as I acknowledge the work of feminists in reconstituting knowledge, I imagine us going forward, growing old (I
hope), or being grotesque in other ways. I see us viewed by ourselves
and others, in our bodies and in our work, in ways that are continu-

ously shifting the terms of viewing, so that looking at us, there will be a new question, the question that never occurred to Bakhtin in front of the Kerch terracotta figurines—

Why are these old hags laughing?

N O T E S

I wish to thank Nancy Fitch and Catherine Portuges for their careful readings of an earlier version of this essay.

1. Mikhail Bakhtin, *Rabelais and His World*, trans. Helene Iswolsky (Bloomington: Indiana University Press, 1984). An earlier edition of this translation was published in 1968 by MIT Press. References to *Rabelais and His World* will be identified as *RW* and included in the text. Also important for discussions of language and carnival are *The Dialogical Imagination: Four Essays*, ed. Michael Holquist (Austin: University of Texas Press, 1981), and *Problems of Dostoevskii's Poetics*, trans. R. W. Rotsel (Ann Arbor: University of Michigan Press, 1973). For other works attributed to Bakhtin, see P. N. Medvedev and M. M. Bakhtin, *The Formal Method in Literary Scholarship: A Critical Introduction to Sociological Poetics*, trans. Albert J. Wehrle (Baltimore: Johns Hopkins University Press, 1978), and V. N. Volosinov, *Freudianism: A Marxist Critique* (New York; Academic Press, 1976).

2. I am indebted to Peter Stallybrass, whose forthcoming book with Allon White, *The Politics and Poetics of Transgression*, contains a rigorous historical and critical introduction to carnival as political discourse.

3. See Julia Kristeva, *La Révolution du langage poétique: l'avant-garde à la fin du 19e siècle: Lautréamont et Mallarmé* (Paris: Seuil, 1977) and *Polylogue* (Paris: Seuil, 1977); and Teresa de Lauretis, *Alice Doesn't: Feminism, Semiotics, Cinema* (Bloomington: Indiana University Press, 1984).

4. Mary Douglas, *Purity and Danger; An Analysis of Concepts of Pollution and Taboo* (London: Routledge and Kegan Paul, 1966); Victor Turner, *From Ritual to Theater; The Human Seriousness of Play* (New York: Performing Arts Journal Publications, 1982) and *The Ritual Process: Structure and Anti-structure* (Chicago: University of Chicago Press, 1968). Clifford Geertz, *The Interpretation of Cultures* (New York: Basic Books, 1973).

5. Natalie Zemon Davis, "Women on Top," in her *Society and Culture in Early Modern France* (Stanford: Stanford University Press, 1965), pp. 124-52. I am quoting from p. 131.

6. Ibid., p. 148. As Davis points out, this image of the "strong woman" is problematic: "The unruly woman not only directed some of the male festive organizations; she was sometimes their butt. The village scold or the domineering wife might be ducked in the pond or pulled through the streets muzzled or branked or in creel" (p. 140).

7. Maurice Agulhon, *Marianne into Battle: Republican Imagery and Symbolism in France, 1789-1880* (Cambridge: Cambridge University Press, 1981); Eric Hobsbawm, "Man and Woman in Socialist Iconography," *History Workshop: A Journal of Socialist Historians*, no. 6 (Autumn 1978), pp. 107-121. See also replies to Hobsbawm by Maurice Agulhon and by feminist historians Sally Alexander, Anna Davin, and Eve Hostettler in *History Workshop*, no. 8 (Autumn 1978), pp. 167-83. For an interesting exchange on the topic, see Neil

Hertz, "Medusa's Head: Male Hysteria under Political Pressure," *Representations* 4 (Fall 1983): 55-73, and the comments that follow it by Catherine Gallagher and Joel Fineman, pp. 55-72.

8. Victor Turner, "Frame, Flow, and Reflection: Ritual and Drama as Public Liminality," in *Performance in Postmodern Culture*, ed. Michel Benamou and Charles Caramello, Center for Twentieth Century Studies, Theories of Contemporary Culture, vol. 1 (Madison: Coda Press, 1977), pp. 35-55. As Turner puts it, "The danger here is not simply that of female 'unruliness.' This unruliness itself is the mark of the ultraliminal, of the perilous realm of possibility of 'anything *may* go' which threatens any social order and seems the more theatening, the *more* that order *seems* rigorous and secure. . . . The subversive potential of the carnivalized feminine principle becomes evident in times of social change when its manifestations move out of the liminal world of Mardi Gras into the political arena itself" (pp. 41-42). Emmanuel Le Roy Ladurie, *Carnival at Romans*, trans. Mary Feeneg (New York: Braziller, 1979).

9. Paul Céline, quoted in Julia Kristeva, *Powers of Horror: An Essay on Abjection*, trans. Leon S. Roudiez (New York: Columbia University Press, 1982), p. 169.

10. Kristeva, *Powers of Horror*, pp. 155-56. See also chapter 8, "Those Females Who Can Wreck the Infinite" (pp.157-73).

11. I am grateful to Ann Rosalind Jones for this insight. For an excellent critique of Kristeva's most recent work, see her "Julia Kristeva on Femininity: The Limits of a Semiotic Politics," *Feminist Review*, no. 18 (Winter 1984), pp. 56-73.

12. "His fascination with Jews, which was full of hatred and which he maintained to the end of his life, the simple-minded anti-Semitism that besots the tumultuous pages of the pamphlets, are no accident; they thwart the disintegration of identity that is coextensive with a scription that affects the most archaic distinctions, that bridges the gaps insuring life and meaning. Céline's anti-Semitism, like political commitment, for others—like, as a matter of fact, any political commitment, to the extent that it settles the subject within a socially justified illusion—is a security blanket" (Kristeva, *Powers of Horror*, pp. 136-37).

13. Writing, or "literature," is a "vision of the apocalypse that seems to me rooted no matter what its socio-historical condition might be, on the fragile border (borderline cases) where identities (subject/object, etc.) do not exist or only barely so—doubly, fuzzy, heterogeneous, animal, metamorphosed, altered, abject" (ibid., p. 207).

14. Stallybrass and White, *Politics and Poetics*, p. 21.

15. Michèle Richman, "Sex and Signs: The Language of French Feminist Criticism," *Language and Style* 13 (Fall 1980): 62-80.

16. Hélène Cixous, quoted in ibid., p. 74. The work of Luce Irigaray and Michèle Montrelay is especially important to this discussion.

17. The dangers of essentialism in posing the female body, whether in relation to representation or in relation to "women's history," have been well stated, so well stated, in fact, that "antiessentialism" may well be the greatest inhibition to work in cultural theory and politics at the moment, and must be displaced. For an account of recent debates around the female body and film, see Constance Penley, "Feminism, Film, and Theory and the Bachelor Machine," *M/F*, no. 10 (1985), pp. 39-61.

18. Catherine Clément, quoted in Richman, "Sex and Signs," p. 69.

19. Luce Irigaray, *The Sex Which Is Not One*, trans. Catherine Porter (Ithaca, N.Y.: Cornell University Press, 1985), p. 76.

20. Jacques Lacan, *Feminine Sexuality: Jacques Lacan and the "Ecole Freudienne,"* ed, Juliet Mitchell and Jacqueline Rose, trans. Jacqueline Rose (New York: W. W. Norton, 1982), p. 84.

21. Ibid., p. 85.

22. Mary Ann Doane, "Film and Masquerade: Theorizing the Female Spectator," *Screen* 23, nos. 3/4 (Sept./Oct. 1982): 74-87, and "Woman's Stake: Filming the Female Body," *October* 17 (Summer 1981): 23-36. See also Kaja Silverman, "*Histoire d'O*: The Construction of a Female Subject," in *Pleasure and Danger: Exploring Female Sexuality*, ed. Carole S. Vance (Boston: Routledge and Kegan Paul, 1984), pp. 320-49, and "Changing the Fantasmatic Scene," *Framework* 20 (1983): 27-36. For a discussion of masquerade in relation to postmodernism, see Craig Owens, "Posing," in *Difference: On Representation and Sexuality Catalog* (New York; New Museum of Contemporary Art, 1985).

23. Doane, "Film and Masquerade," p. 87.

24. Gayatri Spivak, "Displacement and the Discourse of Woman," in *Displacement: Derrida and After*, ed. Mark Krupnick, Center for Twentieth Century Studies, Theories of Contemporary Culture, vol. 4 (Bloomington: Indiana University Press, 1983), p. 186.

25. Spivak, p. 170. As Spivak quotes Derrida, "She is twice model, in a contradictory fashion, at once lauded and condemned. . . . (First), like writing. . . . But, insofar as she does not believe, herself, in truth . . . she is again the model, this time the good model, or rather the bad model as good model: she plays dissimulation, ornament, lying, art, the artistic philosophy . . ." (p. 171).

26. Dick Hebdige, *Subculture: The Meaning of Style* (London: Methuen, 1979); Homi Bhabha, "Of Mimicry and Man: The Ambivalence of Colonial Discourse," *October* 28 (Spring 1984): 125-33. Conversely, both Hebdige and Bhabha have largely ignored gender difference.

27. Elaine Showalter, "Critical Cross-Dressing: Male Feminists and the Woman of the Year," *Raritan* 3 no. 2 (Fall 1983): 130-49.

28. James Creech, Peggy Kamuf, and Jane Todd, "Deconstruction in America: An Interview with Jacques Derrida," *Critical Exchange* 17 (Winter 1985): 30. I wish to thank Theodore M. Norton for alerting me to the hilarious possibilities of this interview.

29. Derrida says, "So let's just say that the most insistent and the most organized motif in my texts is neither feminist nor phallocentric. And that at a certain point I try to show that the two are tantamount to the same thing" (ibid., p. 31).

CONTRIBUTORS

JESSICA BENJAMIN is a sociologist and psychoanalyst who works in New York City. Her essays and reviews have appeared in the *Psychoanalytic Review, New German Critique, Telos, Signs*, and numerous collections of essays in feminist studies. Her forthcoming book *The Bonds of Love* will be published by Pantheon in 1987.

RUTH BLEIER, Professor of Neurophysiology and Chair of Women's Studies at the University of Wisconsin-Madison, is the author of *Science and Gender: A Critique of Biology and Its Theories on Women* (1984). Her essays on science and gender have appeared in *Signs* and the *University of Michigan Papers in Women's Studies*.

TERESA DE LAURETIS, Professor of History of Consciousness at the University of California, Santa Cruz, is coeditor of *The Cinematic Apparatus* with Stephen Heath (1980), and the author of *La sintassi del desiderio* (1976), *Umberto Eco* (1981), and *Alice Doesn't: Feminism, Semiotics, Cinema* (1984).

LINDA GORDON, Professor History at the University of Wisconsin-Madison, is coeditor of *America's Working Women: A Documentary History*, with Rosalyn Baxandall and Susan Reverby (1976), and the author of *Woman's Body, Woman's Right: A Social History of Birth Control in America* (1976) and *Cossack Rebellions: Social Turmoil in the Sixteenth-Century Ukraine* (1983).

EVELYN FOX KELLER, Professor of Mathematics and Humanities at Northeastern University, is the author of *A Feeling for the Organism: The Life and Work of Barbara McClintock* (1983) and *Reflections on Gender and Science* (1985), as well as articles in mathematical biology, theoretical physics, and molecular biology.

BIDDY MARTIN, Assistant Professor of German Literature and Women's Studies at Cornell University, has published articles on contemporary German literature, feminist theory, and Lou Andreas-Salomé in *Studies in Twentieth-Century Literature, New German Critique,* and several collections of essays.

NANCY K. MILLER, Professor of Women's Studies and Director of the Women's Studies Program at Barnard College, is the author of *The Heroine's Text: Readings in the French and English Novel, 1722-1782* (1980) and editor of *The Poetics of Gender* (1986).

TANIA MODLESKI, Associate Professor of English, teaches literature and film at the University of Wisconsin-Milwaukee. She is the author of *Loving with a Vengeance: Mass-Produced Fantasies for Women* (1982) and editor of *Studies in Entertainment: Critical Approaches to Mass Culture* (1986).

CHANDRA TALPADE MOHANTY, Mellon Fellow in Women's Studies at Cornell University, has published essays and reviews in *Women's Studies International Forum, Journal of Teacher Education,* and *boundary 2.* She is currently working on a book entitled *Under Western Eyes: Feminist Scholarship and Colonial Discourses.*

CHERRÍE MORAGA is a Chicana poet, born in Los Angeles and presently living in California. She is a cofounder of Kitchen Table: Women of Color Press (New York), coeditor of *This Bridge Called My Back: Writings by Radical Women of Color* (1981) and *Cuentos: Stories by Latinas* (1983), and the author of *Loving in the War Years: Lo que nunca pasó por sus labios* (1983) and *Giving Up the Ghost* (1986).

SONDRA O'NEALE, Assistant Professor of American Literature at Emory University, teaches black American literature and black women's studies. She has published articles in *Melus, Southern Exposure,* and *Obsidian* and is the author of a forthcoming book entitled *Growing in Light: The Development of the Black Woman as Writer, Character, and Reader in American Fiction.*

SHEILA RADFORD-HILL is Director of Training for Chicago Area Project, a network of twenty-seven community-based organizations. She also teaches courses in Afro-American fiction, black women's literature, and black drama at the University of Illinois at Chicago. She has published articles in *First World* and *Freedom Ways,* and several advocacy reports.

MARY RUSSO, Associate Professor of Literature and Critical Theory at Hampshire College, has contributed essays in literary and cultural criticism to *Yale Italian Studies, Quaderni d'italianistica,* and numerous anthologies. She is currently completing a book on women as spectacle.

CARROLL SMITH-ROSENBERG, Professor of History and Psychiatry and Director of the Women's Studies Program at the University of Pennsylvania, is the author of *Religion and the Rise of the American City* (1971), *Disorderly Conduct: Visions of Gender in Victorian America* (1985), and *The Body Politic* (forthcoming from Alfred A. Knopf).

Theories of Contemporary Culture